*Your*

# MY LIFE

# *Your Death is*
# MY LIFE

The true life story of Bill Earl,
a Funeral Director in Plymouth,
known as
*Earl of Plymouth*

Headstone Publications

First published in 2004
by Headstone Publications
Earl House
Outland Road
Plymouth
PL2 3BZ

Printed by Latimer Trend & Co Ltd, Plymouth

# Contents

# Preface

My thanks go out to all those who have contributed to my biography, without whom, this book would never have been printed, especially with my poor memory these days.

A special thanks to Chris Barkell, who put the back bone into this book, and Carole, who put the flesh into my biography.

Much of what has been written, has even made me sit up and laugh, making me realise, how much I had forgotten.

I particularly acknowledge my wife, family, staff and the many friends I made whilst on my travels around the world.

Note, for confidentiality, a few names may have been changed. Purely because of memory, it is possible, the dates could be a little out, however, be assured, it is precious little.

I leave you with this final thought, 'Welcome to my world, wont you come on in?'

*Bill Earl*

# Foreword

There are many people in this world who are more than willing to offer advice, often without substance. You hear them suggesting that, "you should do it like this", or "I wouldn't do that". They lecture others and interfere in business, which should be of no concern of theirs. They are known as 'busy-bodies', or 'know-it-alls'.

What makes matters worse is that these, 'know-it-alls' never listen to the advice of others and seldom learn from those around them. They have an answer for everything and yet cannot believe that anyone else could know better.

There are few people with truly inquisitive minds. When we are born, we all ask "Why?", "Why?", and "Why?" again, in the process of growing through childhood to adolescence. Unfortunately our society seems to stifle the enquiring mind and most people grow out of asking "Why?" long before they reach adulthood. We can all learn from each other, from our environment and from our experiences, as well as from the usual sources of education, such as books, radio, television, etc. What a shame that most of those learning opportunities go to waste!

There was a man, who thought he knew everything. He would 'poke his nose' into everyone else's business. He told his colleagues where to take their holidays, his neighbours which plants to grow in their gardens, teachers the subjects his children should be taught, and other motorists how they should drive. He had very few deep conversations, as he seldom listened. He never sought advice or help, as he believed nobody else had any to offer. He never observed others and what they were doing, unless he wanted to tell them how to do it better. He only read 'light' novels and tabloid newspapers. He watched television and listened to the radio for entertainment only.

*One day, this man went for a parachute jump and his parachute never opened! His death certificate should have read, "died of ignorance", because although he knew it all, he actually knew nothing!*

There is another man, a man who has spent all of his life searching for knowledge, learning from his experiences and those of the people around him. He has been on a lifelong quest for wisdom and the answer to the question, "Why?". He has readily shared his wisdom with others and draws great joy from helping people from whom he has drawn knowledge. That man is the subject of this book, he was born William Arthur Earl on 4th May 1920, and is affectionately known as, "Earl of Plymouth", but that's another story.

I have been privileged to know Bill for many years, and to be asked to help write his biography. To me, he will always be "The Earl of Wisdom". Read and enjoy, but, most importantly, learn.

*Chris Barkell*

# Introduction

This is a true story of a very well known Plymouth "Character", a retired 83 year old funeral director.

This remarkable, colourful man, Bill Earl, known as Earl of Plymouth (which in itself, shows a strong personality), successfully started many businesses from nothing, travelled around the world five times like a Michael Palin, growing plants from his travels like a 'budding' Alan Titchmarsh. Bill's life story contains many hilarious 'grave' experiences, and conversely serious questions about funerals all answered within this book. There are Chinese proverbs, and Bill Earl's words of Wisdom, like a King Solomon. All Bill's sayings are contained within this book, with much much more.

This is a unique biography, each chapter different, and full of variety, like the bones of a skeleton, I invite you to chew it over, it's certainly tasty. Everyone should have a skeleton in their cupboard.

Bill's one of the hardest working men I've ever known. His brain never stops. The ideas he comes up with, and carries out is unbelievable. No wonder he's made such a success of each and every business he's had, making it known to all and sundry, one's business, is only as good as one's staff.

Known for his hard work, and one who used the fruits of it to help the needy. Nothing for him to carry out a funeral without making a charge, and explaining to others, to remember, 'nothing is cheap, or a bargain, if not needed'.

When different ones tell Bill, they've done this and had that, it would be so easy to say, I know, I've done it all, owned almost every decent make of car, one's heard of, and many one's never heard of, but money was never Bill's guide, even though he made a tremendous amount of it, many called him, the richest man in Plymouth. He'd get most annoyed, never wanting to be known in that way.

His biggest regret, was when he retired, he didn't know what to do, his business was his life. Even now, he willingly carries out the odd funeral, if the deceased or family are known to him.

It's other people and friends who talk about Bill's achievements, he'd rather be able to carry on for many years to come, just as a Devonshire 'Dumpling'. Sadly, like everybody else, that's not possible, but may he have many many more happy years, from one who knows him inside out.

*Carole Barkell*

# Tribute

I first Bill Earl some 26 years ago, whilst working for the Local Evening Herald and Regional Morning Newspapers in Plymouth. Our business relationship quickly developed into a personal friendship between Bill, Carole, myself and wife Pat.

Bill, is a man who has done so much, for so long, for so many people, in a truly caring, professional, dedicated and sympathetic manner.

A man, who in his business life, strives for perfection and achieves it. A man, who doesn't treat you differently, if you are rich or poor, a peer of the realm, or someone from a two up and two down in a small village.

Bill Earl, a man who works tirelessly for charity and good causes, who would never say no to anyone who needs help, advice or assistance. A man who loves to laugh, and to make others laugh to.

Bill Earl, a man who will never let you down, will always do what he says, when he says he will do it. In his own words, "Sometimes Early but never late".

A man, who in my experience, has never had a bad word to say about anyone, nor, has ever knowingly done harm to anyone.

Bill Earl, a small man with the heart of a giant, an ordinary man, a self made man, an uncomplicated man, who lives life to the full.

A man, my wife and I are proud, honoured and lucky, to call 'A Friend'.

*John Marriott*

# 1
# Early Days

**Character Building and Childhood Memories**

It was a sunny morning in May. Everything was peaceful at 18B Bedford Street, Ford, which is an area of Plymouth between the city centre and Devonport. The area consisted mainly of large old terraced houses with a few farms on the outskirts, and was very much a working class suburb of the city. It was 1920 so few vehicles were about at that time of the morning. However there were some comings and goings at the Earl household, as the three children were eagerly awaiting the news from their father and mother's bedroom, where Mrs Earl was in labour and about to give birth to the subject of this life story, Bill. Who could have foretold the travels, learnings and friendships that were in store for this little baby boy? The news was conveyed by the doctor to Bill's father, who in turn passed the joyous news of a baby brother to his other three children. Their excitement meant that the news was soon throughout the streets of Ford, and perhaps across Plymouth; the news that there was a new "Earl of Plymouth".

Two years later Bill's younger brother, Gordon, was born. He was the last of the "Earls" born into the family at Bedford Street, Ford. Bill always teased his brother that mother took one look at Gordon when he was born and said, "That's it. I've had enough, no more! That's finished." Bill would even tease that his mother had wanted to send Gordon back from where he had come from! It was amazing therefore that these brothers retained a great love and respect for each other right through until the end of Gordon's days. Bill forgives himself his habit of teasing by remembering always that it all happened when he was so young, and that, after all, when he was born he was only a baby!

He was always a dare devil, when he was 11 years old, he took his brother, Gordon's, brand new bicycle, and ran away to Penwithick, visiting the cousins he loved. He was so worried, thinking he was being followed, whist cycling the forty odd mile journey, not daring to stop.

Mum and Dad

From Penwithick, he'd cycle about five miles to St. Austell, to the local dance. Happily staying with his Uncle Phil, who worked in the clay works, he taught Bill a lot about nature, something he never forgot. Wondering whether he would lose his nerve, he had taken a return ticket on the ferry, sensible thinking, even at that early age.

Bill's father was a disciplinarian; a hard, strict and fair man, who never allowed any of his five children to play in the streets. They had to play in his father's nearby fields; now full of houses and known as Swilly. The fields attached to his farm were used to play football and other sports on Saturdays. During the week they would hold whippet racing competitions.

These whippet races involved rows of seven foot high wire netting, running the length of the field; maybe two, or three hundred yards. Each dog racing separately in its own lane, unable to cross the wire netting to reach the other dogs. The owners of each dog stood at the end of the field, waving handkerchiefs to attract the attention of their animals, encouraging them to race swiftly to them, as they were released simultaneously by

Bill as a Boy

individuals at the other end of the field. Much later in Bill's life, having travelled the world, he had never encountered again such dog racing. He advertised in the local paper to hear if anyone remembered such events. Bill was disappointed not to receive any response, but he realises he was only a young lad when attending these events, and that he had reached his eighties by the time he advertised therefore, the adults who may have attended such races would have been very old, and more likely to have passed on.

Bill's father used the fields for grazing horses, including the butcher's delivery horse and cart. Deliveries were made that way in those days, and the Earl household received regular deliveries from that same butcher, whose cart had a green tarpaulin over the rear. Bill believed the butcher's name to have been Kershaw, or something similar. The farm, he thinks, was known as Keel Park. A name, well known in Plymouth today.

Bill always remembers his Uncle Sid's blind horse, Joey. Bill, only a school-boy, used to do a vegetable round Saturdays. Whenever the ice-cream man, 'Johno', rang his hand bell, Joey would prick up his ears, and though blind, would start making toward the ice-cream cart, where Bill always bought Joey his own ice-cream cornet. Though blind, Bill only had to go in the field and quietly say, 'Joey', and he would come directly to Bill, who would then harness him. There was a quarry adjoining the field, and though the horse used the field for many years, he eventually fell in and killed himself.

Bill fondly remembers his family's large black dog named Rover. It had four white socks. It was a cross between a sheepdog and a retriever. He was such a well-trained pet that when Bill's mother wanted eggs she would give the dog an open tin can, normally used for milk. He would hold the can, by the handle, in his mouth and run from their home in Bedford Street to the farm, travelling across hedges and fields until he arrived at the farmhouse door, where the farmer, Mr. Yandall, would carefully place fresh eggs into the can, pat the dog and send him on his return journey. The dog would carefully, yet quickly, cross the fields and hedges returning home with all the eggs in perfect condition. Never did he crack even one! Upon reaching home he would place the tin can and its delicate contents in the porch, then lie on guard until relieved of his duties by a member of the family.

When the family eventually left Ford and moved to a different business house in St. Budeaux, another suburb of Plymouth, close to the River Tamar and the ferry to Cornwall, they took their beloved dog with them. Though they built fences around the back garden, nothing kept him in. He had been so used to running free in the fields near Ford, he could not be contained within their garden fences. The dog found a new area to roam, in Ham Woods, owned by Doctor Trelawney Ross. Only when it could roam freely was the dog at ease.

At St. Budeaux Bill and his family lived opposite his school. Being called Earl his school friends called him "Early for short, but not for long". However, in those days of Bill's childhood he was always late for school, despite living so close. His friends would joke about it and exclaim, upon his late arrival, "Come on Early, late again!" A far cry from the Bill Earl of today, whose motto is, "sometimes Early, but never late", and he lives up to that punctuality.

Bill always remembers his school days fondly, as he had some hilarious times, which, later in life, still made him smile. Bill recalls his early experiences of the opposite sex, prior to leaving school at the age of fourteen. Most boys took their lunch to school with them, but Bill, living so close, would run home each lunchtime. He recalls arranging regularly to meet the girl who worked in their house; in fact, whilst other boys were having

The three brothers, Tommy, Gordon, Bill

sandwiches for lunch, Bill was having, what one might call, last night's chips!

Whilst at St. Budeaux Bill's parents opened fish and chip shops. They also ran a mobile shop, the very first fish and chip van in the city. It was an old (old, even for those days) model T Ford with a sign on the side, "Our motto is cleanliness". Amazingly the van continued for many years, despite looking like something out of the ark! It provided a valuable source of income for the Earl family and also welcome lunches and suppers for many working class families throughout the area. It was a novelty as well as a convenience, perhaps the early fore-runner to convenience food? This fish and chip van went to various estates. One of the rounds is now known as Swilly, which was previously his dad's farm and football fields. The CWS Jam factory relied on their fish and chip lunches on Fridays. The mobile also attended other places, such as Tavistock's Goose Fair. On one occasion the van's lights failed, returning to Plymouth, and they had to follow other vehicles closely for as long as they could, in order to see the road.

At the St. Budeaux shop a staircase ran down from the living accommodation to the back of the shop. Each evening, as bed-time approached, Bill and his younger brother, Gordon, would go down to the door leading into the back of the shop. They would quietly open it, shout "chips" to their father, close it again and sit on the bottom stair awaiting their feast. The children were never allowed in the shop, so this was as near as the two brothers could get.

The shop was close to a popular dance hall. At the interval, which was around Bill's bed-time, many customers would be queuing. Their father would serve all his customers, often selling all his chips. Being a strict and hard man, he would open the door and say, "Sorry boys, none left", and send the boys to bed without their chip supper.

A fine example of Bill's father's strictness and his sharp mind (something which Bill obviously inherited) took place on a few occasions when Bill's class was kept into detention at school. Often the teacher would become annoyed because the class was noisy and, despite warnings, would not remain quiet. The punishment was thirty minutes detention for the whole class. As mentioned earlier, Bill's family lived directly opposite the school. Therefore Bill used to be home by five minutes past four each day, taking only a few minutes to say goodnight to his friends and walk the short distance. It was quite apparent when he was late, particularly when it was half an hour late! When Bill returned home on such occasions his dad would ask where he had been. Bill would explain he had come straight from school, but through the class misbehaving they had been detained for thirty minutes. His father, having listened to this information would then instruct Bill that he was to go to school thirty minutes late the next morning. His instructions included Bill having to advise the teacher he was thirty minutes late arriving at school because he had been thirty minutes late home the day before. This not only caused Bill embarrassment when going to school, but also ensured he would be caught out if he had told his father a lie as to his whereabouts, for the half an hour from four o'clock to four thirty the day before. Bill never told a lie. His father was so strict. He soon learned if he had tried he would have been easily found out.

Often, whilst living with the family in St. Budeaux, Bill would go out dancing when his dad thought he was in bed asleep. When returning home late Bill would creep carefully up the creaking stairs, like a crab, hoping his father would not hear him. Mr. Earl senior, with his exceptionally deep voice, would almost always shout, "Who's that?". Bill, as sharp as a razor, and always one for a quick answer, would innocently reply, "It's alright, Dad, it's only me going down to the toilet." Bill would turn around and make his way to the outside toilet. He never failed to get away with this little scam. Before returning to his bed, which he shared with his brother, Gordon, Bill would purposely stand for a short while barefoot on the cold canvas floor. He loved to aggravate his brother, and with his icy cold feet he would purposely rest them on Gordon's back as soon as he entered the bed, so as to wake him with a start.

Gordon was a hairdressing apprentice at this time and mixed with some pretty young girls. Regularly he would remark to Bill about them, as boys do. Having woken Gordon with his cold feet, Bill would proceed to make matters worse by reminding Gordon of one of his pretty friends. When he had Gordon's complete attention he would land the "sucker punch" – "I went out with her tonight, and …. I put a smile on her face!" Gordon would fume and Bill just laughed and laughed.

On other occasions Bill would contrive to rudely awaken the deep sleeping Gordon in mischievous ways. Bill always kept a bottle of Masons Jafferade under the bed, and sometimes, when feeling particularly devilish, he would shake up the fizzy drink, place the nozzle next to Gordon's face, and open it. It would, of course, pop and fizz all over the alarmed Gordon, who would swear at Bill. Bill would tell his brother off for swearing and threaten to tell their mother, just to wind him up a little bit more. When Gordon went to sleep again Bill would reach for his bottle once more. He would quietly and swiftly stick the cold bottle down the legs of Gordon's pyjamas – poor Gordon!! And what a commotion!

### A motto Bill Learnt:- Always Mean What You Say

Bill, in later life, appreciated many of his father's ideas regarding instilling obedience in his children. If any of his sons or daughters misbehaved they would not be smacked but told they were not permitted to go out to play for a week (a punishment known as "grounding" in this day and age, but little known or used in the 1920's or 1930's). No matter the mood of Bill's father if he had "grounded" Bill there would be no respite.

On one such occasion Bill's friends were outside his house calling out for him to come out to play. They had a strange, almost owl-like hoot they would use to attract Bill's attention, hooting, "Bi—ll Eaaaarrrlllll", in a high pitch. Bill's father had been in an extremely good mood that morning so Bill approached him and asked politely if he could go out with his friends. A request to which his father responded with a question, "Did I say you had to stay in for a week?" Bill obviously replied in the affirmative, to which his father replied, "When I say you've got to stay in that's what I mean." Bill would never dare to ask again. Although he felt very sorry for himself at the time he later realised this was a far more effective form of punishment than any amount of smacking. Bill also learned from his father that if you say something, mean it and stick to it. Right up until this day Bill is well known for always sticking to his word. If he says he will do something, he does it. If he says he will meet you somewhere at a particular time, he is there and punctual.

### The Old Clyno, motto:- Where there's a Will, there's a Way

Often Bill's father would call the family together and tell them that he was going to take them all out on a mystery trip. The family car was an old Clyno, not one which has been seen or heard of for many years. The family would all climb into the car, often with a stick of rock each, and wait in anticipation of the mystery trip. They would sit there for some time and wait and wait. Sometimes they would sit there all afternoon and the car would not move an inch. That was their mystery trip! On another occasion the mystery trip involved walking from their home in St. Budeaux to the Saltash ferry. They travelled on the ferry into Cornwall and then walked to the top of Fore Street where they entered Victoria Park. They sat in the park all afternoon and then returned home.

Bill also gained his resourcefulness from his father, and determination, not to just give up, stay and think first, before making a move. In this case, they had already stopped, and couldn't move. Bill was only a little boy at the time. They were all out in the country, far from anywhere in their car, an old 1920 Clyno. It had hand operated windscreen wipers, a triangle on the rear, reading, four wheel brakes. Whether they worked, or not, was dubious. With a dry radiator, the engine seemed red hot. Removing its' top, it almost blew his Dad's hat off. The roads were very quiet in those days, to make it worse, they were miles from anywhere, without a drop of water, what were they going to do? Bill's father had the answer right away, 'widdle' in Bill's seaside bucket. Good job there were six of them. Anyway, it got them home. Then, they couldn't make up their minds, whether to refill the radiator, or scrap the car. After all, they'd paid £25 for it!!

### Some of the History of Plymouth, as Bill knew it As A Child

During the 83 years Bill lived in Plymouth, the tram depot at Camels Head, housed a tram running from the city centre to St. Budeaux. That depot became a garage, and during the war, a fire service station, for various fire appliances. Firemen named it 'Stinkville', and indeed, had the name, 'Stinkville', marked in very large letters on the side of that fire station, overlooking, what had been the sea, where boats regularly moored. When the tide went out, it left nothing but, thick black, stinking mud. After taking many years of land-fill, the sea was no more and the site became, as it is now, the large Dockyard and Royal Navy car park.

Opposite Camels Head school, was a cinema, known as 'Camels Head Bughouse', where Bill spent much time as a boy, in the projection room. The only music for films, mostly cowboy pictures, eg. Ken Maynard & Tom Hicks, was from a piano. The pianist rapidly playing, according to the speed of the film. That in itself, would be enough to make you laugh these days. Admittance to Saturday matinees, was either 2 pence, or 4 pence, in old money.

The Ford Palladium in St. Levans Road, now a DIY store, was also known as 'A Bughouse'. Bill says, what a noisy rumpus it was there at Saturday Matinees, but good old days for all that.

Another of Bill's escapades, during his youth, and definitely off the record, was to occasionally drive a train too and from Millbay Station, which was opposite the Duke of Cornwall Hotel, a short distance, to Plymouth's North Road Station. Actually, they were only shunting, at night. It was an experience he never forgets.

In days gone by, Millbay Station (which no longer exists), was kept busy by many liners anchored in Plymouth Sound, whose passengers used that station, as the beginning of their train journey to London. Back in those days, it was steam trains.

Bill remembers the trams that used to run, during his childhood. Worst part about them, he says, were the tram lines. Cyclists had to ride over them at a 45 degree angle, otherwise the lines would throw them off, especially in bad weather. In those days, many motor vehicles ran on solid rubber tyres. Eventually, the tyres were pulled off the wheels, by the tram lines, before they were worn out.

A joke was, that if an Austin Seven got caught in the tram lines, it had to drive all the way back to Milehouse Tram Depot, to get out of the lines. (Now known as Milehouse Bus Depot.)

The trams, because of the lines, had to stop in the middle of the road, to allow passengers to get on and off. This was very dangerous.

Around 1930, Bill remembers, Plymouth, Devonport & Stonehouse tram drivers, went on strike. Those who disobeyed the strike, and drove the trams, had all sorts of missiles thrown at them.

He remembers cars, dodging in and out of the electric standards in the middle of Albert Road, that held the overhead power cables for the trams, in order to get ahead of the trams, though breaking the law.

## Cutting Hair for Short, But not for 'Long'

Bill's family had a ladies and gents hairdressing salon, and public baths at 6d a time, plus an extra towel for a 1d. For a short while, Bill worked in the business, and remembers all too well, of a few farmers, who would only have a shave once a week, Saturdays. With a week's tough heavy growth, poor Bill had to lather their faces, with shaving brush and soap, for such a long time, trying to soften their beards, that Bill had worked up such a lather, he didn't know where to put the soap, there was so much, it would fall off the hard faces of the farmers. The beards and growths, were so tough, he even had to rub oil into their faces from the beginning.

A popular request in those days, was for Bill to give a certain farmer a weekly relaxing shave. We all make mistakes, and Bill was only a little boy. Generally, all went well, however, one day Bill nicked the farmer, with the cut throat razor causing a little blood to be drawn. One couldn't help laughing, Bill had the answer, he quickly reassured the old farmer saying, "I'm so sorry sir, but that was a little uprising on your face, but I've straightened it out for you now". Bill got away with it every time, and still laughs about it to this day.

In those days, 1934, Permanent Waving, was becoming very popular, and so, more and more females, were having their long hair cut off, to enable them to have the remainder permed. Even though Bill didn't really like the job, he thought it better than continuing at the school, he left aged 14.

However, even in those early days, Bill had an eye to business and showmanship, so he would use all the long cuts of hair, by washing and shampooing it, then perming same, after which he set it, curled the ends, and displayed it, together with a little coloured ribbon to show it off in the shop window. There's no doubt about it, Bill was always good at anything he touched, and a real hard worker.

## Starting Work

Still only 14, Bill's father, knowing his son wasn't really interested in hairdressing, got Bill a job with a builder and decorator. After a short time, Bill's father overheard Bill saying, he didn't really like the job, and was going to do everything wrong, to get the sack. It was then, that his father gave him a talking to, and Bill never forgot it. His father told him, it was up to him, and explained, you have to make up your mind, as to whether you want to be someone's lacky for the rest of your life, or get a profession or trade behind you, explaining, that a lacky is just a labourer, doing a job anybody can do, saying, you don't need brains to sweep the road, or shovel sand etc.

Apparently, Bill's Father gave Bill, a complete new outlook on life, and so, he went to Technical night school, for as many evenings in the week, that the school allowed, and that was more than any other boy in the school.

After Bill's very short apprenticeship, he got a job on St. Budeaux council estate, where two men had to emulsion (Wallpamure in those days) two houses, right through, in a day. The foreman, who had two of his own sons working there, soon realised, Bill was a good fast worker, and so he had him for a mate, knowing, whenever he left Bill on his own, he would work even faster. He left Bill each morning, saying, he had to meet the sand lorry. Bill soon learnt, that meeting the sand lorry, simply meant, he spent a couple of hours, each morning, in the Trelawny Public House, St. Budeaux, drinking with his pals. Bill didn't care, he simply worked faster, to make up for it. The idea was, to complete one house in the morning, and one room in the next house, before lunch, breaking the back of it, making the afternoon easier. Infact, they always finished the second house by 4p.m., when they would both lock themselves in an empty house, until packing up at 5p.m.

After a while, Bill began to realise, he was loosing all he had learnt, eg., wall papering & graining etc., so he got a job with Taylor & Woodrows, where all kinds of decorating, graining and paper hanging was required, but Bill with all the others was stood off for a while, until the next lot of houses were built. In the meantime, Bill did a very special 1st class job of decorating a room, which included panelling the large ceiling and graining the woodwork, after which, he used the room itself, as a very attractive 'show room', and made an exhibition of it, available for viewing at all times to the public.

This was Bill's start, wherein he became, his own boss, having started his own business, he never worked for a building, or decorating firm anymore.

Bill often laughs, thinking back to those far off days, and quips, with a big smile on his face, that if ever one saw a large, heavily laden handcart, with ladders and planks etc., piled sky high, looking as if no-one was pushing it, that was Bill ha! ha!!

## Driving Lorry to Bull Point

During Bill's early days, he used to drive a lorry, delivering armament etc., to Bull Point armament Depot. The time came, when he knew he should be earning more money, for the job he was doing and asked his boss for a pay rise. His boss, an artful dodger, would try, this way and that, to get out of paying more money. He was the agent for Southern Railway Yard, St. Budeaux, and doing very nicely out of the contract. However, he tried various ways, to get out of paying Bill more money. What he didn't know, was, Bill was no fool himself. He had a mate with him all the time, on the lorry, earning less than him. The boss suggested, it would be a good idea, and nice for him, if Bill taught him to drive. Bill, already wary of his boss's tricks, retorted, "What, teach him, so that he can have my job. You must be joking." What a brave answer Bill gave, jobs were hard to come by at that time.

Bill had an agreement with his mate, and decided, from there on, he would not assist with the unloading. The mate, and Bill got on well together. Next morning, unloading at Bull Point, Bill stayed in the cab, drinking his cocoa, and enjoying his snack. One of the Bull Point workers, asked Bill, why he wasn't helping. Bill simply replied, he was the driver, and not paid for unloading lorries. It was a case of the wits being pitted against each other, as to who was going to win? Word soon spread, Bill immediately having the backing of the whole of the Southern Railway Yard staff, including the lorry drivers, who were all underpaid.

After Bill's lorry was fully loaded, Bill went to the employer's office, telling them the lorry was fully loaded, in the garage, where it would remain, until he agreed to the extra money demanded for all his workers, giving them a fair wage. The boss, seeing Bill had outwitted him, agreed with the demands for all his staff. Bill was thanked by the workers, for looking after them, and not just himself. The original wage co-ordinator, I think.

## Family Move To large Country Estate

If Bill's memory serves him correct, when he was a little boy going to school, back in the year 1928, he remembers being taught, that there was a relative to The Earl of MountEdgcumbe family, known as Lady Ernestine MountEdgcumbe, who lived in a large country house estate. The children were taught from the legend, that the people thought she had died back at that time, when really she was only in a trance. The butler tried to cut the expensive ring off her finger, when she suddenly sat up before him. The frightened man, immediately ran off and committed suicide by drowning in a large pond in the grounds. It must be remembered, Bill was only eight when he was told this story.

These memories stayed with him up to a point, when he gradually thought no more of them, that is, until, an unforeseen occurrence happened. He and his family took over the estate, which was always understood to be that of the late Lady Ernestine MountEdgcumbe, and called, as Bill's always known it, 'Honeycombe House', or 'Estate', where he

Honeycombe', the family home during the Second World War

lived in about 1938, when many of the things he had been taught as a child, seemed to 'come to life', by presenting themselves in a natural way.

Bill understood, Lady Ernestine was a rather large lady, and because of same, even right back in those days, had a lift to enable her to go to one of the rooms in a tower, where, he was told, she used to study. The tower etc., exists to this day. The odd and interesting thing is, he used to go to that tower, and from one room to another, until reaching the flat roof, where one could see the beautiful countryside, and The Royal Albert Bridge, where it crosses the River Tamar at Saltash. Climbing to the roof, Bill had to use crutches, because of war injuries and burns sustained on the very day 20th March 1941, the King and Queen came to Plymouth, after their 10 day tour of Devon & Cornwall, when, he had also been with them.

There is a fairly large pool on the estate, big enough for a full size boat. (where the butler could have drowned). There is a memorial headstone and plinth, engraved, to the memory of Lady Ernestine's pet dog.

They had two large kitchens, one in each of the two wings of the house. In one of the kitchen's, there were four or five wall plaques, approx. 3 ft 6" × 2 ft 6", which read, in large Old English, 'No maid servant shall encourage any outside man servant into the house. Any maid servant who shall breaketh a cup, shall forfeit three pence of her wages, and so on, with all sorts of restrictions and orders, such as, Lady Ernestine's horse and carriage will parade in front of the house each Sunday morning at such and such a time, to be followed by the servants' carriages, to form a cortege to Calstock Church.'

There was a very large room, especially decorated for the King, who had dined there. There were two fireplaces in that room and a 36 ft long oak table. The house contained a large banqueting hall, where Bill, as a keen ballroom dancer advertised, just once, that he would be giving an exhibition of modern ballroom dancing. After that, Bill ran a regular dance night, taking a band home from Plymouth. He used to have a regular attendance each week of around two hundred people. There was a very large fireplace in both the banqueting hall and front entrance. In each case, the two extremely large chimneys had built in foot places, to enable one to climb up to sweep the chimney. I suspect, little boys in those days. Each of the fireplaces was large enough to burn a settee.

A small farm was attached to the rear of the house. Bill remembers generating their own electricity, starting the generator by switching on two light switches and then switching one off in the house. They even had their own fire service with fire appliances, hoses and reels etc.

Now, it's known as Honicombe Holiday Centre, for the enjoyment of many, on this lovely, quiet, country estate.

## Bill Joined The Royal Corps of Signals

Bill was in his early twenties, when war was declared, and like most young men, he was called up, to fight for his country, joining, The Royal Corps of Signals. Each morning, Bill, with the rest of his group, had to be on Parade 7.30a.m. This particular Monday morning, Bill wasn't there, he was still in bed, or should I say, he was lying on a flat mattress filled with straw on the slate floor of an old cowshed (just as all the other soldiers had to sleep). Sergeant in charge asked him, why wasn't he on Parade. Bill replied, that he'd had a bad night suffering with asthma.

Eventually, Bill was sent from Osset, where he was stationed, to a hospital in Leeds. He was told to take a return ticket, as he wouldn't be staying, it was only for a check up.

Bill took a peep, over the Medical Officer's shoulder, whilst he was writing, asking, 'is this man fit for overseas service?' That made Bill think. Arriving at the hospital, and handing over the note, Bill was given a white shirt, a blue coat which was a mile too long for him (infact he had to stoop down, to put his hands in the very large pockets ha! Ha!!) and red tie. This combination was known as, 'hospital blues'. Bill quickly spoke up, saying, that they must be making a mistake, as he wasn't going to be staying there. After all, he'd only come to see the specialist. Yes, was the response, but the specialist only visited the hospital on Wednesdays. Undeterred, Bill became quite a character, staying a fairly long time.

It's a well known fact, he has an insatiable appetite, so instead of having his lunch in the ward with the others. He had to go to the large dining hall, where they lined up, just as in the prisons. However, after all was said and done, one was allowed to serve themselves, as much as they liked.

Whilst in hospital, they were given different jobs. Bill didn't like that, but as the saying goes, 'you're in the army now' Bill didn't care about any of the jobs they tried to satisfy him with. Bill, thinking he would find a way out of that, bearing in mind, one of his mottoes was, 'always turn all adversities to one's own advantage'. As will be seen, he did. He's sorry about it now, but glad he did it then ha! ha!

This being an emergency hospital, one side was sadly for those mentally affected by wartime experiences. For this reason, all the fittings were made of brass, example, the bars across the windows, and special fittings in the toilets etc., all to prevent suicide.

No wonder Bill said to himself, 'This is no good to me, I am getting out of here', and he did.

First job he was given, was cleaning all the brass, eg., door fittings, locks, bolts & windows etc. Bill, determined to rid himself of such tedious jobs, would put more 'brasso' on the woodwork, than the brass. They soon got the message, and took' the silly old fool' off the job. Instead, he was

Bill in the Royal Corps of Signals

given the job of polishing the endless wooden floors. He was presented with a large heavy polisher, on the end of a broom handle. He only did this once, when he was asked to polish floors again, his quick answer was, 'What, with my feet', adding, it was breaking his back. They thought, 'poor old sod', and took him off that job as well.

Instead, they gave him a more simple task, an enormous tin of floor polish, explaining, all he had to do was, slide the tin along the floor, no need to lift it, and simply use the stick in the tin to flick the polish onto the floor. You can imagine, Bill made a fine job of that, infact, it took them a month, manhandling the large polisher, trying to get it to shine. However, some good came out of Bill's work, no one ever slipped down on that floor again.

Thinking hard, what could they give this 'silly old fool' to do next. They decided to send him to the cookhouse, with all the lovely civilian nurses. This was right up Bill's street. Always a devil for the opposite sex, he was very excited, and so were some of the nurses, well, at least the one he took a fancy to. Bill was supposed to be 'spud bashing'. True, he was bashing, but there didn't seem to be any extra spuds. Never sure whether he had been sent there for punishment, or, as a Punchinello, neither of which made any difference.

Still turning all adversities to his advantage, this hospital, like Bill, was self supporting. The patients all partook of their evening dinner in the ward, where there was a glowing fire. I can visualise Bill, tripping off to the nurses' little kitchen, asking nurse, if he could borrow her frying pan.

Bill's mates, asked him one day, how he came to have so many eggs. Bill quickly retorted, he was continually receiving food parcels from home. Knowing the enormous appetite Bill had, and the extra large pockets in his coat, they understood, only too well.

The trouble with Bill, who kept telling the nurses, he was too ill to do this job, or the other, including, pushing the big floor polisher, he also had a poor memory. The moment Bill heard the strict tempo of Victor Silvester and his dance orchestra, the poor old chap would unthinkingly, hop out of bed, wrapping his arms around his favourite nurse, or any other, that happened to be around, and he would merrily dance up and down the length of the sparsely furnished ward, well, except for the beds, which were very convenient, when the nurse suddenly got tired. Then Bill would help himself, to another nurse, continuing, with his much loved ballroom dancing.

If one of the patients in the ward was, eg., a corporal or sergeant, they had to display their stripes, on the end of their bed. Bill, who was superior to all others, or so he thought, didn't need to display any stripes, 'after all, he was a private', keeping himself to himself, ha.ha.

There was one corporal in their ward, for some unknown reason, no-one seemed to like him. Bill, always up to his old tricks, would wait, till he went to the toilet, then sneak over to this poor man's bed, pull back some of the bedding, and gently sprinkle sneezing powder, between the sheets, and on the pillowcase. The corporal, couldn't reprimand Bill, for sneezing.

Before going into the army, Bill told his parents, that the next time they saw him, he would have stripes, he did, but not on his arm.

Bill was put off, as soon as he joined the army, when he noticed, that when asked whether he wanted tea, coffee or cocoa, to his amazement, it all came out of the same pot, and he was already suffering with diarrhoea (talk about running).

Reminds Bill of the story he heard at that time, of a soldier, who, no matter where he was, whether on guard, or on the firing range, whenever he saw a piece of paper, he would drop whatever he was doing, and run after it. He was the laughing stock of the platoon. However, the last laugh was on his mates, those who would have given anything to get out of the service. The one who kept chasing the paper, went to the rest of them, explaining, that the piece of paper he was now holding, was the piece he had really been chasing, it was his discharge paper.

Bill's was a very big Mess. Each morning, an officer would walk up and down, repeating, 'any complaints, any complaints'. Apparently, the one wishing to make a complaint, had to sit at the end of the long table, but no one, had the nerve to stand up and complain, they weren't getting enough. They thought, the one making the complaint, would be put on a charge. Looking at it from a commonsense point of view, Bill thought, it would be stupid, putting one on a charge, just because he'd made a complaint. Bill, always wanting to find out for himself, asked if he could sit on the end the following morning. He did. Next morning, as usual, 'any complaints, any complaints'. Smartly standing up, which wasn't very noticeable for Bill. He quickly answered the officer, 'Yes sir'. He said, 'What's the complaint?' Bill replied, 'It's not half enough'. The officer's immediate response was, to take their plates around again, for another full helping. Interesting to note, all those that had laughed at Bill, because of his intention, gladly went around again, and had another full helping.

Next day, now that they had more nerve, 'Jam Face', who was named such because, he always pinched all the jam, decided, he would make a complaint. He did. The officer enquired, 'What's the problem?' Jam Face replied, that the porridge tasted soapy. 'Do you mind?', asked the officer, 'if I taste a little'. 'No sir'. To cut a long story short, he was put on charge, for making a frivolous complaint.

When Bill joined the Royal Corps of Signals, knowing of his vast driving experience, and having taught his Father to drive when he was going to school (he left school at 14 yrs), the army put him down, as a driving instructor, and so, after a few days in the army, the sergeant shouted, 'Anyone able to drive, fall out'. Of course, several of these new recruits did, only to be told, to take the shovels, and fill the lorry with all the rubbish.

That was the first and last time, Bill volunteered, to this day.

Unfortunately, he was invalided out of the army, which is when Bill continued with his taxi work. More about his taxi work later.

## Caught in the Blitz

Bill, back in Plymouth, but not out of trouble from the raging war, he's the only one alive, out of 16, that were in an air raid shelter, that had a direct hit. Ballards Institute which housed many soldiers, was situated opposite the large shelter.

That fateful evening of the bombing, Bill, his girlfriend, and another friend were together in a cinema. The film was stopped, whilst the warning came on the screen, bombing was in progress. Incendiary bombs were raining on Plymouth, it wasn't long before the cinema caught fire, with bombs coming through the roof.

The trio running from the cinema, couldn't believe their eyes, there before them was the awesome sight, the whole of the City of Plymouth was flattened and in a blaze of fire.

Bill, quickly thinking of somewhere safe for them to take refuge from the German war planes, buzzing just above them, directed his friends to the garage, underneath the Ballards Institute, Bill, thinking to himself, that the walls being at least 4 feet thick, would give them a safe haven.

It wasn't long before Ballards caught fire. Bill and the other two, started running for the shelter, dropping flat on the ground, each time they heard the whistling of a bomb, remembering to keep their chins off the road, otherwise, the sheer vibration could knock one out.

I am sure, Bill will never forget that day of the Blitz, for it was also the very day, Bill, who had been on a 10 day tour to Devon and Cornwall, with the King and Queen, returned to Plymouth. Bill was usually driving the second car, behind the Royals.

When in the relative safety of the shelter, Bill kept telling his girlfriend, and the other friend, to keep praying to God. Bill kept repeating, don't stop, as God wont allow you to be killed, whilst holding a conversation with him. That shelter, suddenly had a direct hit, and that little trio were the only ones alive, out of 16.

Bill was the worst of the three, having had his right shoe blown off, his moustache, all his hair, and some of his clothes burnt off. Both his hands were terribly burnt.

An ambulance, driven by a WRAC, was on its' way to collect Bill, when it was blown in halves. That brave woman driver, calmly collected another ambulance, which eventually took Bill to Stoke Damerel Emergency Hospital.

That night, Bill's mother had a premonition, that Bill had been injured. She spent the whole of the next day (having come in from their estate at Honnicombe House, Gunnislake, a good 18 miles away), going to every hospital in Plymouth. She eventually found Bill under a bed in Stoke Damerel Hospital. Yes "under the bed", because by now, he had lost his nerve.

Following day, a special hospital train for the wounded, made its' way to Birmingham, though not allowed to go into the station, because of keeping the public moral up. Instead, many coaches met the train, in a siding. The most serious cases, such as Bill's, ambulances were provided.

They were all taken to a hospital, next to the Austin Motor Works, "above all places". Several days passed, before Bill remembered his dear mother had found him under the bed at Stoke Damerel.

After some days, of laying in agonising pain in bed, Bill managed to just lift himself up enough in bed, to see his face in a mirror. It was the shock of his life. Worse was to come. A doctor came to Bill and said, quote, 'I am sorry old chap, but we are going to have to take your foot off'.

Bill just didn't know what to do, he was so shocked, on top of which, he'd lost his nerve, and going through his head all the time was, how badly placed the hospital was, next to those motor works, a prime target for a German bomb. Under the horrific circumstances, it was more than enough to send one insane. On top of which, night after night, jumping incendiary bombs etc., were attacking all around him, poor Bill had had enough. He used to pull the bedding over his head, which made it so terribly hot.

After another of those terrible bombing nights, Bill, injured, and burnt as he was, tried desperately to make an arrangement to return home to the peace and quiet of, their beautiful country mansion house, that had been the estate of the late Ernestine MountEdgecombe. This is where Bill was hoping he would be able relax, and recuperate from his ordeal, far away from any bombing raids. However, it wasn't possible to hire a taxi, to go all that way to his home at Gunnislake, infact, he couldn't even get a taxi to the station, until at last, a sympathetic nurse, realising how desperate Bill needed to get home, volunteered to take out the passenger seat of her little Morris eight, and take him to the station.

As well as his badly crushed foot, he'd broken his leg as well, and could only keep it out stiff in plaster. To be able to do this, he had to sit on a crutch. When they arrived at the train station, it was only to find, due to the bombing, it was closed. Bill couldn't believe his bad luck, but undeterred, the nurse very kindly took him to another station.

That nurse, looked high and low, for someone going to Plymouth, to keep Bill company, and look after him, for really, he was too badly injured to travel. At last, she found a young man going to Exeter, not bad, 44 miles from Plymouth. Thankfully, the young man, agreed to sit with Bill in the empty compartment of the carriage. Handing Bill a jam jar, to enable him to urinate, the kindly nurse wished Bill a good journey and full recovery.

Bill was terrified on that train journey home. True to say, the only time he wasn't worried, was when the train was going through tunnels.

The girlfriend, who had been with Bill in the shelter, died at the estate. Having lost her father, who himself had a direct hit, her cause of death was given as, quinsy and double shock.

What was so surprising was the fact, that Bill's other friend Jack, who had survived the direct hit, when the three of them were in the air raid shelter, had told Bill, to stop moaning, saying he had broken his leg, which of course, Bill naturally thought was true. Infact, when Bill arrived at North Road Station, on what Bill thinks, was the midnight train, he was met by, none other than his friend, Jack Chapman, now the late Jack Chapman.

Well, at least Bill was home at last, to recover from his injuries, and soon to commence business in earnest, with no more interruptions.

# 2
# Whose Car is it, Anyway?

Bill was madly infatuated by cars from a very young age. In fact he cannot recall a time when he wasn't! He was only ten years old when he first started to spend all of his spare time, weekends and school holidays, at Steve Dyers Garage in St. Budeaux. The garage had a fleet of cars and hearses which were hired out to funeral directors. This type of business was known as, 'carriage-masters'. Often, in those days, a funeral director did not own cars or a hearse, but would hire them as and when required. It was from these early experiences, that Bill not only developed his love for cars, but also grew towards his career in funeral directing. Some Sunday mornings Bill would ride in the hearse when there was to be a funeral in Torpoint, or Saltash. He would travel all the way to the house, alight and then start walking back towards the ferry. He would then be picked up by the hearse when it was making the return journey and he would be given a ride back to the garage in St. Budeaux.

Bill really was infatuated by cars. At a young age he could tell the make of car approaching just by the sound of its engine. He spent many hours admiring cars and learning about them. Before he left school, at the age of fourteen, he taught his father to drive the Clyno car his father owned, as he, had already learned to drive a car regularly on a farm, with competence.

**Taxi Business**

It only seemed natural, when Bill was discharged from the Royal Cor of Signals, to start running a taxi business. It was still wartime, he had as many as 16 cars at one time.

Bill had a good grounding in the vehicle business, after spending much of his childhood, helping out at Dyers Garage, now he was going to put all he'd learnt into practice.

The drivers would meet at The Toc H, for tea and talk over the day's events. Because of the shortage of glasses, he fondly remembers drinking out of jam jars.

Bill in the beginning

Keeping all those men on the road, and making sure they were honest. Bill said to them, 'Look, I'm working, just like you are, I know how much money I take, therefore, your takings should be about the same as mine', it worked.

During those days, the cars were only allowed to travel within a small radius. At night with the black covers on the headlamps, it was hard to see. Plymouth, with its' strong connection with the navy, army, marines and the air-force, had a vibrant night life, especially with the Americans in town as well. Bill ran a very successful business.

He remembers, amongst many funny experiences back at that time. A black, American soldier, asked if Bill could take him to his barracks at Totnes, 25 miles away. Taxis were only allowed a 10 mile radius, never-theless, business was business, so he took his paying passenger. There was also a young lady, that wanted to go back to her home within Plymouth, but was happy to go to Totnes first. Bill, always with an eye for beautiful ladies, asked if she would like to sit in the front, rather than in the back with a stranger. She gladly accepted, squeezing between Bill, and one of

21

his driver's, Claud, whose car was off the road. As often happened in those days. A driver would go for a ride with Bill for the fun of it.

Eventfully reaching Totnes, Bill looking up a one way street, leading to the top of the town, asked the American, "Where's your camp?" "Up the top of this road, buddy". Bill not knowing of another way, took a quick look around, seeing all was clear, quickly put his powerful car into gear, and raced up the street.

When he reached the top, he thought, at last I've made it. Now all he needed was his money, and a quick run back to Plymouth. But it wasn't going to be that easy.

The soldier jumped out, saying, "I'm just going in the camp, to get the money to pay the fare". Bill waited, but he didn't return.

The sentry, asked what was Bill hanging around for. On hearing what happened, Bill unable to describe what his fare looked like, the sentry and other soldiers that had gathered around by now, felt sorry for Bill. He ended up with chocolate, corned beef, beans, cigarettes, silk stockings and all the other goodies, that only the Americans had at that time.

Bill might not have been paid in cash, but he'd certainly made up with it in kind. He finally dropped the young lady passenger home, who'd also received many gifts, plus many admiring looks from the soldiers.

Bill was kept very busy making runs to Convent Garden, at £50 a trip, paid in advance (a small fortune in those days), selling locally grown daffodils, returning full up with other goodies, needed at home. Taxis were only allowed a 10 mile radius, hence the incentive of being paid in advance. The flowers were stuffed in the luggage boot, almost as if they had been stood on, but all that was necessary on arrival, was to put aspirins in the water, they came up, to coin a phrase, 'as fresh as a daisy'.

In those days, people travelling to London, would stuff flowers in violin cases, suitcases etc., as they were worth so much in the City.

The flowers came from the famous growing area of, The Tamar Valley. Bill's trips were a tremendous help to the many growers.

Never missing an opportunity, Bill, 'turning all adversities to your own advantage', had an old disused hearse. In the glass part, he grew the most wonderful crop of tomatoes, which sold at a good price. A greenhouse with a difference!! He used this unique 'greenhouse', until he eventually sold the vehicle for scrap.

**Taxi Service to Whitsands**

Due to petrol rationing during the war, people, unable to run their cars, would holiday at nearby Whitsands chalets. Bill using another motto of his, 'not leaving a stone unturned', placed continuous adverts, which read, "Whitsands, Bovisands, or any other sands, why hire a 4 seater, when you can hire one of Earl of Plymouth's 7 seaters, with all your luggage, for the same price".

Bill built up such a business, he was able to take one family over on eg., the 4p.m. Torpoint ferry, then pick up another family, he had taken over the previous week, and bring them back on the 5.30 ferry. In other words, Bill was one of the original people to introduce the motto, 'two for the price of one', to Bill's advantage. People paid £1 10s each way, so Bill's journey paid him £3, unlike taxi firms, who had an empty cab one way, and therefore, only earnt £1 10s.

Bearing in mind, Bill was only in his early twenties at this time, he was already making his name, as a hard working astute business man.

## Buying Rolls Royces

Bill's advancement in business was so rapid, it's almost unheard of, especially as he had started from absolutely nothing.

From a little boy, right through his life, though one of five children, Bill was always the one with money, due to nothing more than sheer hard work, and the determination to succeed.

Every decision made, was wholly and solely by himself, knowing, if he made the wrong move, whether mechanical or otherwise, he would have been the one to foot the bill.

To save wasting time of often having to go to London to view a Rolls Royce, he would arrange to see many, on the same day, eg., one every hour, but always at Paddington Station, then, should he not make a purchase, he'd hop on a train, and it was, home again.

It must be remembered, Bill was dealing with, thousands and thousands of pounds, with nobody, eg., a mechanic, to help or advise him. One false move could have been disastrous.

One instance, Bill will never forget, was being met early one morning at Paddington, by a smartly dressed chauffeur, gloves, hat, britches, the lot, and like the Rolls Royce Sedanka-da-Ville (not sure of the spelling), which was an absolutely shinning example of this prestigiously outstanding, gleaming, Rolls Royce. However, Bill conscious of the fact, 'all that glistens is not gold', would have bought it on its' glistening face value. He decided to leave it to his better judgement, insisting he went for a trial run. The problem was, finding a quiet spot in London, to enable him to listen to the engine. Having found one, he immediately realised, the engine was running a little faster than normal tick over. Bill asked the chauffeur, for a screwdriver. He didn't have one. Never one to be beaten, Bill replied, it didn't matter, he could manage without it. Taking a sixpenny piece out of his pocket, he used same to slow down the engine, enabling Bill to ascertain, that the small ends were knocking. Bill was cute enough, not to tell

Cars, cars

and more cars. *Photo courtesy of Evening Herald*

the chauffeur, until after he drove him back to Paddington, where he was met by another chauffeur for the same purpose, meaning, to test drive another Rolls Royce. Infact, he had five test drives that day, and eventually ended up purchasing three of them.

## Bill Becomes a Carriage Master

Bill having so many cars, and with his past experience with his old friend, Steve Dyer naturally progressed to become a carriage master supplying funeral directors with their cars, this was another business opportunity he could see opening up. In the early days, there were over 100 funeral directors in Plymouth, known as 'builders & undertakers', who knew little more, than simply putting a body in the coffin. Bill used to say, one minute they were sticking somebody's chimney up, next minute, laying someone's loved one out.

## Extending garage under lady's garden

Extending his fleet, Bill purchased the longest Rolls Royce, he had ever seen. With his enterprising brain, he could see plenty of potential for this special vehicle. He had it stripped down, and custom built, to his own design, for dual purpose. One minute it was a gleaming Rolls Royce hearse, next, an outstanding beautiful Rolls Royce limousine for the bride. In effect, he purchased two very valuable vehicles, for the price of one, with an added advantage, whenever he came to sell it, he'd have two completely diverse markets for prospective buyers, he could sell it either as a hearse, or Rolls Royce limousine.

As a hearse, this gleaming vehicle, would be seen with a cross on the radiator, removable roof rail for the flowers, and a coffin in the rear. After the funeral, there was a 5 minute transformation, the same vehicle would be seen leaving the garage, minus roof rail and silver cross on radiator, which had now been replaced with the Rolls Royce Lady, flowing white satin ribbons. The interior boasted, finely upholstered seats in luxurious cream leather, deep pile red carpet, and all the bridal trimmings, one had come to expect from Bill's highly respected firm.

There was one draw back, with this long sleek beauty, or should we say, two. The garage was too short for the car, or the car was too long for the garage, if you see what I mean.

However, as the well known saying goes; 'No need to fear, Billy's here'. Immediately turning 'all adversities to his advantage', he'd thought of a wonderful idea.

Those who know the area in Plymouth, of "Ker Street, Devonport", will know of the large, mansion type houses, with their very long gardens. Bill's garage, was at the end of one of these gardens, in the next street, called Mount Street. There, proudly sat Bill's garage, with a workshop up over, the floor of which, was at the same level as the long garden it backed on to.

His inventive idea, was to lengthen his garage, by burrowing up under the garden. Brilliant thought Bill, problem solved.

One of Bill's many fleets of cars

With a light hearted swing in his step, off went Bill to Noyces, the scrap metal works, on Plymouth's Barbican, where he purchased iron girders, to reinforce the garage extension, under the garden.

Bill, with Brian, his trusty employee, enthusiastically started digging a big hole in the back wall of the garage, and under the unsuspecting lady's garden. Things were going really well, Bill wondering, why he hadn't thought of this before, the first girder slide into place effortlessly. However, this happy state of affairs, was not to last.

It started raining 'cats and dogs', day after day, as the saying goes. This was the beginning of the 'downfall' of Bill's extended garage.

With the girder in place, next job was to slide in some corrugated iron, but with all the rain, the bigger the hole in the wall was getting. Bill was frantically using more and more corrugated iron sheets. He'd already used up the ones he'd purchased, and was now using corrugated sheets from a condemned house, next door. Each time they needed more sheets, Brian climbed out of the roof window, in the workshop, quickly collected them, and ran back. Well, with the torrential rain, continually pouring down, the earth running out of the hole, which was getting bigger and bigger, Bill wondered where and when his garage extension would end.

Brian was going out of the roof, again, again and again, however this time was different. He came back with his usual sheets of iron, wearing a big wide grin on his face, saying, 'That woman's chicken run's got a bloody great pit in it'.

'Yes', said Bill, 'And by the look of things, the B. fowls will soon be down here as well. I've already found a couple of eggs'.

But for the rain, Bill's underground garage extension, would have been very successful. They estimated, they could have had an extension, 50 ft long at least, without anyone being wiser, including the owner of the house.

Next job for the intrepid pair, was to try to do the impossible, fit all the stones etc., back from whence they came. Infact, as readers know, this can't be done. Bill had so many stones etc., left over, to say nothing of the feathers and eggs. He had to hire a lorry, to take it away.

Eventually, the garage, and garden were back to normal. As Bill said, the project only failed through an act of God, but he still had the problem of getting his long Rolls Royce in the garage, what could he do?

Don't worry, not one to give up, Bill's mind was already at work, and another decision made. They removed the enormous garage doors, together with the large, heavy door jams, and posts etc., repositioned them on the outside wall of the garage, and in effect, extended the garage, out into the street.

Walking on the pavement, and reaching Bill's garage, one had to step out, to pass the building, especially if pushing a pram.

Not to be deterred, and wanting to make his workmanship look less obvious, Bill carefully positioned troughs of pretty flowers around the posts. What a character!

## Built a Hearse

Bill badly wanted another hearse, but it was during the 2nd World War, cars, and even parts, were hard to get hold of. Not one to be beaten, Bill sat down and designed a hearse, then went ahead, having it built in his spare time, and at night in his own garage, using the labour of "body builders" (excuse the pun), from Milehouse Corporation Bus Depot. It was a large Humber Snipe, used to carry the firemen, and towed an ARP trailer pump during air raids for the fire service.

They dismantled the large sheet metal van body, Bill with his keen mind, full of ideas, reused the sheet metal in the building of his embalming mortuary. This way, not only did he have a new hearse, but had the satisfaction, nothing was wasted, with the added advantage of a new mortuary as well, the first in Plymouth. You could say, two deals for the price of one.

## Bill Becomes A Funeral Director

Bill becoming so involved with these undertakers, he decided, this wasn't good enough, he was going to change the way funerals were carried out. Having travelled the world, particularly USA, he took a leaf from their book, and decided to study, passed his exams, becoming a qualified embalmer, the first in Devon & Cornwall.

27

Bill says, the funeral business is one of the hardest to get into, especially, as he started from nothing, never borrowing a penny in his life. Most funeral directors, had their business passed on down through the generations, with a loyal clientele. As Bill often remarks, don't think one can put a sign up, and expect business to come in, it isn't like that.

### Private Ambulance

Ahead of time in another aspect. He was first to have a cream private ambulance, marked as such, for removing persons from hospitals and nursing homes etc., rather than the usual hearse or black van, suggesting death. This way, old people didn't know whether he was taking someone for massage or some other reason, which didn't upset patients living in various nursing homes. A thoughtful kind way in which Bill kept striving ahead.

### Crossing Saltash Ferry

What a magnificent sight it was, seven black Rolls Royce limousines and a Rolls Royce hearse all in line, driving slowly along the road. It was also a sight tinged with a little sadness for the poor departed occupant. Earl of Plymouth funeral service was sure to turn heads wherever they went, and in those days, the mid 50's through the 60's, the business was touching all parts of Plymouth and spreading its fingers into Cornwall.

Bills fleet coming off the Saltash Ferry

It was a regular event for the team to have to drive across the ferry to Saltash for a funeral. Bill Earl was the only person ever to drive 8 Rolls Royces, including the hearse, onto the Saltash ferry, which, with 8 such large vehicles on board, the ferry appeared quite small. Whenever Bill and his team of drivers approached the ferry with a coffin in the hearse they were immediately beckoned to the front of the queue. Thus avoiding an embarrassing delay for the cortege, or any additional discomfort for the other drivers in the queues.

Driving into Saltash from Devonport, where the Earl of Plymouth chapels were situated, was easy because there was always a coffin in the hearse. However, to return to Plymouth from the funeral was a different matter. Queues could delay drivers for hours, time which with a growing business, Bill could ill afford. Eight drivers and their vehicles, plus additional staff, depending on the size of the funeral, sitting idly in a queue of traffic was no way to run a business!

Quick-thinking Bill only allowed the queues to delay his Rolls Royces once. After that he always carried an empty coffin in the bottom of the hearse. When the funeral was over, and before his cars returned to the Saltash side of the ferry crossing for the journey back to base, the empty coffin was raised into position and the awesome procession of seven limousines and a hearse looked, for all intents and purposes, as if it was a cortege heading for another funeral service. This time, in Saltash, the ferrymen beckoned the team of drivers to the front of the queue. Thus each time they returned from Saltash they avoided any delays.

Bill still smiles to himself these days remembering that little scam, and also with some pride when recalling the sight of such a magnificent fleet.

## Grey Cars

At one time, thinking of ways to make funerals a little less sombre, Bill decided to have the whole of his large fleet of limousines, painted grey. This was a serious decision and a gamble for its' success, bearing in mind, all other funeral director's vehicles, at that time, throughout the whole of Britain, were black He did this, by taking them all off the road, and in the meantime, he hired a hearse and cars. It really was a brave risk to take. Bill lost sleep, turning over and over in his bed, not knowing how the new look would be accepted by the public, until one day, he said to himself, well, if it's no good, I'll have them all done black again.

He never forgot the first funeral he carried out, it was from a house, high up, on a mountain of steps. Arriving on the morning of the funeral, with all his grey fleet, Bill gingerly walked up the steps, with much trepidation, and rang the door bell. A lady answered, and at the same time, looked down the steep steps, and to Bill's amazement and sheer delight, she gasped, 'oh, what a delight, how much nicer than seeing the drab black cars'. Her remark made Bill's day, and he's never looked back since that time.

It quickly spread throughout the city, that the Earl of Plymouth has a brand new fleet of vehicles, like no other funeral concern. It seemed, that almost before one could say Jack Robinson, everybody in the town knew about it. When the Evening Herald reporters got hold of the story, they immediately telephoned Bill to ask the question, 'Why grey?' Bill, with his well known quick witted responses, simply replied, by asking the reporters, 'Why black?' To which they replied, "Because it's a sign of mourning", when Bill quipped, "Tell me, where in the Bible does one see black for mourning?", adding, "There's only one reference I know referring to mourning, and that's white, which was a sign of rejoicing, for the one who had gone to a better place".

What an answer, but Bill had certainly stood his ground. Where he went, many followed, as they have. Funeral fleets today can be seen in many variations on the morbid 'black'.

## Cars & Number Plates

In the interest of those Bill served, always ahead of his time, he had a very distinguished looking sign, 3 ft in length, reading 'Funeral', on the front of the hearse. On each end of the sign was a subdued maroon flashing light, making sure all cars in the funeral cortege were not split by inconsiderate drivers, Bill also had many magnetic signs, one for the bonnet of every car, including private cars attending the funeral. These magnetic signs were simply, solid blue metallic flags, on a short pole that moved according to wind direction, having 'Funeral' printed on both sides.

In addition to this, all vehicles drove with dipped headlights. After the funeral, it was Brian's responsibility to collect all flags, and check headlights were switched off.

To further implement his scheme, Bill had a simple, short indiscreet advert in the local newspaper, reading, 'Headlights on Funerals', we do this because breaking up a funeral cortege causes distress. Earl of Plymouth.

Bill always remembers, a car ran into a Co-op funeral cortege, on Mutley Plain. First thing the police remarked was, had you had your lights on, like Earl of Plymouth, this wouldn't have happened.

Bill, continued to make the most of his name, instead of spending thousands of pounds for private number plates, each of his cars, simply bore the name, 'Earl of Plymouth', on the number plates, of each car. The Western Evening Herald often commented on various remarks made by readers, eg., a family of children running into their home, shouting, daddy,

daddy, quick, the Earl of Plymouth is driving up the road, come, see all his smashing cars. (Talk about me, good if you can, bad if you must, but talk about me.) That's Bill's motto, and it worked.

## Various Fleets During His Lifetime

Bill had many fleets of cars during his lifetime. He had large fleets of American Packhards, Cadilacs, Galaxies, Ambassadors and a fleet of

Funeral just after the war

More of Bills fleet of cars

More cars ...

and more cars

eight Rolls Royce limousines, including a Rolls Phantom, purchased from Lord Mildmay. The fleets of 7.5 litre American Galaxy limousines, and a whole fleet of American Ambassadors were purchased from American Motor Corporation, all with consecutive numbers. In each case, he purchased them through Canada, that way, he saved a lot of tax. That old business brain of his was always ticking over, like the cars!

32

Two of the American 'Silver Fox' fleet

Having continually advertised his fleet of Rolls Royce limousines for brides, what was he going to say now, that he also has so many American cars. It could so easily have appeared like contradiction. So, he then also advertised, 'Brides be different, go American'. That way, Bill completely covered all and each of his three fleets.

Imagine the publicity, surprise and pride caused to Bill and his staff when reading the following in a local newspaper, "One day the outstanding fleet was seen going up the road, each with "Earl of Plymouth" on its number plate. Many people had contacted The Evening Herald, reporting, they'd seen Earl of Plymouth in the city, and what stylish cars he owned.

That's Bill's many cars covered, now to Bill's outstanding businesses.

# 3
# Getting Down to Business

**Some of the Businesses Bill Successfully Started From Scratch**

It's true to say, every business Bill started, was from scratch, with shear determination and hard work. Bill proved for himself, the longer one lives, the more knowledge and experience one accumulates. There's a saying; Jack of all trades, master of none. Often, that's true, but not always, in his case, he became a master of many. Infact, the competent person is capable of becoming proficient in several walks of life, infact, the more one does, the more experience one gains.

Some of the businesses, Bill's successfully owned during his lifetime are:- Editor of his own newspaper called Devonport Gazette, Owner and founder of Earl of Plymouth Funeral Service, Founder and owner of Driving School, Partner of Ladies & Gents Hairdressing and Public Baths, his own building & decorating business, agent for Norwich Union, Earl of Plymouth General Supplies save pounds pounds pounds (selling eg., lawn mowers, refrigerators), made to measure suits & off the peg, Taxi business, said to have had the largest wedding car business in Britain (27 weddings on a Saturday), Writer & Critic, coffin maker, qualified embalmer, florist, instigated The Double Value Funeral Bonds, etc.

**A World Renowned Funeral Director**

Bill Earl's had such a vast experience and enthusiasm, that I, the writer, hardly know where to start. He spent so much of his long life studying and learning all he could, in the sole interest of those he served. He studied the different religions and burial customs, all over the world, with one aim, to increase his knowledge, thus giving a better service to the bereaved. Having been around the world 5 times, he told me, he was glad to unwind.

He studied, by staying and living in Sri Lanka, all Scandinavian countries, Italy, Japan, New Zealand, Australia, China, Hong Kong, Singapore, Canada (Toronto & Ottawa), Malta, Spain, Africa, Germany, Gibraltar, India, Thailand, Greece, Cyprus, Turkey, USA, you name it, he's been there, all for practical and educational experiences, in the sole interest of those he served. This is what contributed in making him such a progressive businessman, always ahead of his time. Where he went, others followed, often, many years later. Example, Bill trying to lift the sombre feeling of funerals, was 1st to have an all grey fleet of hearses and cars. 1st to have a private ambulance. 1st to employ a qualified florist, who taught Bill's staff the art of making floral wreaths etc. 1st, thanks to Bill's son, to have their own monumental masons department. 1st to have a Rolls Royce fleet of hearses and limousines. 1st, and the only firm in the world to have funeral bonds, that doubled their value immediately, eg., £500 bond immediately doubled its' value to £1,000. 1st to have their own consecrated funeral chapels, for holding funeral services.

To say least, Bill had such a wealth of business experiences, that I, the writer, know of no-one to compare.

He was honoured to have led several processions, in the name of Earl of Plymouth, England. Example, he led The Memorial Day Procession in USA, the Centenary Fire Service Procession in Lambertville, USA, etc., wherein during his speech, he thanked them for the honour bestowed upon Earl of Plymouth, England, saying what a pleasure it was, adding, after all, one cannot do too many of these in a lifetime, can one? Bill also did similar for OFSA (Ontario Funeral Service Association), Canada.

**Bill, The Business Child**

Bill always had a business brain. Even when quite young he was thinking of how to make money. He kept homing pigeons and, from time to time, would sell a few to his school friends, who would take their new prized homing pigeons home, but were careless, in not keeping them in long enough to establish a sense of their 'change of address'. They would then release them, only to return home to Bill. He was quick to learn these pigeons were a regular source of income as he could sell the same one many times and his school friends were none the wiser, just thinking that they had been careless in losing their newly acquired pigeons.

Also whilst Bill was still at school he would play marbles in his playtimes. He not only enjoyed the game, but it provided him with a thriving little business. Imagine the scene in a grassy schoolyard in St. Budeaux, Plymouth in the early 1930's. A number of young schoolboys crowded into one corner of the playground; usually a bare patch. All had their long shorts stretched tight against their legs as they crouched to watch. Most would have their white shirts hanging out at the back. The rules were simple; draw a circle and mark the centre, where everyone placed their marbles. Each player would then take turns to roll another marble at the circle. The marbles knocked out of the circle were theirs to keep, those remaining were fair game for the next player. The game was about to commence, as all the boys taking part had placed their marbles in the circle. Then came the decision as to who would start. "I'll go first," shouted Bill, as he did every time. The other boys watched in amazement as Bill rolled his marble towards the congested circle. He could not miss, there were so many marbles in the circle. Seven, eight, nine, or more, flew out of the circle and ended up in Bill's pockets.

Incredibly Bill was permitted to go first game after game and his winnings grew and grew. When the other boys ran short of marbles, but wanted to continue playing, Bill was there with a supply for sale. This continued for a number of years and supplied Bill with a regular, albeit small income, and, more importantly provided him with some more experience and knowledge in the field of business.

Yet Bill, even as a little boy, was always so kind and generous, as he is to this day.

## Bill Started From Nothing, How Did He Do It?

"I don't know of one funeral director, that started from nothing".

"I do, it was Bill Earl, and he told me how he did it." He knew that putting a brass plate on his house, engraved, 'Funeral Director', would have no affect, it could stay there forever, without one result. Bill put his thinking cap on, realising, to become recognised, one must be seen doing funerals. It was Builders and Undertakers, that did the funerals then as a side line, perhaps, only 4 or 5 a year, that's how they started, and how they remained, never specialising. Consequently, whatever state the body was in, that's how it remained, and was simply placed in the coffin, in its' same state. The Undertaker, saying to the family, "if he or she begins to 'turn', let me know, and I'll fasten the cover down". That's because, the deceased was usually kept in the house until day of funeral.

Many old folk will remember, that often, through the body not having had professional treatment, or refrigeration, it would burst, due to the internal organs putrefying and decaying, thus generating an unpleasant gas, hence the smells associated with dead bodies. Then, the common procedure was, for the undertaker to pour a full sack of sawdust in the coffin with the deceased, and fasten the cover, which only hid what was still taking place, not hygienic, you will agree. For the same reason, meaning, seeping body fluids, the interior of coffins were always sealed in the making, with boiling hot pitch, which was made to run around and seal the joints between the bottom and sides of the coffin, still done today. However, if disposal is to be by cremation, the law is, as pitch gives off too much black smoke from the cremator, it must not be used, instead a sealing paste is utilised. Though Bill's firm made all their own coffins, except for a very few, it's true to say, most funeral directors today, don't make coffins or with respect, even know how. Interestingly enough, as far as Bill was concerned, having always professionally treated the body, he never needed to seal the coffins at all, he was determined none of the unpleasant happenings, described above would occur with him.

Bill was different, he wanted to specialise, making it his profession. He would say to the family, after having given the deceased a simple treatment on the bed, somewhat like giving a blood transfusion (embalming), "he or she wont 'turn' now, as far as I am concerned, those old fashion days are gone". Though Bill didn't mention it, he was infact, the first qualified embalmer (MBES and later MBIE), in Devon and Cornwall.

To make himself recognised, he obtained the contract for Paupers funerals. Bill, embalming all the bodies for the paupers funerals for nothing, thus gaining experience. I know Bill kept a book, not showing how much profit he made, on the contrary, it showed how much he lost, but he looked at it as the price of the advertisement it had given him. From then on, he obtained other contracts eg., Royal Air force, Prison contracts etc., and with the excellence of his work, rapidly made his name, a household one. Consequently, everybody knew of Earl of Plymouth. Infact, his postal address was simply, 'Earl of Plymouth, England'.

## What's In A Name

Bill used his name to great advantage for his business. Perhaps, in some small way, it's been useful to others, if only for the fact, it's easy to remember.

Bill, never one to give in, his accountant informed him, the law insists, business names must be registered, and asked Bill for the name. 'Earl of Plymouth', Bill replied. The accountant said, they wont accept that. "You're a defeatist", retorted Bill, "You haven't even tried yet. Please do as I've instructed".

Through Bill's insistence, his firm is known and registered as, 'Earl of Plymouth, England'. Consequently, being well known all over the world, his mail arrives from the four corners of the Earth, simply addressed, 'Earl of Plymouth, England'.

An amusing happening came from The Earl of Plymouth, whose first name is, would you believe it, 'Other'. He complained, he'd received a full kit of a serviceman, who had died.

'Other' Earl argued that Bill should alter his name, to which Bill replied, that he didn't have his name thrown at him, he was born with it, the same as his father. It could be said, Bill was, Earl of Plymouth, whereas he was only the 'Other' Earl.

MIRROR, Wednesday, July 28, 1993

## END OF THE PEERS SHOW

*THE Mirror is campaigning to get hereditary peers kicked out of the House of Lords.*
*Their presence in Parliament is undemocratic and they are not suitable people to run our lives. Each day we will introduce you to one of them. Here is the latest living dinosaur.*

# EARL OF PLYMOUTH

### By NIC NORTH

**HAVE pity on the third Earl of Plymouth – he moaned in 1985 that it cost him £40,000 a year to live in his stately home.**

"And that's not in a very grand way," the toff complained.

Still, home is magnificent Oakly Park, near Ludlow, Shropshire, rather than a two-up two-down semi.

A year earlier the Eton-educated aristocrat embarked on one of his biggest crusades – to ban a Devon undertaker from taking his name in vain.

The cheeky Plymouth-based funeral director, Bill Earl, called his company Earl of Plymouth Funeral Services.

CRUSADE: The Earl

### Killed

He claimed his firm was "chosen funeral directors to Her Majesty's Services".

The **REAL** Earl of Plymouth, 69, who is married with four children, claimed that as a result, the kitbag of a serviceman killed in the Far East had once been sent to his Knightsbridge flat. "It was simply addressed to the Earl of Plymouth, England," he said.

"My family were most upset."

For reasons not laid down on record, the Earl of Plymouth's first name is Other. His others include Ivor and Windsor-Clive.

Motto: I Trust In God.

Courtesy of *The Daily Mirror*

Newspaper cutting about the 'other' Earl

Bill had solicitors letters, saying, the Other Earl would agree to Bill's suggestion, of either, putting a coma after The, Earl of Plymouth, or put a bracket, (Earl) of Plymouth, either way, was of no disadvantage to Bill.

Bill decided to oblige, providing, he allowed Bill a sum of money to allow him to alter all his advertising. The Other Earl's solicitor, offered Bill either £10, or £12, he forgets which.

Bill immediately wrote back, saying, the ridiculously small amount of money offered, showed how unimportant the name was, telling them, he wouldn't do anything, neither coma, or bracket. The name of Bill's firm has continued to this day, and is still, as always, Earl of Plymouth, England. True to say, Bill never had any trouble with him, or anyone.

His name has opened many doors all over the world. Interesting point, attending an Ontario Funeral Service Association conference, the funeral directors said, if any of them had such an impressive name, as Earl of Plymouth, that would be a hundred dollars on the bill before starting.

Albert Road Chapel

One of the stained glass windows that Bill made

Early Chapels               Early Chapels

### Earl of Plymouth Chapels

Bill, starting from nothing, his business had a humble beginning, with his first 'little' chapel in Mount Street, where in an effort to make this little chapel look authentic, Bill employed an excellent artist to do a drawing, of a church organ, showing the pipes and keyboard etc. It looked so real, giving a Holy, churchlike atmosphere. Bill would leave the light on night times, enabling passers by to look and admire.

Even as far back as those post war days, Bill was so far seeing, trying to improve on the meagre service given by the many builders & undertakers. He did. Whereas Bill used to say, they were sticking up someone's chimney one minute, and still with a pencil in their ear, and overalls on, the next minute they were laying out someone's loved one. That was no good to Bill. He made a sincere profession of it, studying all his life, in an effort to continually improve the service he offered.

The business expanded. Young Bill was now married, living at Albert Road, Devonport, a three story terraced house, in the middle of a busy shopping area, close to the Dockyard, the main employer in Plymouth, a strategic area, always thronging with people.

41

## Early Chapels

With his eye to business, he soon started to alter the front of his home, in readiness for his expanding funeral concern, Earl of Plymouth.

For a while his wife and son lived in the same house, though it was gradually being taken over by the funeral business, until one day, there wasn't enough room for both his business and family to live in the same building. Eventually Bill moved out, as every inch of Albert Road, was converted into consecrated Chapels, where thousands of services were held.

Earl of Plymouth were, and still are possibly the Only Funeral Concern in Devon & Cornwall to hold funeral services in their own private chapels, consecrated and dedicated for that purpose, where more than one service of different denominations, can take place at the same time.

In 1988, Bill took a massive step, purchasing the freehold of approximately quarter of an acre in Wolseley Road, building probably the largest and most distinctive group of chapels in Britain. All in the same building, adjacent to a large roundabout, in the busy city of Plymouth. Some funeral director friends of Bill's from distant countries, came to visit him, and to see the Chapels.

Bill, with the help of his son, designed all the Chapels. Bill personally making each of the thirty six, 4 ft high, beautiful, stained glass windows, which emitted a rich combination of warm lighting giving a holy atmosphere. With one flick of a switch, all the windows lit up, and at the same time, the background organ music played, thus breaking the silence, for families paying their last respects. In addition there are electric organs played by professional organists, during services.

Funeral Chapels at Wolsley Road

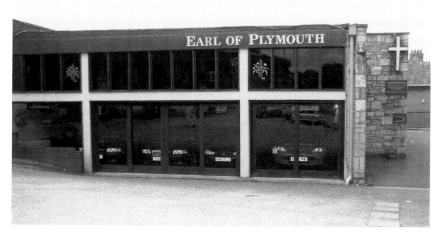

Funeral Chapels at Wolsley Road

Entering the building, one steps into a large and beautiful central hall, covered in rich red carpet, with an ever running fountain in the centre. The Italian porcelain fountain, is enhanced by a Roman lady, standing at the top of three tiered porcelain bowls, surrounded by a circular garden of pretty flowers, where one can quietly sit and compose themselves, before facing the busy world again. Leading off the central hall, are the various chapels, arranging rooms, flower room, offices, minister's changing room

Entrance Hall with Ever Running Fountain

Dedication of the new Chapels

etc., all on the same level, making it suitable for the disabled. The whole building's, centrally heated for the comfort of mourners.

Incorporated in the building is a glass showroom for his limousines, strategically placed along the side of the building, allowing the public to admire his fleet. There is a new purpose built mortuary, with every

Dedication of the new Chapels

modern device necessary, including huge refrigeration units. Still under the one roof, the rear of the building holds a very large workshop, with double doors for deliveries, not forgetting a comfortable room for the staff to relax at break time.

The building was officially opened and consecrated, on Bill's retirement in 1988, the Lord & Lady Mayoress were present, together with the Bishop of Plymouth, Reverend Peter Williamson, Circuit Methodist Minister, and Canon Bead Davis, representing the Roman Catholic Church, and several other dignitaries.

Dedication of the new Chapels

He has many treasured memories of well wishers' cards, letters and presents, received on the opening of what can only be described as, ultra modern, fully equipped Funeral Chapels, combining offices, workshop, floral department, mortuary and garage etc. One example is; 'We, your staff, thank you for your enjoyable presentation dinner, together, with the pleasant company, for the whole of the evening. We wish you all the success you deserve, after your hard work, over the years. Each of us, are as proud of "Earl of Plymouth's" fine reputation, as you must be, yourself. You must now learn to relax, but knowing you, that will be hard'.

Bill certainly achieved his life long quest by that day in 1988, having purposely built, probably the best funeral home in Britain, for the comfort of the bereaved, incorporating every little detail to fulfil his dream, and his well known advertisements, which said, 'One call, we do it all', and they certainly did.


# EMBALMING

Bill always says, the one and only reason for having a funeral, is because we have a body. That being the case, surely then, first and foremost, it's the body that should get all the attention, as already indicated, the only reason for the funeral. Example, the body could be in a solid gold coffin, but that wouldn't mean a thing, if the deceased was in a bad state.

## Embalming In London

Bill lived in London to study for his practical and theory part of embalming. Eventually, he formed a close and friendly association with the well renowned Lear Embalming Service, and also with the firm of Sir John Kenyon Funeral Service. This firm carried out the Royal Family funerals.

Bill, never one to lose an opportunity, always grasped at any possible advantage, so, when the chance came his way, he eventually did embalming for Lears, and, Sir John Kenyon's firm.

A further advantage, Bill grasped, was, instead of staying at a hotel, Bill chose to live with the family of Kenyon's head embalmer. This way, as was the case right through life with Bill, he was almost married to his chosen profession.

Bill, though successfully running his own funeral business, approached Kenyons, and asked them to let him freely give his services to Kenyons, asking them to call on Bill, from every branch of the profession, thus giving Bill, some of the most wonderful experiences possible in the funeral profession. Bill went on many millionaires' funerals whilst involved with the Kenyons.

The Lear Embalming Service, employed male and female embalmers, for the only purpose, of embalming bodies for the funeral firms, that didn't have their own embalmers. Each Lear operator, drove a van, with all their equipment for embalming. In comparison, the amount of embalming done in Devon and Cornwall, was so small, it didn't warrant them employing a full time operator, instead, all embalming was passed on to Bill, who acted for Lears, all adding to Bill's already superior experience. Bill went on many Millionaire's funerals, whilst involved with the Kenyons.

## Jews & Embalming

Jews, especially the orthodox, did not usually accept embalming, however, in many incidences, they requested same. It's the old story, give
people a choice, and they will usually chose, that which looks the best.

Bill, another JR Hartley trying to trace his lost book. *Courtesy of The
Western Evening Herald*

Bill knows of many Jewish friends, especially in USA, who choose to be embalmed, and of course, these days, they do have Jewish Funeral Homes, one of whom, presented Bill with a beautiful book, which he cherishes very much, wherein the sender in his own words, recorded, 'it was a pleasure of a visit, and a joy to compare thoughts'.

## Ancient & Modern Embalming

Many years ago, Bill wrote a book he entitled, 'Ancient & Modern Embalming'. Much has happened to Bill since then, with strokes, heart failures, and various ups and downs, that he's forgotten what he did with it, or who printed it. Though many remembered the book from all those years ago, they too can't remember the printer. The search for the book attracted local and national newspapers, and TV. Proving, most of us fall in the same category as Bill, having a bad memory.

Having had so many enquiries from those genuinely interested, writing and telephoning, wanting to know the differences with ancient and modern embalming, Bill has agreed to satisfy their quest for knowledge, though at his time of life, he can hardly be expected to re-write the complete book. However he has decided, to enclose a short resume, enough to satisfy the many questioners, but before doing so, he wishes to explain; going back in time, when refrigeration for bodies wasn't available, he realised, how very important it was, in the interest of hygiene, that each body was embalmed. Example, if you went home, finding the cat dead infront of the fire, would you leave it there? Of course you wouldn't. Well, it's no different with a human body.

This brings back awful memories to Bill, of the mortuary at old Freedom Fields Hospital, where bodies were simply placed in black boxes, with loose fitting covers. On removing the covers, all too often one would witness, a big black blow fly coming from the orifices of the body, eg., a wide open mouth, the eyes or nostrils etc., where it had already laid eggs, to shortly become maggots. Bill often remarked to the mortuary attendant, that, fly is now probably in a butcher's shop, crawling over sausages.

Most people don't realise how a fly eats. Well, next time you see one, moving parts of its' body on eg., a lump of sugar, it's worth bearing in mind, for a fly to eat; it first eats, then regurgitates, finally swallowing the soup it's made. It doesn't exactly make one's mouth water, does it?

One thing brings Bill to another, too important to leave unsaid. Something most don't realise is, no matter what one smells, eg., dog faeces or roses, a particle of it has to first enter one's nostril. This is why, Bill never believed in masking horrible smells with air fresheners, his answer is, get rid of what's causing the smell, which brings me back to 'Ancient and Modern Embalming'.

The ancient Egyptians, though well advanced in their time and age with embalming, their knowledge did not compare with the scientific knowledge we have today.

The ancient Egyptians reason for embalming, was through a superstitious, religious belief. Believing, after death, the soul went through another cycle of life, eg., as birds and various animals etc., and eventually, to take up its' old abode, and live a new life with the god of the dead, who was named, Osiris, and who they believed, lived and reigned forever. At times, they even altered the features of the deceased to copy various gods, and according to their wealth.

Their method, was to remove the organs, even cleverly removing the brain through the nostrils. Then various chemicals, herbs and spices (too many to mention), were used. The body was then wrapped, and painted with pitch like substances, eg., varnishes, bitumen, and shellacs etc., thus sealing the whole body and mummifying it. The organs, having been removed, were pickled. The whole body was then placed in a wooden container, shaped like the human body.

With modern embalming the organs are not removed. It is done for three reasons. Firstly, that the body remains in a hygienic condition, between death and disposal. Knowing the circularity system in life, pumps blood to every part of the body, the same circularity system is used, by injecting embalming fluid into an artery, pushing out the blood, which is drained from a vein. The embalming fluid, like the blood, reaches every part of the body, and has the powers of destroying all bacteria, therefore destroying that which is trying to destroy the body. Thus the body remains in a restored hygienic condition.

Obviously, if there's been a post-mortem, or a person has been in an accident, the embalming is more complicated, hence Bill's embalming exams, involved learning about the human anatomy, all very necessary, if wanting to fulfil one's profession to the highest standard possible.

Bill always added 'liquorisorib' (think it's the spelling), to the arterial fluid, which is a reddish colour, thus restoring the lifelike appearance, as in life, to the whole body. Bearing in mind, the colouring we have in our bodies, comes from the blood. Example, in life, one can look at two people, both 100% fit, yet one may have bright rosy red cheeks, whereas the other is pale. The reason being, the venules and arterioles happen to be closer to the surface on one person, than the other.

Bill realising how important this treatment was, for restoring the lifelike appearance of the deceased and also for hygienic reasons, he believed in making this service available to rich and poor alike. In other words, looking after the dead, is looking after the living.

To sum up, there are three reasons for modern embalming.

1. Hygienic reasons.
2. To restore the deceased to his or her lifelike appearance, thus lifting the burden for the bereaved, leaving them with treasured memories.
3. So that the body remains in a sanitary condition, between death and disposal. As can be seen, whether cremation or burial, makes no difference. As already explained, it's simply for between death and disposal. Modern embalming, unlike the old Egyptians method, has nothing to do with keeping a body forever. Having said that, Bill has already proved, in another part of the book, that he is able to keep bodies forever. He did it with animals.

## Embalming Greek Orthodox Priest

It was the 1950's when science and technology were still in their infancy. Films such as Frankenstein were popular. Death and dead bodies were things held in fearful respect by most people. One can only guess at the morbid fascination caused by Bill's ability to preserve dead bodies and his openness in displaying them to the medical profession, particularly in Plymouth, USA and Canada. Bill shared his fascination with another embalmer in Australia, who embalmed a Greek Orthodox priest, whose religion forbade him to be dethroned. This presented Bill with yet another experience. On this occasion the method of embalming was to secure the priest in his sitting position, on the throne, by inserting straps through his vestments, maintaining his sitting position for ever. This method of embalming was, as is known to the profession, the "six point injection system". The body, left permanently in the sitting position, had to be transported to an underground burial chamber where he remains sitting to this day. The Australian funeral director learned of Bill through the Australian media, reading of the fact that Earl of Plymouth had been entrusted with the funeral and embalming of the highly respected, late Sir Francis Chichester, the lone yachtsman, who had sailed around the world single-handed, making him famous world-wide.

## Embalming Foxes

Bill and his two close friends, Brian and Peter, from Sheepstor on Dartmoor, regularly went shooting on the moors Sunday mornings. They often "bagged" a fox or two. Bill used some of these dead creatures as subjects for him to embalm. The adult foxes were preserved in beautiful condition, with rusty red coats, big bushy tails and upright, alert ears. These were presented proudly by Bill to an inquisitive pair of doctors. They were kept in a heated greenhouse, together with other such specimens, which had been maintained in perfect condition throughout the previous summers and winters, at over 100 degrees Fahrenheit. The doctors examined the foxes carefully, and try as they may they could not remove even one bristle from their beautiful brushes. Bill used his embalming skills to such good effect that they had been preserved in a life-like state, with absolutely no deterioration to their coats and brushes. Doctors were rightly amazed and were soon followed by others, who wondered at Bill's work.

Attention grew world-wide and full page articles appeared on both sides of the Atlantic in publications of the UK and USA Institutes of Embalmers. Through one of these articles people from the Animal Rights Society traced Bill and were very vocal in their condemnation of him shooting foxes, and apparently permitting one of them to suffer in the interests of his research into methods of embalming. Bill later admitted remorse and apologised for one particular paragraph in the article used by the publications, which had referred to a fox taking as long as two minutes to die from its gunshot wounds. He had mentioned it as a scientific factor in the blood loss of the animal prior to embalming, and had not intended it to cause distress or imply he had no feelings for a suffering creature. He stated he would never do such a thing again, but that his research had proved invaluable. Both were factors in eventually appeasing the Animal Rights Society to an extent whereby he was no longer a target for their actions.

Bill's foxes were so well preserved they have been available for people to examine right up until this day. They look as lifelike as they did fifty years ago, when they were alive! Bill always explained enthusiastically, as he never ever lost his verve for any aspect of his chosen profession, to all interested parties that at no time were any of the organs or viscera removed from his animal subjects.

## Embalming Fish

Bill embalmed not only foxes during this period, when he was rapidly developing as an excellent embalmer, but many other animals as well. Bill promised a local fish and chip shop owner, George, that he would embalm a small whale to be displayed in his shop window. George was sworn to secrecy, not even to tell his own mother, as Bill did not wish to attract any detrimental attention. Prior to starting on the whale, Bill practised on a whiting. This according to Bill was a different kettle of fish altogether! He used his usual pink embalming fluid and the whiting ended up looking like a gurnett, which, of course, is reddish. George hid this unusual specimen behind an indoor, lavatory cistern and forgot about it for many years, until one day the cistern sprung a leak. The fish had been there undetected for nearly a dozen years, as there was no smell. George had completely forgotten about the fish until the plumber exclaimed loudly that he had found a pink fish, George thought it must be a "red herring". He was so amused to find this extremely well preserved whiting he took it to Bill, who examined his forgotten masterpiece, now as stiff as a poker.

Bill recalled this episode many times in later life, often telling the story in some detail. Then he would chuckle, stating he will never forget the look on George's face, when he brought the fish to him. That is that he cannot forget the look of amazement on George's face, not the poker-stiff face of the not-so whiting!

## Embalming Rabbits

Bill was thoroughly engrossed with embalming and also practised on rabbits, only chatting about these with his close, medical friends. One day he received a serious enquiry from Harold Gilbert, for the Who'd Have Thought It public house on the edge of Dartmoor, as to whether he could embalm squirrels. He wanted some to display in the bar as a curiosity feature and thought the quality of Bill's embalming made the animals much more lifelike than being stuffed by any taxidermist. Bill says Harold's peculiar request was yet another story, not yet to be told.

## Embalming a Pet Poodle

One of the most challenging, and surprising, embalmings Bill was ever requested to undertake was when the well known and highly respected accountant, Tom Spinks, asked him about his sixteen hand horse, which he was expecting to die at any time. He kept the horse in a field adjacent to his bungalow at Green Lane, Yelverton, on the edge of Dartmoor. Tom, who also happened to be a partner in a bakery, thought he was "using his loaf" when feeding the horse, day after day, with all the leftover bread, buns, etc. It was no wonder the poor animal suffered badly from the wind! One job satisfaction brings another, so Bill says, but little did he think that one day Tom would jump from his recently embalmed dog to his high horse.

Tom and his wife, Jessie, had a pet poodle for some years. It was brilliant white and had been a well loved member of their family. When it died Bill had been asked to embalm it and bury the body in Tom's and Jessie's garden. The dog's burial casket was made of solid oak, as had been requested by the Spinks. An engraved inscription plate was affixed to the casket. As the poodle had been female the casket was fittingly upholstered in crushed pink satin and silk. The casket, containing the body, was kept in the house until they eventually buried it in a grave in their garden.

The dog, which always used to bark at strangers, would regularly be ordered to lie down and shut up. But the dog had always wanted to have the last word, and therefore, even after a long interval following such an order, it would growl and give a defiant bark. Therefore the coffin name plate read, "Wow wow... wow... wow wow!"

Tom, like Bill, was a close friend of another well known Plymouth businessman, Stafford Williams, owner of the Magnet Restaurant. The three of them would often meet and talk over a meal and a drink together in the upstairs room at the Magnet. When Tom was anticipating the imminent demise of his horse he asked Bill in confidence, and in the presence of Stafford, if he would embalm his beloved horse. He had been so pleased with the result of the embalming of his pet dog that he thought it would be marvellous to be able to preserve his horse in a similar way. Bill, always "up for a challenge", accepted, but he never expected to embalm such a large animal. Bill asked Tom, in all seriousness, because he knew of Tom's inclination to do all sorts of odd things, never to take an elephant for a pet!

## Coffins to Suit All Tastes & Pockets

Occasionally, when family's are selecting a coffin or casket for their loved one, they'll look at Bill and say, 'there's no point in having anything expensive, it's only for cremation, it will only be burnt and wont be seen again'. Bill would agree, adding, "Of course if it's buried, you wont see it again either". Bill's belief was, one should have a choice for burial or cremation. Unlike years ago, when he remembers, purple cloth covered coffins were used when it was for cremation, they were often made up of cheap old wood, knowing it was all going to be covered with purple cloth. May I add this never happened to any of Bill's funerals.

In line with his quest to give the best service possible, Bill always kept a large variety of coffins and caskets in his Selection Room. Even the Co-operative Society often came to Bill, when they wanted a casket. Achieving his ultimate aim, a varied choice to the public. The selection room being very large, contained coffins & caskets, not only from England, but around the world eg., Sri Lanka, Italy, France, Spain, etc., something for every nationality. He even thought of the sadness parents feel at the loss of a child, perhaps, not wanting a dark, heavy looking coffin, all looking too depressing and even more miserable for some families. He had coffins & caskets in pink, edged with gold, for a little girl, and blue for a little boy, tastefully finished, looking more in keeping for the loss of a young one. Having many members of the public belonging to various clubs, he had a casket edged in the local football team's colours, very popular with the ardent football fan. The edging available in any colour to suit the family's requirements.

Part of the selection room

Part of the selection room

Bill always conscious of the various beliefs and customs, would make sure, if example, the funeral was for a Greek Orthodox, that the correct style of cross was affixed to the coffin, with an icon close by, for mourners to kiss, if they so wished. If a Free Mason, the square and compass would be affixed, and so it goes on, but always paying attention to every little detail.

It's not every day, the public go into a selection room, so to lesson the strangeness, Bill made his selection room appear, warm and familiar, more like a furniture showroom, with carpeted floor, paintings on the walls, and strategically placed flowers.

The coffins and caskets were given names, such as Ashley, Bromley, Carlton, Devonshire, all commencing with different letters of the alphabet, each had its' price on an engraved disc. The family were left alone to choose and told, when ready to bring the disc of their choice, to give to the member of staff arranging the funeral. Hence it was easier for the office staff to remember, eg., 'A', or 'B' had been selected. The Chapels too were named, in alphabetical order, eg., Chapel of Ascension, Chapel of Blessings and so on. Again, to make arranging a funeral as fool proof as possible for the staff. Bill was always very strict, everything had to be 100% correct first time. Hence all paperwork was in triplicate. Different staff members checking and re-checking every request made by families were carried out to the letter. Even the sets of funeral arranging cards were in two colours, printed in black for burial, and red for cremation. Then, at a glance, one knew, whether the funeral was burial, or cremation. Every question that one could possibly think of, was included on the arranging card, leaving, as one of his sayings goes, 'no stone unturned', and all carefully thought up, by Bill.

He'd even thought of a special, first call sheet, with all the questions required, when a family first telephone to arrange a funeral. Bill always believing in the personal touch, no answering machines, or central call centres for him. The telephones were manned 24 hours a day every day, by a member of the staff. Thus giving a personal and knowledgeable service at all times, by staff who would be dealing with that family, rather than a tape recorder, which is so impersonal, or someone miles away, who would never meet the family in question.

Bill continuing to give the best service possible, had a book printed, that was presented to families after the funeral, containing comforting words and pictures, giving all details of funeral arrangements and who attended the funeral etc., leaving pages for the family to complete with a family tree. Something that could be treasured forever, a lasting memory

## The One Man Cot

Almost anything of advancement, that any funeral concern has now, Bill already had it many years ago, example, even the 'one man stretcher', whose correct name is, 'the one man cot', from USA.

56

To learn about this wonderfully helpful equipment, Bill first went to the 'Patent House', in Washington, saw exactly how it was constructed, and, as well as becoming the first person to have one, he became an agent for them in Britain.

Bill advertised it, as a piece of equipment, almost as important as the hearse. Bill's first enquirer was, the Co-op. However, Bill said, to be honest, he didn't continue with the agency for two reasons, 1. he was too busy running all his other operations and 2. to be honest, being the first to have a one man cot, and wanting to remain one of the few, rather than the many. When he looks back now, he thinks it was probably a silly decision, but as he says, he was very young then, and determined to be always ahead, with all his advanced ideas.

## Flowers Day Before Funeral

Bill maintains, as the flowers are meant for the deceased, that's where they should be, and at least a day before the funeral, thus enabling families, when paying their last respects, to look at the flowers for as long as they wish, giving them the opportunity to read and absorb messages written on the floral cards. Instead of the usual way, where floral tributes are simply put on the roof of the hearse, to be taken off at the grave-side, when it could be blowing a gale, and tipping down with rain, making it impossible for mourners to read the cards.

Flowers in the sign of a cross

In the beginning it was hard for Bill to get florists to change their ways. Bill was very persistent, having made up his mind, he was right. Some florists made such excuses as, the flowers wouldn't be fresh the next day. Bill, forever quick with his answers would say, 'That doesn't say much for your flowers then, does it!' Of course, Bill knew that some florists would tell their staff, to use those older flowers, as they were only for a funeral, meaning, they're only seen once. However, Bill stuck out, consequently, you can be sure, that when florists deliver to Earl of Plymouth, the flowers are always, to coin a phrase, 'As fresh as a daisy'.

## Taught Staff to make Floral wreaths

Bill offered another service to the bereaved. The families were able to order floral tributes directly from him when making funeral arrangements. One less problem for these stressed people to think about.

Bill was always improving on the best service in town, however, he first employed a florist, making sure she taught all his staff, to make wreaths, and crosses etc., professionally.

Not content just to leave it at that. Full of ideas, he had floral designs made, so that one side was completely different to the other. These were displayed in his window, showing one side one week, the other side the next.

That was the beginning of Bill's successful Floral Department.

## Bill's Tribute To Brian McLoughlin,
## who Bill calls, 'A Man In A Million'

Brian never took a half day off, in the 50 years, he worked for Earl of Plymouth, from age 14.

At 4.30p.m., whilst on an errand, Brian called at Earl of Plymouth's garage, to ask if there was a garage boy's job going. Asked when he could start, he replied, "Right now". He did. Arriving home, his mother clipped his ear for being so long, unaware he'd started work. Infact, he'd been working for a week before she knew.

Progressing from Garage Boy to Manager, Brian worked in every branch of the profession, maintained many fleets of the firm's cars during his working lifetime of 50 years, including a large fleet of Rolls Royce limousines, one of which, he completely dismantled and re-built.

Brian, never took time off in his whole career, preferring to work his holidays, and having the money. He turned his hand to any and everything, whether putting in new drains, building a garage wall, he did it all to perfection, and there was nothing in the funeral profession he couldn't do either, eg., he made coffins, taught others, including Bill's son

Christopher, monumental masonry, and made floral wreaths. The firm also had a driving school, Brian becoming the main instructor.

Bill cannot sing his praises enough, he's a man in a million.

## Airline Costs

Point of interest. Each time a body is sent to Australia, in accordance with airline rules, one always has to pay up front, until the weight of both casket and body are known. The amount overpaid, is returned by cheque.

Rules for sending bodies abroad are stringent, especially to USA. The body having to be embalmed by a qualified embalmer. A certificate signed by the embalmer is sent with the body. Different countries, different rules. Some insist the body is also enclosed in a metal container. Certificates from the Home Office are needed. All in a day's work for the funeral director. With so many people going abroad for holidays, the transport of bodies from one country to another is obviously on the increase.

## Burials In New Orleans

The land in New Orleans is below sea level, making burials, as we know them, out of the question, because of the earth being water logged. Coffins are laid to rest in vaults. To further explain, first, one decides the area to be used. Make a flat cemented surface, upon which stone vaults stand, all the same size. After the coffin is placed in the vault, the front is sealed with a slab, not unlike a headstone. On the front, one can have engraved, the name, age, date of death etc., with a provision for a family floral piece, when the flowers die they are removed, that way, the vaults remain clean, tidy and with respect. This system is used by many European countries and others. Standing, 3 or 4 vaults one on top of the other, looking clean and attractive, it's a very useful system of burial, especially with the constant shortage of land.

## Funerals In Space

Bill, always keeping ahead, as well as providing a varied first class service, was able to offer, those who wished, to have their sacred remains transported into space. Although Bill doesn't want this method for himself, "preferring to stay as he is now". He said, if he did chose it, it would be appropriate as he is always so punctual, hence, whilst orbiting the earth, his family would still be able to set their clocks by him, saying, there he goes, it must be 1p.m. Trust Bill to think of that.

## Presentation of Deceased

To present the deceased in as natural way as possible. Bill often asked for a recent photo of the person. If the family agreed, he would suggest dressing their loved one in their favourite clothes. Looking at the photo, Bill would meticulously copy the hairstyle, use make up if needed, if they wore glasses, then their glasses put on, if eg., they smoked a pipe, place their favourite pipe in their hands. It was these personal touches, that made the presentation of the dead, a labour of love to Bill, especially, when seeing the pleasure on the family's faces. These might seem odd words to use, but it wasn't unusual for a family to remark, "Doesn't he, (or she) look well".

### Funerals Taken from Another Funeral Director & Given To Bill

Not a nice phrase, however, sadly, it's perhaps, the only way to truly explain a few happenings. One might say, good for Bill, but, Bill says it's bad for the offending funeral director, which is why, on principle, Bill wouldn't disclose names.

However, on occasions, Bill's been contacted by bereaved families, who, having used his excellent services in the past, were now involved with the other side of their families, who, shall we say, used a funeral director from their own area, only to experience the difference, when going to view the body. They were, to say least, dissatisfied, upset and disappointed when witnessing the contrast in the way their loved ones were presented for viewing, that they immediately contacted Bill and asked him to completely take over from the other funeral director, collect the deceased and start all over again. I always remember dear old Bill suggesting to the family in his kindly way, it would be nicer for them, to ask the other funeral director to cancel everything and take the deceased to Earl of Plymouth, rather than Bill having to tell them. Also, it would be more professional and less hurtful doing it that way, to the other funeral director.

In all but one such case, Bill had to confirm with the minister that the times of the church service and cemetery etc., would be the same, the only difference being, it will now be carried out by Earl of Plymouth, and not, as originally arranged, by Joe Bloggs Funeral Service. At least the families were again, more than satisfied with Earl of Plymouth, which of course, is why they came to him. Naturally, it was a feather in Bill's cap, who always dealt with such cases, very tactfully.

## VARIOUS FUNERALS & ODD REQUESTS

### Funeral Of Sir Francis Chichester

One of many funerals, Bill's been honoured with, that stands out in his mind, was that of a man, Bill had always admired. It was of the late Sir Francis Chichester, such a highly respected man, not just here in

Plymouth, but all over the world. Although in such ill health, with his sheer determination and perseverance, was the first lone yachtsman, to circumnavigate the world.

On his death, to use Lady Chichester's words, she apparently told the staff at The Royal Naval Hospital, she wanted the best funeral service possible. Going through a printed list with her, pointing out the various firms, she was told, that as she said she wanted the best, then it would have to be Earl of Plymouth.

Bill's first contact with Lady Chichester, was at The Holiday Inn, where they sat together, making the arrangements, for what was obviously going to be a very high profile occasion.

Bill and his staff, had to remove Sir Francis to Earl of Plymouth Chapels, embalming the deceased, and dressing him in his yachting clothes, just as he was known by everybody throughout the world.

He was placed in one of Earl of Plymouth consecrated Chapels, where he reposed, until Lady Chichester said, that in accordance with his wishes, she would like him to leave, on the day of the funeral, from Royal Naval Hospital.

Bill carried out her wishes, and took him to the little Chapel at R.N. Hospital, the day before his funeral.

Bill, in his usual way, visited the little Chapel. He was escorted by a Royal Naval officer, to find a R.N. rating permanently on guard, and Lady Chichester sketching Sir Francis.

Sir Francis Chichester's funeral

She was obviously delighted to see Bill, realising, as she said, Bill was taking so much care over every little detail. She explained, she was sketching her husband, because in life, he wouldn't keep still long enough. Bill went on to explain, he often got requests from families for photographs of the deceased, and that he always used the same professional photographer, because he knew exactly what had to be done. She was so pleased, her eyes lit up, saying, 'Oh, I would never have thought of that', and asked Bill to arrange same.

To ensure, everything went according to plan, they had a full rehearsal, using an empty coffin for going into St. Andrews Church.

Bill always remembers, how pleased Lady Chichester was, when she saw that his fleet of cars were all silver grey, rather than black.

On the day of the funeral, St. Andrews Church, Plymouth, was full. Outside, were literally thousands of people. After a lengthy service, followed a luncheon in Plymouth Guildhall, after which, the large funeral cortege slowly moved off, wending its' way along the country roads over Dartmoor, through Tavistock, and suffice to say, in an area of Oakhampton.

The roads were thronged with people, all the way, bidding their last farewells. Finally arriving at the Churchyard, where his father was once the vicar, they had another service, followed by the committal.

There was such an abundance of floral tributes, that the following day, they had to make several trips from Plymouth to the graveside with the flowers.

Funeral Director friends of Bill's in Australia and all over the world, were telephoning Bill, saying they had watched this important funeral on their TV, and commended Bill for carrying out such excellent arrangements.

## Funeral of a Poor 13 yr old Girl, no one else would do

A very poor family, consisting of a man, wife and 13 year old daughter, all slept in the one bed, in the only room they had, which had a big coal fire burning all the time, the only real comfort these poor souls had.

Their daughter died. As they were Roman Catholics, they rang a Roman Catholic Funeral Director, who called, saw that obviously they hadn't any money, and left.

The family rang Earl of Plymouth Funeral Service, just as Bill, dressed up in a frock tail evening suit, was leaving to give an exhibition of Ballroom dancing, at a diner and dance.

The mother of the child explained the sad facts, telling Bill, she, her husband, and the deceased would have to spend yet another night, with all three of them, in the same room, as the child was still in the only bed they had.

Bill, his heart touched, immediately put the wife, Mrs. Breakle and her husband's minds to rest, assuring them, they wouldn't have to do the same that night, because within half an hour, his men would be there, to take their daughter to one of his Chapels. First thing in the morning, Mr. Earl, would be at their home, to make funeral arrangements. Telling them over and over, not to worry, there would be no charge whatsoever. (This is typical of sentimental Bill, who cried for days when the cat died. A good attribute, not always found in this fast selfish world we live in today.) Even her doctor made a point of wishing to remain anonymous, when giving the family, a little donation.

Taking into consideration, the little girl had already lain in bed over 48 hours, completely covered with blankets, together with a big fire burning night and day, it's true to say, in the kindest way possible, under all the circumstances, putrefaction etc., was suggesting it better, the little girl was not viewed, unless given a treatment (embalming) and facial restoration.

Bill, thinking of this poor family, gave such treatment, after which, the Mum and Dad couldn't thank him enough.

Bill will never forget, that at that time, Randolf Churchill was in the middle of a vast crowd, electioneering for Conservatives, when, to everyone's amazement, Mrs. Breakle, walked right into the middle of the crowd, picked up the microphone, and said, 'What we want, is more people like Mr. Earl', and went on an on, singing his praises.

The best thank you Bill could have, was knowing they'd really appreciated all he'd done.

## His One & Only Friend Was His Canary

A lonely old gentleman, without a friend in the world, except his dear little canary, became so depressed when it died, the old chap committed suicide, but not before leaving instructions, that his beloved canary, was to be attached to his leg, and buried with him.

Bill had always taught his staff, whatever requests were made, irrespective of how odd they may appear, they must be honoured.

I can hear Bill saying, if a family requests their flowers must be upside down, then upside down they must be, 'it's not ours to know the reason why'.

As always, the request was abided by.

## Snooker Player

Another odd request, amongst hundreds of pre-arranged funerals, Bill organised, was of a keen professional snooker player, who made it abundantly clear, that at his demise, he wanted, not only his snooker cue, buried with him, but also his full set of balls.

His wish was of course, eventually fulfilled. Another of the many advantages, of pre-arranging one's own funeral, which came about, through Bill knowing Frankie Fuge and his Ballroom Orchestra, who had played strict tempo several times, to aid Bill, when giving one of his exhibitions of Modern Ballroom dancing. Bill went all over Devon & Cornwall with this famous man.

## Mum & Child Together

A German lady died shortly after childbirth. Bill gave her family all the details, even including the weight of the baby, of eleven pounds four and a quarter ounces.

Asked, if it was possible to delay the funeral for a longish period, allowing various members of the family, scattered throughout the world, to come together, and attend the funeral.

Bill complied to the family's wishes, and having given the necessary professional treatment to mother and child, the family were able to view, the precious pair they had so tragically lost.

The baby boy was placed in mother's arms, in the same coffin. Various ones came, day after day, to Bill's original 'little' chapel.

Perhaps an odd way of putting it, or should one say, the only way of putting it, is to say, the family were so pleased. The child, being big, looked a year old. At the family's request, Bill had photographs taken for them, which went to various parts of the world.

To give readers some idea, the coffin was upholstered in white satin, with a mattress and pillow to fit, plus a white silk eiderdown to match, both mother and child were dressed in the usual night attire. The child, being a boy, was dressed in blue.

Bill says, giving such care to every detail, means much to grieving families. I know Bill receives much satisfaction from giving his expertise to help others in their time of need.

## Lady Wanted to Be Buried As A Bride

A lady, aware of her impending death, requested Bill personally arranged her funeral, and fulfil her wish to be dressed in her own wedding gown, and made up like a bride.

Bill asked the husband for a photograph of her on her wedding day. He then embalmed the lady, and copying her photograph, dressed and made up her face accordingly, with all the usual frills, even to the bridal bouquet.

Having done all he had been asked, she was placed in an oak casket, upholstered in a befitting way, displaying an elegant good looking bride.

I shall always remember Bill explaining to his staff, that though many requests could seem out of the way, unnecessary, even outrageous, it's not their right to know the reason why. In Bill's profession, it's one's duty to do whatever's requested when humanly possible, bearing in mind, each and everyone of us have our own differing opinions about everything, hence, either sea burial, earth burial, cremation, or even outer space. Once again, Bill had sincerely dealt with the request in his usual professional manner. Incidentally, as was more often the case in those days, Bill embalmed the deceased on her bed, and she remained in the house until day of funeral. As was usual, Bill, having finished his professional treatment, informed the family, in this case, the husband, asking, would he now like to see his wife. To put it mildly, the husband was amazed, saying, "She looks just as she did, the day I married her".

She was buried in a brick walled grave covered with a solid stone slab. However, years later, the owner of the grave died. His wishes were, to have been the first one buried in that grave. In which case, there was an exhumation, to allow the two bodies to be in the order, the owner had requested.

Note, the burial ground referred to, is a very old dilapidated overgrown private cemetery, which, through lack of money, they just do not know what's going to happen to it. In which case, if for any reason, the remains had to be re-interred, as was carried out by Earl of Plymouth, with an old cemetery behind Plymouth Corporation Tram depot, it could possibly become confusing, when seeing dates on the engraved inscription plates on each casket.

## Burial of Tiny

'Tiny', as he was affectionately known by all and sundry, was a gentleman, near on 40 stone.

To put it mildly and respectfully, sadly, he looked a mess when Bill collected him from the hospital mortuary. This could have made his wife's last memory of him, not very pleasant, had it not been for the care Bill gave to this lovely man, whom Bill knew well.

Bill embalmed him, giving facial restoration, thus lifting the burden for his wife, leaving her with pleasant lasting memories.

As Bill says, irrespective of how a body may look, it's always the last memory that's remembered. It's true to say, if ever there was a dedicated and caring man, right down to the last detail, it was Bill, who had so much understanding of whatever the religion may be, he understood, and knew what to do.

Tiny's wife and family, couldn't thank Bill enough, for his loving care. However, there was more, and under the circumstances, much more to be taken care of. Earl of Plymouth had to arrange a double sized grave, and a specially made and strengthened coffin, to be carried by twelve bearers.

It was another of the many unusual funerals, Bill was pleased to have successfully completed. Understandably all such funerals incur even more concern than usual.

## Odd Requests

Bill has arranged hundreds of prearranged funerals, with all sorts of odd requests.

One was for a business gentleman, who owned a hotel in Plymouth, and wanted to ensure, his funeral cortege, was led by a full brass band to the Crematorium. Bill couldn't assure him, until he had found a brass band willing to do same. This meant Bill travelling to a little place in Cornwall, called Penwithick. Having painstakingly made all the arrangements, the gentleman made a quick exit to Australia, to avoid paying a vast amount of income tax in this country.

That put an end to his unusual request, and of himself, because sadly, he died in Australia. This was after Bill, had made prearrangements for the gentleman's mother's funeral, whose death preceded his.

Under the difficult circumstances, the son was not able to return to England for his mother's funeral, as the tax man would immediately pounce on him. The mother's funeral service, was held at Earl of Plymouth Chapels. Knowing the son couldn't attend, Bill had the whole service recorded and shown on TV. and sent the video to Australia.

Later, Bill received a very early 4a.m. call from Australia, thanking him for his efforts. At first, he'd telephoned Bill on the business number 4a.m. in the morning. When told Bill wasn't there, having made up his mind he wasn't going to be thwarted, he rang again, this time at Bill's home, when his first words were, 'Bill my boy, you served me well. I can't thank you enough for all you did, for me and my dear mother. You made it feel as if I was there, and attended the funeral, even having my name mentioned at the ceremony'.

Bill felt pleased, he'd helped someone from such a long distance.

## Gun Carriage Funerals

Thankfully, the days of gun carriage funerals, have almost gone, cutting out the long walks for the ratings, with the inevitable traffic hold-ups, to say nothing of the cars carrying the mourners, from over heating. Infact, such funerals, these days, with the ever increasing traffic, should, in Bill's view, be discouraged.

For those unfamiliar with such walking funerals, perhaps never having seen same, it's where the coffin of a service person, is draped in the Union Jack, placed on a gun carriage, and drawn at slow walking pace, by service personnel, as shown on TV from time to time, eg., that of the late

Sir Winston Churchill's funeral. At the graveside, or outside the door of the crematorium Chapel, a bugler blows, 'The Last Post' for finalising the committal service.

## Funeral of Ron

Bill had to arrange the funeral of Ron, someone Bill knew well. Bill's last question to Ron's wife was, what day and time would you like to see Ron. She replied, oh, I don't want to see him, I'd rather remember him as he was. Ron's wife went away and thought about it, she telephoned the next day, asking to speak to Bill. She told him, she had changed her mind, and decided yes, she would like to pay her last respects, and see Ron.

Later that day, Bill, whom she knew very well, was waiting for her at the prescribed time, and accompanied her into the chapel. When she saw Ron so nicely dressed, with his favourite suit and tie, together with matching pocket handkerchief. She exclaimed, "Oh, how wonderful he looks Bill, I am so glad now, that I came to see him, he looks just like I always knew him. Had I known, Billy, that he was going to look like that, I would have had him done sooner". She thanked Bill so much, he ended up shedding a few tears himself.

Bill's received numerous remarks like this, after the bereaved have seen their loved ones, so nicely dressed and properly cared for, Bill always took so much time and care in his work.

One of Bill's printed sayings, in their mortuary is, 'always treat each deceased person with care and respect at all times, as if the family were stood immediately behind you'. This way, a new employee was instantly and constantly reminded of the perfection and respect Bill demanded from his employees, for the families using Bill's service.

## Two Odd Requests

Another odd request, was from a lady who contacted Bill, asking, could he bury her car with her. She'd only had her brand new Mercedes two days. That funeral, hasn't taken place yet. A good advert for Mercedes, a lady who can't bear to be parted from her car, even when dead.

Another odd one, was a lady who knew Bill all her life, but when she died, she made the request known that she didn't want Bill to see her naked.

## Man Who Cut His Throat

Like everywhere in society, there's a black sheep. Bill could go on and on, but as he says, that's not the reason for this biography. Hopefully, readers will enjoy gaining useful knowledge, mingled with plenty of laughter and humour, when reading this, bearing in mind of course, business is business. The following, is one instance, Bill will never forget.

For those not knowing; the rule is, when there's an unexpected death, murder, suicide, accident, foul play etc., it becomes, what is commonly known as, 'A Coroner's Post-mortem', wherein the coroner's officer becomes involved, and reports his findings to the coroner.

To keep a semblance of fairness, coroner's officers are supposed to be above reproach, to do this, they should ask the next of kin, the name of the funeral director, they wish to use. At such a time, naturally, many are unable to act rationally, leaving the decision to the officer, whose job it is, to chose the nearest funeral director to the area, simply to remove the deceased to the mortuary, in preparation for a coroner's post-mortem. Which funeral director eventually carried out the funeral, is of no concern to the Coroner's Officer, he shouldn't have any say in the matter. If, on the other hand, it was more than obvious there wasn't any money to pay for the funeral, eg., the body dead for many days, the deceased lived in run down conditions, with obviously, no-one to take charge, or pay for the funeral, the coroner's officer should use the funeral director, who held the contract for 'Paupers' funerals.

It must be noted, the standard cost of a coroner's removal, whether pauper's funeral, or ordinary funeral, are all paid the full standard fee. One particular officer, Bill remembers back at that time, didn't ever do as he should. He was always passing funerals to a funeral director friend he had. Bill says, he could write a book about him and his sly ways, but what's the good. He made life very difficult for Bill, just starting in business.

The Coroner's Officer, was called to a house for a suicide case. The deceased, was still sat upright, in a high back chair, having used a cut throat razor, to cut his throat. As is normal, in this sort of case, the heart continues beating for a short period, pumping the blood out, which naturally flows to the floor, quickly coagulating into, a pyramid, of say, a gallon lump of coagulated blood. Not a nice sight, even for those used to dealing with such occurrences. The coroner's officer, aware of all these facts, having been to the house after the death, didn't have the decency to warn Earl of Plymouth funeral staff, what to expect, or the shock.

Interesting to note, that on that rather messy occasion, the Coroner's Officer, this time, didn't put the removal of The Coroner's case, into the hands of his funeral director friend!

Naturally, Bill's men, went to the house in the usual manner to remove the body in the normal way. What a shock, seeing this poor man, in such a state. Unable to remove him in the normal manner, rigor mortis having set in. They had to go back to the chapels, collecting special means for straightening out the body, and of course stretcher, gloves etc., before returning to carry out this unusual removal. Bill always felt, and knew, that this particular coroner's officer was mean, corrupt and uncaring, not to pre-warn them.

## Speedway Rider

There was a well known Speedway Rider who wanted a photograph of himself, placed in his coffin. Not any old photograph, it had to be of him, photographed whilst taking part in a racing event, passing all the other riders, whilst rounding a corner on the track. Needless to say, he had his wish, because, 'He Always Wanted To Be Up Front', even at the end.

## Motor Bike Funeral

Bill carried out a funeral, many years ago, of a female, using a motor bike and a sidecar, as a hearse. Bill said, he didn't like it at the time, but as he used to say, 'Not ours to know the reason why'.

## Fairground Funerals

Earl of Plymouth have conducted many Fairground family's funerals, each standing out in Bill's mind. On such occasions, it was obvious, the families had a very close bond with each other. The funerals, were invariably very large, ordering an abundance of floral pieces, with various designs, made up to imitate eg., steam traction engines, dodgems, and various other amusement rides, besides copying various side stalls etc. Often, there were so many floral tributes, that in addition to the usual methods of transporting the flowers, at times they were taken to the cemetery, using their own transport, open flat bottom lorries. The masses of flowers looked so attractive, they were equally as good as those in the Jersey flower festival.

Here in Plymouth, many of the fairground families, spend their winter months, with their huge caravans, and lorries etc., parked in a sheltered large Fort, enabling them to remain together, and also carry out necessary maintenance work. Of course, some own their own well kept property here. Bill remembers one family, he was called to visit, that lived in the Stoke area of Plymouth, whose property was, 'one to behold'. Just like everything these travelling people owned, it was immaculate. Bill says, he could write a book about these lovely people.

## Bill Takes Funeral Service

I know, I was there. Jim and Paula, well known to Bill, asked him to take the funeral service of Jim's sister, who, knowing her time was near, told her brother Jim, she did not want to be taken into church when her time came, but wanted Bill to "do her service". Bill did, to the satisfaction of the family.

Incidentally, conducting graveside services, is something else, Bill's done.

Bill's noted over the years, that many have attended church funeral services, not understanding what was said. In the case of Roman Catholics, up until some years ago, the service was in Latin, which most Catholics themselves, did not understand. Reminds Bill, that years ago, doctors wrote prescriptions in Latin, but the bill, always in English.

I repeat Bill's thoughts, that if you have a religion, and are happy with it, then stick with it, because no one knows who is right and who's wrong. He's said, that if he was an atheist, he would still have his children attend Sunday school, because, as he says, if it doesn't do them any good, it won't do them any harm.

## Burials At Sea
Of all the burials Bill has had to arrange at sea, the one that stands out in his mind most, was having to arrange for a very high ranking deceased officer, with the shell oil company to be brought back to England, in a sealed coffin.

Though the officer had been dead for quite a while, the wife insisted, the coffin was to be unsealed, to enable her to pay her last respects, by viewing the body. Bill tried to warn her, that because of the time lapse since her husband's death, that the deceased would more than likely be in a bad state. He was, in a bad state. Bill thought, in no way must she see him as he was. The funeral directors abroad, knowing the inside shell was to be sealed, not seeming to bother, or showing any semblance of care, just shoved him inside in any old way.

That officer's wife, will never know the hours Bill spent, embalming him for hygienic reasons, together with the fantastic amount of facial restoration that was required, which is a hard task when there's been such a wait between death and eventual disposal. The delay partly caused by the sea passage to England, when again there was a further delay, because, unlike most people imagine, the Navy doesn't send a battleship, or any other ship out to sea, simply because of a burial. Instead, the funeral had to be further delayed, until a ship was going to sea.

Helping the family in every way possible, Bill suggested that the funeral service should go ahead in accordance with the family's Roman Catholic faith, therefore, the deceased was received into the R.C. Cathedral on the eve of the funeral, prior to Requiem Mass the following morning. After which, to all intents and purposes, for the benefit of the family, they then placed the coffin, in the hearse in the normal way, and as far as the mourners were concerned, they left the church for the cemetery, whereas infact, the coffin was taken back to one of Bill's Chapels, where the deceased reposed, until finally, a ship was made available, then Bill went with it for the sea burial.

Leaving Devonport early morning, Bill was made welcome in the Ship's Officers' Lounge, where, having had coffee, was left sitting comfortably reading the daily newspapers. Bill realised, the ship had been sailing, for what seemed a long time, when suddenly, the continuous roar of the ship's engines ceased, and all was quiet. The Padre and Officers came for Bill and escorted him to a special burial platform, where the coffin rested.

Bill had personally supervised and interceded in the specially prepared coffin, to ensure it immediately sank, having made special, undetectable air escapes in the coffin, to facilitate, its' sudden disappearance, into the turbulent English Channel, even more important, as they were so far out in the deep.

This having been done, Bill returned to the warmth, and comfort of the officers' lounge, with a warming cup of coffee, and continued to read the newspapers. After what seemed a very long time, with the continual roar of the engines, Bill began thinking and hoping, they had forgotten all about him. With his usual quick thinking business mind, he conjured up thoughts of the free advertising effect it could have. He was hoping, the ship was on a non stop trip to Australia.

Infact, they had completely forgotten all about him, telling Bill, they had to flash back a message for a ship to come and collect him, and as he says, it "really was a fair sized ship", it must have cost a fortune.

It turned out to be a very long, and interesting day, when at one time, with such confusion, Bill said he didn't know, whether he was coming or going. However, when he eventually arrived home, it was dark, and Bill was very tired, but he was disappointed, as he had really thought he was on the way to much warmer climates.

A few days later, a nice commendation came to Bill, in a letter from the Navy, saying, of all the burials they had had at sea, his firm's were the only ones, that always sank immediately.

## Upright

Bill had several cases, where the deceased, having left a wish, that their body was to be taken out of the house upright. In each case, having embalmed the body, in accordance with their wishes, the coffin stood upright in the corner of the room they had chosen, until the day of the funeral. Bill's words again, 'It's not ours to know the reason why'.

## Motor Bike Accidents

Hard thing to talk about, but a serious one, that must be said. Bill, unintentionally, made a name for himself, by always restoring the deceased to lifelike appearance, even when badly disfigured. News quickly travels. A motor bike association, sadly lost one of their team, who suffered a fatal accident, leaving the rider disfigured. Another of the team members, knowing of Bill's capabilities, advised next of kin to talk to Bill, before doing anything.

From there on, if ever a fatal accident, Bill's name always came to the fore.

## Who Said Rolls Royces Never Break Down

The late owner of a well known Theatre, was being taken to the cemetery, in a Rolls Royce hearse, which incidentally, did not belong to Earl of Plymouth, it broke down, and had to be towed to the cemetery, by above all, a gas lorry. An embarrassing situation to say least, but one that couldn't be helped, and as Bill always says, everything mechanical, wears out and can break down.

## 13 Grave Spaces

A well known businessman, having used Bill's services several times, came to Earl of Plymouth Chapels, to speak to Bill. Apparently he wanted to purchase, thirteen freehold graves. Had Bill not known the gent, he would probably have thought, something's odd about this, especially as the number was 13. However, after discussion, it was clear, his family not being natives of UK, or of Christian faith, wanted to be buried in unconsecrated ground, where eventually his whole family would be buried in the same area.

Bill, having arranged and paid for all the freehold graves, which was a very substantial amount of money, obtained each of the grave deeds, and was satisfied, having done all that was requested, and sent his account to solicitors, as instructed. A transaction well done thought Bill. Then, to his surprise, he was informed of changed wishes. The gent had now decided, he wanted all his wishes changed, enabling the same instructions and provisions, but, at a different cemetery. Bill, fortunately realised, both cemeteries happened to belong to the same company, and so, after a considerable amount of thought, was able to rearrange everything to the family's entire satisfaction. The family sent Bill a very touching letter of thanks.

## The R.C. Widow, Who Needed Help

Bill is always ready, to go out of his way to help those who seek his advice, which he genuinely gives.

Several months had lapsed since Bill had conducted the funeral of Mr. Grey, when, out of the blue, his widow asked if Bill could visit her, she didn't know where to turn financially. Bill agreed to do all he could to help. He drove to one of the poorer parts of Plymouth, to a street of run down terraced houses. The lady, a Roman Catholic, complained, that she had a weekly outlay for a taxi to take her too and from the church she was used to attending. Bill, knowing full well, there was a Roman Catholic Church, close by to the middle aged lady's home, pointed out that the first saving she could make, was by walking to the local church instead. Mrs. Grey further surprised Bill, by saying she had to pay the minister several pounds, before he'd say a mass for her departed husband. Bill, immediately corrected her, saying, there's no such thing as having to pay for a mass, and as a Roman Catholic, she should be more than aware of that. Simply explain matters to the priest, telling him, you want a mass said. Bill visited the priest on her behalf, asking him to visit the lady, which he did, agreeing with all Bill had said.

Next, he looked in her deep freeze, which was empty, except for some fish. A further shock was in store, when she explained, the fish was for her cat, she couldn't afford to put anything in the freezer for herself. She apparently, bought the fish once a week, and had it delivered all the way from the fish market. Bill pointed out, that as her circumstances had changed, she should sell the freezer, and feed her pet cat as cheaply as possible, specially as she admitted, she only kept the freezer because of the cat.

By the time Bill had finished, he had saved this widow many pounds, in many ways. She was truly grateful, and continued to keep in touch with Bill, even after her re-marriage and safely back on her feet. Infact, she never fails to send him a Xmas card, though he has never sent her one.

Bill has acted in a similar manner to many, who needed and sought his help. Many elderly people, have enjoyed happy vacations through Bill's help. When one dies, leaving the partner, alone in the area, often with family and friends miles away, they have asked Bill for his advice, he will always say, before making a rash move, sleep on it first, don't do anything in a hurry. Wise words indeed.

## Two Odd Experiences
### Thought He Was At The Dentist
One of many experiences, that are laughable; a gentleman, rang the door bell of the Funeral Chapels one morning. Bill's wife, Carole, answered the call, and, as was usual, asked the gent to come into the office, he said he had a 10a.m. appointment, which seemed odd, because Bill didn't use an appointment system in his delicate type of business. Bill, who was in an adjoining office, asked Carole to tell the gent, Mr. Earl

wont be a second, he's on the telephone With the same, he asked, "Who did you say?" "Mr. Earl", she replied. The elderly gent quickly stood up, saying, "I thought this place looked different, I don't want Mr. Earl, I'm not ready for this place yet." He ran out saying, "I only wanted the dentist."

### Lady That 'Shit' Herself

Mrs. Alford, the senior secretary, always advised new office staff, when starting work for Earl of Plymouth, that if ever they were stuck for a reply, not to worry, go to Mr. Earl, as he always has an immediate answer for everything. Coincidentally, within minutes of Mrs Alford giving this useful information to a new girl, a lady came to the door, which was answered by Mrs. Alford, who was asked by the lady (Mr. Earl dislikes this kind of talk), quote. 'Can I use your toilet, as I've shit myself?'

Mrs. Alford, not knowing what to say, ran straight to Bill, knowing, he wouldn't like anybody like that on his premises, she recounted 'exactly' what had been said. As usual, like a flash, Bill quick with the answer, said, tell her, they go across the road to Agnes Westons with problems like yours (It's a hotel for sailors).

The woman, who already "had the runs", made a 'quick movement, and ran ... like hellfire'.

## Don't Remove The Wrong Body

Called to a religious home operated by nuns, that all of E of P staff were very familiar with, the nuns simply told the men, what ward the deceased was on. Usually, curtains were drawn around the one to be removed. This time, they failed to draw the curtains. The men, looking around and seeing (we say this with the utmost respect), a very elderly lady lying there. The dear old soul's head was on one side, her mouth wide open and eyes closed. The men thought this was the person they had been called to remove, but suddenly realised, she was only asleep. The body infact, was in the next bed. How embarrassing it could have been, but for the fact she was asleep, and oblivious to the event.

## Ask Bill The Funeral Director

An elderly lady, in one of Bill's Chapels, paying her respects, was heard saying to another, referring to the deceased, 'Doesn't he look long, do you think they stretch them?' An optical illusion of course.

Reminds Bill of many years ago, exchanging views with a funeral director in USA. He was asked, what's the first thing you do when going to a house to arrange a funeral. Measure the body, Bill replied. Whatever for? To know what size to make the coffin of course.

The enquirer replied, with a smile, you don't measure the person, when purchasing a bed, do you?

The American funeral director was correct *in his case*, but it must be remembered, they use caskets, which are rectangular, and all made to standard size. Infact, more like a bed.

Bill having been a funeral director, all his life, having made and taught others to make coffins and caskets, says, in his opinion, a casket is by far more practical in every way. Example, it's easier to lay out a body, with the deceased's head slightly turned to one side, making a more natural and acceptable appearance, because a casket is more adaptable, like a bed. It's more simply made, and of course one can embellish it as much as desired.

## Bill Makes His Own Casket

Many ask Bill, does he want burial, or cremation. To which he replies, 'To be honest, I am quite happy as I am'. Obviously, not in a hurry to leave this world, he has infact made his own casket, in his bedroom, ready for his pre-arranged funeral. It is of dark wood, tastefully decorated with a longitudinal mirror, and the usual gold coloured finishing touches. It really does look good. The newspaper had photos taken of it, they were so interested.

Bill's a man, that doesn't like anybody, or anything, to be stood idle, and so his casket, proudly stands in his bedroom, holding his treasured fancy waistcoats, trousers and made to measure shoes. In place of the usual breastplate, is an engraved gold inscription plaque, reading, 'Bill Earl, Funeral Director and Friend to many, this is Your Life'.

Bill, well known as one, always ready for a laugh and joke, takes his profession very seriously, and with genuine feeling. However, he always sees the funny side of anything.

Bill asked his wife, Carole to bring Brian to Bill's bedroom, to show him the casket. Brian is a friend of Bill's, whom he uses as a part time bearer.

Brian stood back, admiring Bill's work, saying, it's lovely, fantastic, and to think, he made it in the bedroom, without any vice etc. Yes, said Carole, have a look at the inside, which is equally as good. On opening the door, Brian saw Bill stood there, nicely dressed, collar & tie, pocket handkerchief etc., with a pleasant smile on his face. Brian gasped, 'oh!', fell to the floor on one knee, with uncontrollable laughter.

## More Questions Answered

Bill, with his usual kindly, and familiar words, whenever talking of eg., pre-arranged funerals etc., says, always remember, no one can see what

The casket Bill made in his bedroom for himself

is before them, and no one goes any sooner, through talking about it. Hence Bill has pre-arranged many hundreds of funerals, besides his own, and that of his wife. Thus making sure, one gets his, or her own wishes, as well as arranging it, when there's no sadness, making life easier for those left behind.

Another of Bill's sayings is,' There's two places he wants to keep out of, one is the cemetery, the other is, his own Chapels'. Having said that, he's not afraid of dying, it's just that, he doesn't want to be there at the time.

The following questions, you've always wanted to ask, but didn't like to. Bill Earl, with long, world-wide, professional experience, promises to answer, 100% truthfully, every question he's been asked.

After cremation, can one be sure of getting the correct ashes? Bill understands people putting the question that way, however, he taught all his staff, ashes come from the fire place, but these are the sacred remains of a loved one. Yes, you can be "absolutely assured" of getting the correct remains.

It's not true that a body sits up during cremation. The only slight possible movement, is, as the coffin burns, it naturally 'gives' a little, and of course, the body 'gives' with it. Bearing in mind, unlike a casket, a coffin is smaller one end.

Yes, every coffin or casket is burnt to dust, and all fittings, handles etc., have to be fully combustible.

Various ways of disposing of the sacred remains are; they can be scattered to the four winds. In one's garden, or infact anywhere within reason. They can be sent to outer space, kept at home in a suitable container, or buried at sea.

*Seeing the lighter side, and assuming nobody reading this, is affected in any way, if the remains are of one who was too lazy to work when living, they could decide to put them in an egg timer, with an inscription saying: 'he/she never did anything in life for us, so he/she can work for us now.'*

## Hoax Wedding and Funeral

There are those who try to play tricks on others. Bill is usually cute enough to immediately see through any hoax whether wedding car bookings, or even hoax funerals, here are a couple of such instances.

The telephone rang, a gentleman wanting to book eight cars for a wedding at West Hoe. After asking a couple of questions, Bill immediately sensed all was not correct, and said he'd call at the house to help, and get written instructions. The young man insisted, he didn't want Bill to call, saying, he'd give the details when the cars arrived on day of the wedding. This wasn't good enough for Bill, who called at the house and found there wasn't to be a wedding. Bill, was too wise for him.

Another time, a gentleman rang saying his wife had died, could Bill send a hearse to the house to collect the body. Bill, too quick for the hoaxer, saw through him after a couple of questions. Apparently, he had had an argument with his wife. Bill decided to teach this nasty man a lesson. He sent him a bill for the hearse and four men being sent to the address, and made him pay up. An expensive joke. I don't think he'll try that again. Bill then warned all other funeral directors.

## Starting The Wedding Business

The hearse is the most expensive vehicle to purchase, tax and insure. It can only be used for one purpose, thus spending most of its' time in the garage. This was the reason funeral directors, didn't own a hearse and cars, but hired, from what's known as, 'carriage masters'.

In Bill Earl's case, with his usual enterprising outlook, realising his whole fleet, already taxed and insured, spent most of its' time, including Saturdays and Sundays in the garage, he decided to do something about it. So he concentrated on more ceremonial work, such as weddings, christenings, and also VIP chauffeuring. He ended up with the biggest wedding business in Britain, doing as many as twenty seven on some Saturdays, hiring as many as forty to fifty cars from other sources, guaranteeing each bride would have one of the special Earl of Plymouth Bridal cars, complete with driver in chauffeur's livery.

Bill scanned the engagement columns of local papers, then sent out his printed forms to newly engaged couples, which read, "I gazed into the crystal, and saw you were getting wed, I also saw some writing, this is what it said, if you want to live and thrive, be sure to ring Plymouth 5415, as I gazed on, an omen I espied, which meant good fortune will attend you, if you ring Plymouth 5415".

That was just one of the ways he built up his terrific wedding business. Bill advertised nightly in his local paper, The Western Evening Herald, the advert read:- "Wherever you see Rolls Royce, you see Earl of Plymouth, wherever you see Earl of Plymouth, you see Rolls Royce". This went on for a long time, bringing in much business.

One day, Mr. Vielvoy, Western Evening Herald's advertising manager, contacted Bill saying, his nightly adverts would have to cease, as someone who now owned a Rolls Royce, complained.

Bill, always ready with an instant answer replied, leave it to him, he would have a replacement advert in Mr. Vielvoy's office, that afternoon. He did, it simply read, 'Wherever you see Rolls Royce, whose is it?' Immediately underneath it read, "Brides, for Rolls Royce limousines, contact Earl of Plymouth. Bridal car draped with flowers. Photographer and receptions catered for. One call we do it all, 11 telephones one number 52624."

Because of continual advertising, "wherever you see Rolls Royce, it's Earl of Plymouth", and with the fact that Bill had purchased the very famous, well known, Lord Mildmay's Rolls Royce limousine, with its' own cocktail cabinet, 12 cylinder, 24 spark plugs, 32 gallon petrol tank (red carpet treatment, every time Bill filled up), microphone in rear to speak to chauffeur etc., together with his advertising in eg., Western Evening Herald, Western Morning News, Sunday Independent etc., the

Bills Favourite paper. *Photo Courtesy of Evening Herald*

inspector of taxes asked, had Bill gone into selling cars. Bill, quick witted as ever, replied in writing through his accountant Mr. Goodman, tell him, Mr. Earl's comment was, it must be a good advert, as even the tax inspector picked it up, but tell him, not to go to London, as then he would feel, Mr. Earl was fiddling the books.

Bill had only that week, taken delivery of his brand new fleet of American Ambassador limousines. He'd already taken the opportunity to advertise their arrival by saying, 'Brides be different, go American, with one of Earl of Plymouth's stylish, American limousines, interior lined with lush white fur, and deep red carpet, smart livery chauffeur driven'.

Well, as you can imagine, these long sleek silver beauties, were fully booked, 12 months and more, in advance.

Bill proudly drove one of them on its' first wedding, one Saturday morning. Having taken the bride into church, he explained to Ken, one of his drivers, he was going back to the office in Albert Road, to check with Mrs. Alford, one of his secretaries, whether any funerals had come in, during his absence, as that was one of the Saturdays he had 27 weddings, making it a long time to be away from his office. That's how keen Bill was, always thinking of his profession. He carefully parked his brand new outstanding limousine on the road, adjacent to his premises, opposite Agnes Weston's. Having checked all was well, he walked back outside, finding to his astonishment, his beautiful car was nowhere to be seen. He couldn't believe it, pacing up and down the street, making sure he hadn't made a mistake and parked further away, but no, it had been stolen. Bill quickly took the only car left, the hearse, telling his drivers waiting at the church, one would have to make an extra journey on this wedding, explaining his car had been stolen.

Most people, would have immediately contacted the police, but not Bill, who never misses an opportunity of, 'turning all adversities to his own advantage'. He first rang, all the national, and local Sunday newspapers, TV channels etc., thus getting maximum FREE publicity, and lastly, rang the police.

Bill's car was found 150 miles away, when it ran out of petrol. The thief gave himself up to the police (would you believe it). The police drove him the 150 miles back to Plymouth. Bill paid another driver to go with him, to collect the car, costing Bill money, and a lot of petrol. Who says crime doesn't pay!!

Are people funny or peculiar? After all that publicity, would you believe it, the phone never stopped ringing, every bride wanted the car that had been stolen. What could Bill do, bearing in mind, all his fleet had consecutive numbers!!

Apparently, the thief, who was a double Decker bus driver, said, he stole the car, because he'd had a row with his wife. Bill's immediate remark was, then why didn't he steal a double deck bus. Wait for it, a fortnight later, he did and a little while after that, he stole another car, but this time, he caught it on fire, because he didn't like the owner.

Bill said, 'Aren't I glad he liked me.'

Answering the telephone, the staff were taught to say, 'Earl of Plymouth here, can I help you?' Whether the person on the other end wanted to make funeral arrangements, which is a sad occasion, or wedding car arrangements, that method of answering covered both, same telephone number and same staff. A thoughtful move on Bill's part.

Forms for weddings were sent in duplicate, one copy needing to be returned immediately, including full details of wedding and a booking fee, which was the price of the bridal car. Three weeks before the wedding, balance to be paid in full. The idea of booking fee, rather than a deposit is, it's non refundable. Bill's cars were very popular, booked more than twelve months in advance.

One experience. Bill encountered, a couple having already booked his cars, sent back the second form three weeks before the wedding with the balance, but they had changed the time of ceremony, without informing Bill. The difference was only noticed when checking original signed form. The change of time meant, there was no way he could do that wedding, other than the time booked. Bill banked the cheque, after all, he had reserved the cars for months. The groom was furious, not comprehending, it wasn't Bill's fault. The young man engaged a solicitor, who said, after reading Bill's signed wedding forms, there's nothing the couple could do. The wording on the form was Bill's idea, as he always said, one must make everything watertight, no refund allowed. I always remember Bill saying to the young man, 'You're just starting a new life aren't you?' 'Yes', he said. Bill replied, 'Well let this be your first lesson'.

## Driving School

Bill, having acquired a great deal of knowledge about cars, whether maintenance, or driving skills. He had been signed up in the army as a driving instructor, as well as gaining driving competence from his funeral concern, and operating a successful taxi business etc. Bill, noting a large number of driving schools popping up here and there, owned by such people as, Vospers Motor Company etc. Always with an eye to business, he couldn't ascertain how such schools could be profitable. Not one to be beaten, always ready to try something new when the opportunity arose, decided, as he already owned a fleet of taxis, he'd use one of those, starting his driving school with little outlay. He could then, find out for himself, how profitable, this type of business was. A professionally made sign was affixed to the front of the car, marked, 'Earl of Plymouth, Driving School. Dual Controlled. AA and RAC', with an 'L' plate placed either end of the sign.

Bill, with his outstanding reputation, was soon inundated with bookings for driving instruction. It wasn't all plain sailing. There were those who, through jealousy, tried to stop Bill, by writing to the media, engaging solicitors etc., trying to stop Bill using AA and RAC. It was all to no avail, and at their expense, Bill never spent a penny, arguing, all his fleet were AA and RAC covered. Of course, the more the controversy was brought to the limelight, the more free advertising he received, fulfilling one of his sayings, 'Talk about me, good if you can, bad if you must, but talk about me'. In the meantime the public were booking more and more lessons. Soon, Bill was only able to accept weekend and evening bookings, for fear of his new business venture interfering with his funeral business. He could easily have used more cars, but soon realised the profit was greatest for large garage organisations, who bought their cars trade price, and had the opportunity to sell them cheaper to the newly qualified driver, who naturally preferred to drive a car they were used to. Therefore, each of the large car dealers had a new car each year for nothing, giving them even more profit.

Having proved his point and making a success of the business, he sold it, lock stock and barrel, to Mr. Good. All goes to prove, whichever way one looks at it, Bill had plenty of "Drive".

## Starting Newspaper Business

Challenge has always stirred something in Bill. Whether it's a competitive thing, a test of intellect, or just that he takes it upon himself as a personal quest to overcome such obstacles. He certainly likes the thrill of taking up a challenge and takes satisfaction in seeing others acknowledge that he got it right! Don't get me wrong, Bill doesn't jump in with both feet regardless of the magnitude of the challenge, but if he does take up the gauntlet, which is more often than not, you can rest assured he has carefully considered the odds and is pretty well sure he can accomplish it.

It was not surprising then, that one day, in the early 1960's, whilst busy running his funeral business from Albert Road in Devonport, he suddenly awoke to the ultimate in an entrepreneur's challenge, to start a business without any money.

Bill considered the challenge long and hard. He was determined to prove he could start a business without any capital, and he did so, by encouraging customers to part with cash up front. Bill didn't want to invest any cash. In surprisingly quick time he was inspired and thought about a commodity very dear to his heart, advertising and publicity. He considered a group of businesses which could use assistance in this area, and thought of businessmen who would find any offer from Bill Earl credible. It was so brilliant, yet so simple, a free advertising newspaper for businesses in his area, Devonport.

The following day he set off, dressed in his dark work suit, armed with nothing other than his speed of thought and sales ability. He called upon various businesses, eg., retailers and convinced them of the need to advertise, the importance of "flying the flag" for their business. He explained he, Bill Earl, was starting a free newspaper to provide advertising for the businesses in Devonport to the consumers in surrounding houses and neighbouring areas. His first customer bought into the idea, agreed to advertise, and then parted with a few pounds, according to the amount of space he wanted. The business had started!

Besides his funeral concern, Bill had now become, owner and editor of his own newspaper.

One of the first customers, was the highly respected Stidever Bros., gents outfitters, Albert Road.

Knowing the cost of printing his Devonport Gazettes, then having obtained a special price from the Post Office for delivering same. The law was, that all newspapers had to print a certain amount of "copy" besides advertising. The latter is what would pay for the paper and give Bill a profit. Copy was not going to provide any problems as Devonport is steeped in news and history; with the HM Dockyard, RN Barracks, Mount Wise, Scouts, churches, old people's homes, nursing homes, etc. Bill, proved the point, of starting a business without any capital whatsoever.

## An Appropriate End To This Serious Chapter
*A "Funny" Funeral*

Many years ago, there was a special meeting arranged, where every funeral director in the area, was asked to be present. Bill's employees asked Bill and his wife, that as this was such an auspicious occasion, would they take the phone calls for the business that evening. They agreed, hoping, there wouldn't be any calls. Infact, they had one of the most unusual calls, Bill had ever had, in the whole of his long established career.

Having settled down, to watch an interesting TV programme, the telephone rang. The caller, was a gentleman, obviously upset, and highly strung. He lived in one of the higher class areas, informing Bill, he was an antiques dealer. He knew exactly what he wanted. He requested, that he wanted the body removed to Earl of Plymouth Chapels immediately, using the hearse, definitely not a removal vehicle, or one of Bill's private ambulances. Judging by the terms he used, he appeared to fully understand the funeral profession, saying, he didn't want Bill to use a removal shell, that he must come to the house with a casket, and the very best at that.

That was the end of Bill and Carole's quiet night in. Carole immediately dressed in her usual black trouser suit. They drove down to their chapels, putting a solid mahogany casket in their Rolls Royce hearse, and went up the short drive to the detached house. Bill said, he'd go in first, to make sure everything was alright. Having done this, Bill and Carole, carried the casket into the large hallway.

Bill asked the gent, which room the deceased was in. He replied, 'Just go upstairs, it's the first room facing you'. Bill went up the wide staircase into the room, as instructed. To Bill's surprise, there was no body to be seen. Bill thought to himself, the poor old chap was so upset, he must have made a mistake. Bill went down the stairs, tactfully explaining, there was no one there. The gent, then became very irate, assuring Bill, beyond doubt, the deceased was definitely in that room. By now, to say least, Bill too, was getting irate, Carole wondering whatever was going on, seeing Bill going up and down the stairs. This time when Bill entered the room, he wondered, whether the deceased had become so emaciated, that the outer form couldn't be seen through the bedding and heavy eiderdown, so he lifted the bedclothes, to look, but there was nothing in the bed. Next, he looked under the bed, infact, he looked everywhere, even in the fitted wardrobes. Eventually, the gent came up, pointing to a very ornate gold cage, in the corner of the room, where the old gent's best friend, Percy the Parrot, lay dead, reminding Bill, to treat his departed friend, with the utmost respect.

Bill was absolutely flabbergasted, for the parrot's legs were absolutely covered with diamond rings, seeing is believing. Bill and Carole then had to carry the solid mahogany casket upstairs into the bedroom, arrange the lovely velvet pillow, gently placing Percy on it in the casket, having first closed his eye, he only had one. The old gent watching, like a 'hawk' all the time, as Carole caught hold of its' wings, and Bill its' two legs, gently placing, the valuable, brightly coloured, large parrot complete with so many diamond rings on its' legs (they had never seen anything like it in their lives), on the velvet pillow, and closing the top.

Try to picture the scene. Bill 5 ft 3" took the foot end of the casket, Carole is 5 ft 8" took the head of the casket, which meant, when Bill was six stairs down, Carole was still standing upright on the top stair. The moment they began their descent, there was an almighty loud bang, which nearly made them drop the casket, until they realised, Percy had fallen off his pillow (not his perch, he'd already done that), and slid from top of the casket to the bottom. The old gent was very upset, saying, "Mind my Percy". With difficulty, they eventually got the casket to the hearse.

Next, Bill had to make the funeral arrangements. The old gent, making it abundantly clear, it had to be exactly the same, as an ordinary funeral. It was difficult at first, Bill could hardly believe, what was being said. However, the old gent knew exactly what he wanted, and had plenty of money to pay for it, having already given Bill a thousand pounds in advance, which Bill hadn't even asked for.

The service, was to be at the graveside, in a Plymouth Cemetery. The greatest shock of all, was when he requested the hearse and thirteen limousines were to leave from his house. What was Bill to do? After all, he had the money, which reminded Bill, as he always taught his staff, "Not ours to know the reason why", but our job to do all that's requested. Always telling them, if a family requests all the flowers to be upside down, then upside down, they must be. However, Bill did question the number of cars, suggesting, it would perhaps be better, he told Bill the number of people, and let Bill work out the number of cars he'd require. He nearly shot Bill's head off, reminding him, he was paying, and knew what he wanted, even asking Bill, if he wanted some more on account.

Well, he was Percy's only mourner, and wanted all the cars to line up, before leaving the house for the cemetery. Everything was perfect on the day, until the committal part at the graveside service, when, having lowered the casket into the grave, and said, 'Rest In Peace', the elderly gent, suddenly asked for all the valuable jewellery that was on the Parrot's legs. Shocked, Bill quickly replied, 'You didn't ask me to remove the jewels, and in any event, it would be hard to take them off'. The old gent, quickly explained, they were worth, thousands and thousands of pounds, and he wanted them off, now, quickly.

Well, as Bill said, this was the funniest job he'd ever had in the whole of his career. Imagine the scene, with the old gent ranting and raving, Bill hanging over the grave, pulling Percy's leg, just as he's pulling yours.

The book wouldn't be complete, without this enclosure, Bill's favourite tale, which he never tires of reciting.

# 4
# Brushes with the Law

Petrol rationing during the war made it extremely difficult for Bill to make enough money to keep his fleet of Packard hearses and large 7 seater Packard limousines on the road. Bill had only recently come out of the Royal Corps of Signals and had bought, at a very young age, the business of R. Boughards Garage & Car Hire in Emma Place, Stonehouse. He was trying very hard to establish his business at this particularly difficult time.

In those war days it was builders and undertakers who carried out funerals, none of whom owned a hearse or, in fact, any suitable funeral cars. Therefore they had to hire their vehicles from a local supplier, known as the Carriage Masters. Bill had quickly established himself as one of the Carriage Masters for Plymouth. He soon spotted that the only real way to keep operating his separate funeral and taxi fleets was to obtain enough petrol through alternative sources. He could not afford to use all of his petrol coupons on taxis as he would inevitably require some for funerals.

So, out of the blue, an opportunity presented itself. Bill knew a petrol tanker driver, who was letting some car owners purchase petrol "off the record". Never one to miss such an opportunity Bill made the tanker driver a partner in his business, convincing him that it would be more advantageous for both of them if he supplied this "off the record" petrol to Bill's fleets. This was Bill's opportunity to establish his business during the period of petrol rationing, during and after the war. His business kept running whilst others ground to a halt.

This "scam" continued for a long time until one day Bill returned from a funeral to find two detectives waiting for him. They had seen a 40 gallon drum in Bill's garage and wanted to know what it contained. Bill replied that the drum was empty. It had been empty when he left the garage earlier that day, and it had been there for weeks. They asked Bill to push the drum with his foot, whereupon he found it to be heavy and full. They requested to know its contents, to which Bill replied that he did not know.

Gordon, Bill's younger brother, once recalled the story and said that he could clearly remember Bill's face as he jumped out of his hearse, full of life, only to be confronted by the two very tall detectives. Bill had looked up at them with a cheeky grin on his face and asked, "Hello, Sir, and what can I do for you?" His face had visibly dropped when he had been asked to move the drum with his foot. Quick, as usual though, Bill responded that that particular drum must have been dropped there in his absence. The detective enquired as to the reason anyone should do such a thing. Once again, as quick as a flash, Bill suggested that, maybe, somebody was trying to get him into trouble.

The next day another detective called upon Bill and informed him that first he was going to speak to Bill as a friend, and then, after that, he would talk to him as a police officer. He proceeded to tell Bill the story. Apparently three people were involved, the loader of the petrol, the tanker driver and Bill!

Bill reminded the policeman he had said first, that he was going to treat Bill as a friend. The policeman agreed. Bill said, in which case, tell me what the other two culprits had told him. The policeman told Bill everything. Bill agreed with the whole story. Later this was helpful in supporting his defence; what little there was of it!

At court Bill was considered to be a very young man to be running such a business, particularly in such hard and worrying times. Bill's honesty stood him in very good stead, just as it has done for the whole of his life, and his straightforwardness with the detective had also been admired. Thus Bill was fined just £10 and allowed to continue to run his very demanding business.

## Legally Parked Car

One of Bill's cars was parked outside Agnes Weston, opposite his chapels, in Albert Road, when the police called, telling Bill, he must move his car, as Miss Carr, the lady in charge of Agnes Westons had made a complaint to the police.

Bill's immediate response to the policeman was, "Please hear me out first, and then, if you insist, I will move it." "O.K." Bill explained, "No one has any more right to park their own car, outside their own door, than anyone else", adding, "In your own interest, take note. Providing I am not causing any obstruction, you have no right to tell me to move. Now, you tell me, do you insist I have to move the car, if so, I'll do it, but I must warn you, I will take the matter further. I respectfully tell you now, in your own interest, you will lose".

The police officer asked to use Bill's phone, and rang the police station, telling the sergeant, all Bill had said. The seargent said, "Then don't tell him he has to move."

To Bill's surprise, the inspector of police, called on him two days after, simply to confirm all Bill had said was correct.

An interesting happening took place several months after, when Bill returned home from a long stay in USA. On the Queen Elizabeth, where he met and became friendly with, an American couple, who were only going to stay in London, decided, after Bill's kind invitation, to extend their holiday, staying at Bill's residence as his guests.

Apparently, during Bill's long absence from UK, a parking rule had come into force outside Agnes Westons, stating, "Parking not permitted between the hours of 9a.m. and 5p.m.".

At 10a.m. on Bill's first day home, a policeman came to his door, stating, Bill had committed an offence, by parking his Rolls Royce outside Agnes Westons, after 9a.m.. Bill's reply was, 'A', he didn't know of the new restriction, as it has been enforced whilst he was in USA, and 'B', it wasn't him that parked there, it was an American couple staying with him, whom he'd lent his Rolls Royce to, to give them a thrill.

The policeman, who didn't seem to believe a word Bill said, asked for their address. Bill, went into the lounge, where his American friends were relaxing, recounting the story, probably prompting them with a reply for the policeman ha! Ha!! They introduced themselves to the policeman, giving their address, in Hollywood. Which is where, Bill stayed with them, the following year, even though, on saying goodbye to them at Plymouth Railway Station, he added, "No good saying one thing and meaning another. I don't suppose we'll ever meet again". Yet the following year, Bill spent many months with them in USA. The friendship had begun. Even teaching them, the art of making a Cornish Pasty!!

As for Bill and parking his Rolls Royce illegally, he got away with it, yet again.

## Police Make a U-Turn

Bill, always a law abiding citizen, drove up the busy one way street from his home, doing a U-turn at the first set of traffic lights enabling him to travel in the opposite direction. This particular day, Bill clamed he had legally done a U-turn, just after a police car had passed the junction, Bill then following the police car.

It wasn't long, before the car had its' blue light flashing, signalling Bill to pull in. The policeman told Bill he pulled him in, because of the U-turn, and was going to issue a fixed penalty. Bill then asked him by saying, "Would you agree, that the last man any driver would want to upset is a policeman?" He agreed. Then Bill said, "You're wrong for pulling me in", adding, "I've given you the chance." He didn't heed Bill's warning and issued the ticket. Bill laughed in a polite manner, saying, "Oh, I thought you were going to let me off."

Bill paid the fine immediately, having already made up his mind he was going to fight the case, which he did. Suffice to say, he won.

Result, Bill had a cheque with compensation repaid to him personally at his home by the chief constable, together with an apology.

Not one to gloat over success, Bill, having taken the numbers of the two policemen that stopped him, wrote to the one that issued the fixed penalty, explaining, he didn't think any less of him, having made a mistake, on the contrary, Bill said, he looked upon the police as one's friend, his only regret was, that more people didn't do so. Assuring him, there was no hard feeling whatsoever. The odd and interesting thing about this is, that though Bill is always out and about, he has never seen that policeman since, which has concerned Bill a bit, because the last thing he would have wanted, was for the policeman to have lost his job Hopefully, he didn't.

I always feel, Bill would have made an excellent lawyer.

## Wine From France

Bill fondly remembers, being stopped at customs, on his way home from France. He was towing a very large caravan, infact, the largest legally allowed to be towed. He was asked how many bottles of wine he had. Always known for speaking the truth, "Only the one", said Bill. The customs officer waved the family on, little knowing that one bottle of wine was nearly 5 ft tall, strapped in the caravan wardrobe, and later used as a decorative standard lamp.

Similar happened with his bottles of brandy, and Martini. Each time, he told the customs, he only had the one bottle, but what a size those bottles were, each containing at least two gallons.

## Cases Won, But Never Lost

Bill's a modern day Rumpole of the Bailey. If someone's being treated unjustly, he likes nothing better than to take up the case. Here's just a few, with the motto, 'stick up for what is right, and don't give in'.

Pam Glanville, a girl Bill went to school with, and her husband Lou, came to Bill, armed with a huge pile of letters, from a London firm of solicitors, who were trying to stop Lou, successfully claiming compensation from H.M. Dockyard, for asbestosis and bronchitis, from which he was unable to work. Poor Lou, didn't have anybody behind him to help except the Union, who seemed to do precious little. Bill felt so sorry for the couple, knowing they had a mortgage etc., to pay. Seeing the many letters they had, as much as Bill wanted to help, he said, it was impossible for him to go back through all that. I remember it well, and can see the sadness on their faces now. Bill said, "I tell you what, give me the first two or three letters, and the last two or three". Quickly glancing through, he said, "Now listen to me, and do as I say". "O.K. Bill". "Make sure you visit your G.P. every few days complaining, during which time, I can't promise anything, but I will see if there's any way, in which I can help".

The outcome was fantastic, Bill completely reversed the situation. The solicitors were trying to claim, Mr. Glanville was ill because of his bronchitis, not the asbestosis. Bill said nonsense, and fought tooth and nail arguing, bronchitis comes and goes, putting it the other way round, Mr. Glanville has bronchitis because he permanently suffers with asbestosis, and will for the rest of his life. After much correspondence, Mr. Glanville excitedly telephoned Bill, telling him he'd been offered £3,000 compensation, thanking Bill, saying they were delighted and would accept same. (£3,000 is a lot of money to someone who hasn't any.) Bill advised them not to accept it, pointing out, they have admitted liability, by making the offer. Bill explained, the offer wasn't made because they like you. They reluctantly agreed to leave the matter in Bill's hands. Bill fought on, until he got them £27,000, enough to buy a decent property at that time. They were, to coin a phrase, 'over the moon', made for the rest of their days.

A friend of Bill's had a large, three generation, well established family business. They were faced with a compulsory purchase order on their business premises, together with many other businesses in the same area and the local population. The council wanted to widen the road, knocking down his shop. Bill's friend sought the firm's solicitors advice, who told him, in view of the compulsory purchase order, the council would have to provide him with premises, to enable him continue the family business. This is a long story, but to cut it short, Bill realising his friend had everything to lose, and nothing to gain for his enforced move, gave his friend far superior advice, which was, whatever you do, don't let the council provide you with other premises, tell them that none of you feel like starting all over again at your time of life, and that they must fully compensate you for premises and putting you out of business, thus giving him far more money than doing it the solicitor's way. He decided to do it Bill's way.

This allowed the business friend to look for premises himself, or, not even start again, if he didn't want to. Financially, a far better option, which he gratefully took up. Consequently, he could never thank Bill enough, and did infact purchase suitable premises themselves. There was however, one big difference, with Bill, there was no 'bill', but with the solicitor he first went to, there was a big one. Another satisfied friend. No wonder so many visited Bill for his wisdom, which when carried through, was always beneficial.

The paintwork on Bill's four year old Datsun was in a very poor state. The car had only done "42,000 miles", garaged, and meticulously maintained from new, as is the rest of his fleet. The manufacturers, stated that as it was well out of guarantee, they were not interested, completely washing their hands of the problem, thinking, that was the end of that. Bill, not one to give up, knowing he was having a raw deal, wrote back to Datsun, saying, "Who am I? You may be able to prove me wrong, so not involving you in any expense, this is what I plan to do". He was going to park the car in the middle of the city, immediately outside the press offices, placing a large sign on the car, asking the public to sign a petition, if they agreed with Bill, that this car was in poor condition for its' age. Bill offering half a crown for each signature, saying to himself, eight half crowns to the pound, all going to charity, to a maximum of £500. Datsun, not wanting negative publicity, paid for the whole car to be stripped to bare metal, and re-painted, before Bill put it on show to the public. A lot of thought and perseverance, paying off, even against giant companies. A bit like David and Goliath, showing David can win, if he's like Bill Earl.

Another case involving paintwork on cars, was when Bill decided to have all his black fleet painted 'silver fox'. It was unheard of many years ago, for a funeral director to have anything other than a black fleet. Bill had already spent many sleepless nights, before finally making his decision to change the colour of his very large fleet from the traditional black, a true pioneer. All went well at first, then as the last car was being resprayed, Bill could see the first car hadn't been properly painted. He complained to the garage owner, who re-sprayed the cars again, but with the same disastrous results. Bill noticing the problem on the first car that was sprayed, as the last car was being done. He fought the solicitors tooth and nail, until eventually, he had a letter from the solicitors saying, if the account is not settled within seven days, procedures will be instigated. Bill, who had never used a solicitor, immediately wrote back saying, 'Do not wait the seven days, please proceed today'. Suffice to say, Bill won the case without a solicitor acting for him. If Bill hadn't pointed out the many faults, this garage would have continued with a second rate service to you, the public.

Bill, always liked to keep his properties immaculate, but maintenance free, so he opted to have his funeral premises at Albert Road pebble dashed. All started well, with the exterior chipped right back to the brick and cemented. Then the builders made their mistake. The pebbles on one side of the house were thrown one way with the left hand, on the other half they threw them the other way with the right hand. Bill quickly noticed what they had done, and told them. 'Like teaching a mother how to suck eggs'. The finished job showed their mistake. These traders tried twice more to patch their workmanship, by cementing on top of the first pebbles, and adding more, which only bounced off. Bill ended up fighting the solicitors, and won his case, not paying a penny. No, Bill didn't have a solicitor. A lesson they wouldn't forget, for the bad workmanship.

Bill bought a well known brand of kitchen carpet, it didn't live up to expectation, as advertised. The dirt not coming cleanly away from the carpet. He complained to Trago Mills, "two years after purchase", without a receipt, stating the problem, and branch it was purchased. One of Bill's staff, remarked, Bill didn't stand a 'cat in hell's' chance of getting a refund, after two years, and without a receipt. Bill's office staff said, don't say that, he's never lost a case yet. Not one to give up, he persisted, and had his full refund. His employees were astonished that he was even paid, let alone in cash (not a cheque or credit note). Bill's honesty paid off, and he knew he was in the right. Best of it is, Bill to this day, still has the offending carpet, though at that time, in fairness to Bill, he did send a sample of the carpet to Trago Mills. Infact, the carpet covers the floor in his large sun room.

This is Bill all over, seeing a chance to help Mike Robinson, proprietor of Trago Mills, he did, Mike immediately replied to Bill, saying he couldn't thank him enough. Apparently, Mike wanted to sell pharmaceutical products at reduced prices, however, this apparently, wasn't allowed. Bill, thinking he saw an unfair happening, wrote, telling Mike, all purchases made from the Co-op, were subject to 'The Divy', worth investigating. Competition is now allowed.

A slightly different story. Bill was used to receiving his mail by 7a.m., every morning, thus enabling him to respond to all correspondence immediately. Without informing him, the Royal Mail decided to change the delivery round, his mail not arriving until almost lunch-time. This is no good to me, said Bill, whose never one to easily give in, he fought and fought, result, after much persistence, his mail was specially delivered by van, before 7a.m., every day.

The post office often mixed up Bill's home address mail, delivering it to his Earl of Plymouth chapels, and vice versa, in each case the mail was correctly addressed. Complaining about this inconvenience, which was eventually righted, he now fought for compensation and free postage. He received a cheque for compensation and a pile of stamped and addressed envelopes.

Unknowing to millions of motorists, Bill Earl helped them all, even though none of it affected him personally. Margaret Thatcher the then Prime Minister of Great Britain, was going to bring in a bill, wherein every car owner was going to have to pay a yearly road tax, for owning a car, whether the vehicle was ever used, made no difference. The compulsory road fund tax was to be enforced, purely because, then and now, some fleece the government, by driving their cars, without paying tax. Bill felt this was very unfair, punishing the innocent for the guilty. He was so incensed he wrote a polite letter direct to Lady Thatcher, stating his thoughts. Lady Thatcher kindly acknowledged Bill's letter, thanking him for his interest, and promised, she was now going to give it further thought, and would contact him again later. Finally, she informed him, that after giving the matter more thought, she decided to accept the suggestion Bill made, and would not bring in the new legislation, that had been planned. Laid off cars to this day, do not need to be road taxed, thanks to Bill's intervention.

Bill's two year old flymo grass cutter ceased working. The manufacturers weren't interested, as it was out of guarantee. Bill wrote a nice letter explaining, a guarantee for a mower that spends most of the year in a garden shed is different to most items, that are used every day. He went on to say, with our English summers lasting five months, if we're lucky, the mower is used once a week for twenty weeks. A two year old mower, only used on forty occasions and ceases to work, didn't say much for the mower. Flymo saw the point, repairing Bill's mower, that is used to this day, without anymore problems. It just goes to show, it pays to be a 'cut' above the rest.

Many years ago, Bill's local Lloyds bank was robbed. Amongst other items, the thieves emptied all the customers' private bank safe deposit boxes. The Bank Inspectors were called in to investigate. The manager saying to them, "If all my clients were like Mr. Earl, I wouldn't have any problems". The manager knowing Bill extremely well, after many years of being a loyal customer to that branch, witnessing first hand Bill's honesty and how well he operated his banking accounts and various businesses, he asked Bill outright, what was contained in his box. Bill told him that amongst the many valuable papers, that the thieves did not steal, he had a substantial amount of cash, that they did take. Because Bill was held in such high esteem with the manager, Lloyds Bank agreed to repay Bill the amount he said was contained in his box, although there wasn't any proof whatsoever. All through being so totally honest all his life. Who says, honesty doesn't pay, it certainly saved Bill a lot of problems that day.

Jon, from a little boy, to this day, always ran to Bill, asking his advice, on what is the best way to do, this or that. Even if he hurt himself as a child, he wouldn't listen to anyone else, saying, "I'm going to Dad, he'll know what to do", meaning his step-dad. Suffice to say, Jon's always put his infinite trust in Bill. Neither Jon, or his class mates at school have forgotten, the sound advice he gave, when they were going to write to the headmaster, complaining about their American teacher. Apparently, all the class disliked him. Bill advised Jon, not to write the letter in the usual manner, explaining, in the normal way, the first name will automatically be accepted as the instigator, and could be made an enemy for life. Instead, Bill advised, they write their complaint on a letter in the shape of a circle, with all the signatures going around in a circle. That way, no one would know who had started the complaint. In a circle, there's no beginning, and no end. That is what they did, and succeeded in getting their grievances aired, fairly. Bill reminding Jon, it's not the nationality at fault, it's the personality

Well, there are many more cases like this that Bill has fought, and won, his name being registered as 'Earl of Plymouth' is another mentioned elsewhere in the book, the custody of his two children, yet another case, and so on. The advice we can all learn from Bill, is, we must all stick up for ourselves if we want justice. Don't moan, do something about it. No firm is too big to fight, providing, you know you're in the right and know what you're talking about. Bill would have made an excellent solicitor, making sure justice was carried out.

# 5

# Around the World
# in Eighty Years

Bill Earl's travels, or busman's holidays, give an invaluable insight of this adventurous character. Welcome to Bill Earl's World, won't you come on in!!

Bill, in his first eighty years of life, travelled right around the world no fewer than five times! Most people don't get around it once! He spent much of his time actually living in various countries, learning their customs, religions and different styles of cooking, etc.. Bill thrived on living in different places because there was always so much to learn, and knowledge he could share.

No other funeral director, I've ever known, has spent so much time, in all parts of the world, studying and taking an active part in funerals.

## USA & Canada

Whilst he was in USA, Bill met and spent time with a funeral director whom the courts had tried to summons, because of his advertisement, which read, "We bury beautiful bodies, we buried Marilyn Munroe". The judge made a pertinent point, asking those present, 'Did she have a beautiful body?' The unanimous response was, "Yes". In which case, the advertisement, was deemed true, allowing the advert to continue as it was. An interesting experience for Bill.

Bill visited Kennedy's grave, where there is an ever burning flame. He also visited, the famous Forest Lawn Cemetery, and seen cemeteries that do everything, as well as cemeteries where music seems to come from hidden speakers, behind water fountains etc.

Back to Forest Lawn Cemetery. Their system is, for families who request their full service; they collect the deceased, take it to their own Funeral Home, situated in the Cemetery. Embalm the body, and place it in the Funeral Home to enable viewing. Each room of the American Funeral Homes, are deliberately made to look like the living room of a person's

Around the world in 80 years. *Courtesy of The Evening Herald*

house, giving a warm, cosy, home from home impression. They arrange for the funeral service, in one of their very many churches, of numerous denominations. The cemetery is so large, they run a taxi service from within the grounds. It's the most fantastic cemetery in the world, with so many beautiful churches, and many ornately carved and varied monuments, there is just nothing like it. Too hard, and too much to explain to do it justice.

*Apollo 13*

Bill gave many lectures, particularly in Canada, and at least one in New Orleans. It was on the day, 17th April, 1970, that Apollo 13, commanded by Jim Lovell, splashed down safely after its near disastrous mission to

Studying with students at San Fransisco College of Mortuary Science

the moon. That is how Bill remembered it so well, and because when Jim Lovell was interviewed, Bill, who was always interested in religion, asked Jim the question, "When you were in outer space was your faith in God increased or decreased?" His reply was, "Increased." Many of the hundreds attending the interview later congratulated Bill for asking the best question.

During the early years Bill lived in USA, studying at the San Francisco College of Embalming & Mortuary Science. He also lived in Canada where he studied at Humber College of Mortuary Science & Funeral Directing.

Whilst in USA Bill stayed in several Convents, more Convents than most, his interesting experiences are described later in this chapter.

**Coffins From France**

Holidaying in France with his wife Carole and the two children, Bill noticed a funeral one morning, taking place in a sleepy French village. The many mourners were going into church on this bright sunny summer morning. The Earl family were on their way to a quiet beach in Brittany. Bill suddenly said to his family, after looking lustfully at the funeral procession, look, you 3 will have to wait, because he felt compelled to attend the funeral, to see if there was anything different he could learn. After the service, he made contact with the funeral director, asking to see the best

Bringing a coffin home from France

coffin they had, after explaining he was a funeral director from England.
Having seen their full range, Bill said, there was nothing good enough.
They then showed him a brochure, which had a picture of a very fine casket, in mahogany, with edges trimmed with gold. The same day, Bill,
Carole and the children drove 200 miles each way, to the casket factory.
Bill, and his wife with her limited knowledge of French, eventually managed to make the owners understand what they wanted, and so, a few
hours later, a jubilant Bill left the factory with a magnificent casket safely
secured to the roof rail of one of Bill's very long limousines. Bill placing
an order for more caskets to be delivered directly to his Chapels.

The following day, the family started their homeward journey, on one of
the wettest days they'd ever known, to say nothing of the gale force winds.
As they were driving along, parts of the very strong material used to cover
the casket, were flying past the back windows of the car, due to the exceptional weather, much to the amusement of the children. The casket covering, was somewhat like 6 ply corrugated material. To say least, this was
most disconcerting to Bill, especially, when due to the extraordinary soak-
ing and pounding it had, the pieces kept whizzing past Bill's eyes when

driving. However, when arriving to board the ferry from St. Malo, inspite of everything, nobody seemed to notice anything untoward perched on top of Bill's limousine

Arriving at Weymouth Docks, Bill naturally drove into the 'RED, something to declare department'. The customs asked Bill, if he had anything to declare, to which Bill replied, no, adding, that he didn't think customs would let him through, without wanting to know what was on the roof. Customs then asked, what is it? Told it was a casket, the officer asked, is there anyone in it? When told, no. The customs officer looked concerned, saying, the problem was, the customs office which dealt with all the paperwork needed, was closed. Bill explained, he was only going a little way, because he was staying the night with his brother in law Chris. In which case, could they let him out, and he would come back in the morning to Customs. The reply was, that he dare not let Bill out with the casket, telling Bill he'd have to leave his car behind, with casket on top, and walk out of the ferry terminal. Bill explained, that Earl of Plymouth is well known all over the world, and drew attention to the number plates, each bearing the name, 'Earl of Plymouth', but all to no avail. Bill, quick with a remedy to the problem and not wanting to leave his car behind, asked for 4 men, to unscrew the roof rail, enabling Bill to simply drive forward, leaving the 4 men holding the casket in the air, ready to come back the next day and finish the journey home to Plymouth, after a contended night's sleep. The casket was a talking point in Bill's selection room, different from anything else he had. He sold many of these caskets, making a long lasting business relationship with the French Casket Factory. As for the children, Anita and Jonathan, they never forgot this 'busman's holiday' of Bill's.

## Coffin from Benedorm

Another incident, on how Bill came to import another choice of casket. He, with his wife and family, were holidaying in Benedorm, for a nice relaxing spring break, for a change. Bill, not able to keep himself away from his profession for long, was soon looking in the yellow pages, to discover, the location of the closest funeral director. Ah, not too far away, thought Bill, looking at the address, in the old town, just off the adjoining beach. "Right", says Bill to his bemused family, "We're going for a little stroll tomorrow, just to see the local funeral director, O.K.?" Well, what could his little family say, they'd heard it all before, so knew what would invariably happen.

The next morning dawned hot and sunny, as usual. Off they went, for a little stroll of about 45 minutes, to a modern shop fronted premises. Bill was welcomed with open arms. The Spanish funeral director able to speak fluent English. Bill was shown around the small, but immaculate prem-ises, when his eye caught a rather outstanding casket. Bill couldn't keep his eyes off it. It was of rich mahogany, with intricate carved details all over, its' highly polished wood. Opening the cover, revealed an inner glass cover, allowing one to see the deceased behind glass. Enquiring from the funeral director, he discovered, it was identical to the casket, President Franco had. No wonder it looked so good.

Needless to say, after much deliberation, Bill imported this style of casket, with others, from Spain, to add to his varied collection, for the public to choose from.

The following day, the family had decided to take their car into the coun-try. Unfortunately, they took a wrong turning on the way, and ended out-side a cemetery, very peaceful, and a pleasant change from the busy life in Benedorm. Bill thought it a good place, very picturesque surroundings, in a country setting, to sit and have a picnic. It wasn't long before, who should come along, conducting a funeral? You've guessed it, none other than the funeral director from Benedorm. He smiled and gave a little wave to the family, whom he must have thought were very keen indeed!!

## Sri Lanka & Flying Coffins Home

Always very keen to learn more about his chosen profession, Bill went to live with the owners of the largest funeral business in Colombo, Sri Lanka (then called Ceylon). He would fly, with the owners, from one funeral branch to another. The business was owned by two brothers, one of whom studied for his professional qualifications in London. He, like Bill, had the B.I.E. diploma of the British Institute of Embalmers.

Bill Earl, known all over the world, always advertised "Earl of Plymouth, England, contacts throughout the world, hence simplicity of the postal address". Much of his mail, received from all parts of the world, arrives simply addressed "Earl of Plymouth, England", which is how the initial invitation to Sri Lanka was addressed. The letter began, "My dear Lord". Bill, always thrilled by the chance to learn and excited by oppor-tunities to travel, immediately replied, writing, "I accept, but I am just plain Bill Earl to my friends".

Bill's little business cards, only 3" by 2", reading, "Contacts Throughout The World, Hence Simplicity of Address; Earl of Plymouth, England", have caused amusement the world over, not least in Sri Lanka, as wherever Bill travelled, he would write on the reverse of one, stick a stamp on the front, and place it in a post box. Never did one fail to get to his home address in Plymouth, thus proving how well he's known, and what a useful and inexpensive means of keeping the family up to date with his news and whereabouts from 'anywhere' in the world.

Bill, always interested in religions, knew that all could be found in Sri Lanka. He realised the invitation was a fantastic opportunity afforded to him; one he grasped with both hands which turned out to be the most helpful and wonderful experience he's ever had.

He was able to live with the family funeral concern, who became his very dear life-long friends, as one of a Sri Lankan family, to experience the many wonderful new things in this unusual country, where he was involved in carrying out hundreds (yes, hundreds) of funerals of all types, nationalities, religions, and disposals, whether by funeral pyre, gas cremation, or various other unusual procedures, such as committing a body to be devoured by high flying birds. The embalming and funerals of many different cultures and colours made it a priceless experience for Bill.

One of the brothers, called Maurice, wanted to open a funeral business in Australia, with Bill as his partner. Bill went to Sydney to pave the way. His idea, at that time, was never to have to experience another winter for the rest of his life, by living in Australia during their summers, and in England during theirs. However, matrimonial problems stepped in to Bill's life and the new business partnership never materialised, nor did Bill's dreams of one everlasting summer!

Maurice had to take some capital with him to Australia in order to invest in a funeral business. This was not as simple as it sounds. At that time the natives of Ceylon (Sri Lanka), were not permitted to take any money out of the country. Bill, himself, had to declare how much he was taking into the country when he arrived, and then he had to prove how much he had spent there in order to leave the country. The ironic part of this story is that their money was of no value whatsoever in any other part of the world! Maurice was able to overcome the problem so Bill understood, by purchasing a large consignment of antique furniture, transport it to Australia and then sell it in order to raise the capital required.

Although Bill did not enter into partnership with Maurice, he did spend long periods visiting Australia and often visited Maurice.

Whilst staying in Sri Lanka, Bill ordered caskets from Maurice and Aubrey. They had never exported any of their caskets to Britain before, Bill, always using his business brain, was able to tell his funeral director friends in Sri Lanka, how to fly the caskets made there, to the UK for the price of one.

At the time, the airlines charged according to size of cargo, and not weight. Bill asked his friends to make a casket according to his own design, most of which he learnt through seeing so many caskets, on his many round the world trips.

Bearing in mind, his Sri Lanka friends' caskets were most sought after throughout the world, hence they had a good export market, but, for Bill's idea, they still didn't know how to send two for the price of one, until Bill ordered two of these especially made caskets, of two different sizes. Example, 6 ft 3" × 2 ft, inside, the second one was, 6 ft × 1 ft 10", and then told them, to put one inside the other. No way, they said, it can't be done. Why, Bill asked. They replied, because it wont allow enough room for packing between the caskets, and without the packing, the highly, French polished finish, would get rubbed off during transit. That was until, Bill explained, no packing whatsoever would be required. All you have to do, is carefully put one casket inside the other, without rubbing the sides, then, with one screw either end, screw the bottom of one to the other. "Two for the price of one!!"

To coin a phrase, Bill said, 'there's more than one way of killing a cat'. The two caskets arrived at Heathrow Airport in perfect condition, and that was how further consignments travelled from then on.

To this day, Bill's sincere and most precious friends in Sri Lanka, always have one of The Earl of Plymouth Caskets on display in each of their selection rooms in Sri Lanka.

## Australia

Bill had just attended an Australian Funeral Directors' Conference, at Surfers Paradise, Gold Coast, Australia. Instead of going straight home, he flew to Alice Springs to look at the flying Doctor's base. It really was fascinating seeing their light aircraft in the hanger, ready for take off at a minute's notice, to help, if some distant farmer was in trouble. He also visited The School of The Air. Listening to the teacher talking to her pupils, on the radio, all living miles away. It was very interesting and certainly different. The child is called by his or her first name then by the name of the ranch, or farm, as a means of identification. Homework was sent by post. Probably now, a lot of it is done with the computer. Well, the distances travelled in Outback Australia, are really awe inspiring. There, Bill saw the biggest lorries he'd ever encountered, called Road Trains, the main arctic lorry towing up to three large trailers behind. There isn't a railway line in Northern Australia. It was nothing to see a warning, on leaving a town, saying, fill up with petrol now, no more fuel stations for 250 miles. When leaving to drive somewhere, one should always inform officials where you're going, and expected time of arrival. Then, if you don't arrive, a search party is sent out, without delay. There's no second chance if lost in the Outback, it's vast, empty, dry, hot and dangerous, one wouldn't live long. Having left the town of Alice Springs, seeing Ayers Rock, the herds of wild camels, wide open spaces, with not a house in sight, from horizon, to horizon. Bill, on seeing the usual tin drum on the main road, which heralded the entrance that led down, miles of dirt track

Flying doctor service, Alice Springs

to one of these huge farms he'd heard so much about, fascinated by not being able to see a building in the distance, he decided to drive down one of these dry red dusty tracks. It really was, a good half hour's drive, when the homestead came into view, with it's clutter of wooden bungalows, sheep sheds, water windmills, water tanks and vehicles, all shimmering in the intense heat. The young farmer's wife, with two girls about 6 yr and 8 yr, greeted Bill and his wife Carole.

They were made very welcome, when suddenly, the farmer's wife shouted to the girls, to be quick, it was time for school. Bill watched as the girls went into a room in the bungalow adapted for school use only. They were talking on the two way radio, to that same teacher Bill had visited the day before. He had noticed a chart in the kitchen of the human body, sectioned into numbers and letters. This was used if they needed to call the Flying Doctor. By using the chart, it could be explained exactly to the doctor, where the problem was. A locked medicine chest was kept close by, all medicines, numbered in a similar way. The doctor could say, take tablet X or Y. If someone was really ill, the family had their own airstrip for the Flying Doctor to come. They went shopping three times a year, and flew to the town, in their own plane. If the girls wanted a larger pony to ride, one from the wild herd of ponies was caught, and broken in. They had sheep, thousands of them. They hired hands when it was sheep shearing time. They wouldn't change their life style for anything, and their next door neighbour only lived forty miles away!! The drinking water, was only used for that, drinking. Another tank of water was used for washing etc. Well that was an interesting visit, answering Bill's curiosity about these evasive huge farms. One parting question he couldn't resist asking, "How do you find someone to marry, living so far from anyone?" "No problem", came the quick reply, "We talk to others on the two way radio, if you like the sound of someone, then we arrange to meet". Again, the computer probably comes in useful these days. Bill, satisfied carried on with his travels, to a little town called Kununurra in Western Australia. Population 25,000. The little town was self sufficient, able to grow anything, dairy herds, beef, etc., close to a reservoir called Lake Argyle, which looked, more like the ocean, it was so huge. All in all very fertile land, developing fast. When the town mayor, learnt that Bill was a funeral director, the local dignitaries, begged Bill to stay, and start up business in their town, they were fed up of having to travel 250 miles each way to Darwin to make funeral arrangements. They really were disappointed when Bill thought about it, saying, maybe if he had been younger, he would have taken up the challenge, but it was a bit hot for him there, and he wasn't as young as he used to be. Next stop Darwin, to visit a young funeral director, who rounded up water buffalo in his spare time. Australia was in the process of destroying all the water buffalo that were caught, because it wasn't a native animal to that vast country, and instead, protecting the crocodile that had been mercilessly hunted in the past. The crocodile really is something to be feared, not frightened of humans, a real killer. Bill knew which of the two animals, he'd rather see, and it wasn't the crocodile.

Bill has visited Australia so many times that he had the opportunity to visit every major city except for Perth.

This is a day, Bill and Carole will never forget. They were in a small holiday town, about 300 miles south of Sydney, completely unspoilt, very lush and green. They awoke before sunrise, to accompany their funeral director friend Maurice onto the modern fishing boat, they'd chartered. Although the sun was shinning and the skies blue, the sea was very choppy. The boat headed out deeper into the rough sea, following the radar, which showed where the fish were gathered. It was so rough, the boat rocking from side to side, that poor Bill was knocked off his feet, landing on his back. Bill always recalls Carole saying to him, 'Bill, you should be more careful'. Bill thankful, he hadn't gone over the side. Carole, who'd never fished before, to her surprise caught a shark, that she threw back. There were plenty of fish in the area, so after a successful morning, the fish, mainly barramundi, about 2 ft long, and very sweet tasting, were placed in a polystyrene box, packed with ice, so that they could be eaten that night, on their return to Sydney. They had no sooner got their 'land legs' back, and they were up in the air. That afternoon, a local funeral director, hearing of Bill's visit to the area, took them flying in his small 4 seater plane. It was a very exhilarating experience, with marvellous views of the rocky, empty bush that surrounded this coastal town, the flight lasting about an hour. By the time they drove back to Sydney, where the fresh fish were barbecued, it was a long, but varied and interesting day, certainly a full day, worth remembering.

In Sydney, Bill had had a busy day, having attended a Japanese wedding, decided to take a look at the famous Opera House. There were hundreds of people present, when Bill burst into song. I shall never forget that day, as long as I live. After claps from his appreciative audience, none of whom he knew, to make things worse, or was it, he then started yodelling, which he is very good at, and practices every day, he soon had everyone roaring with laughter. Not many can claim to have sung in the one and only Sydney Opera House.

Once, when Bill and Carole were visiting Australia in the 1980's, they were on a long tour in a massive bus, run by 'Newmans', in which there were only ten passengers and four drivers. The tour took them to a different location in the outback each night.

Some days they would have travelled three hundred miles or more through the vast interior of Australia, known as the 'outback', not a house to be seen, from horizon to horizon, fascinatingly, eerily, void of people. Nobody likes carrying lots of dirty underwear, and Carole was no exception, so they managed to find a way of washing and drying their "smalls" each evening. The Australian passengers on the bus were most intrigued when Bill mentioned that he and Carole were managing to wash and change their underwear every day. They wondered how it could be done, in view of the short stops overnight and the limited facilities. Bill explained to them how in one location they had used the large standard lamp in their bedroom as a clothes drier. Carole had washed their clothes and then carefully placed them over the top of the lamp, which they switched on and left outside the closed curtains, in the window, so as not to keep them awake. The passengers were in hysterics, at these antics. On another night, when there was no such lamp, not to be deterred they used the large ceiling fan. First Bill cleaned the dust from the blades, they then positioned the wet clothes carefully on each blade so as to balance the fan. The clothes were left whirling around all night whilst they slept; Bill had re-invented the spin-dryer! Another night it was extremely hot and Bill, after drying the clothes, placed them in the small deep-freeze compartment of the fridge in his room. Next morning he limped gingerly to the bus. In fact he looked so crippled that the other passengers were extremely worried. They could not see how Bill was going to be able to continue this long and arduous journey. Bill, always the joker, laughed and explained how his frozen pants were so stiff that they had nearly broken his back! It made a nice cold start to a blisteringly hot day.

Before long, it was time to leave Australia, another adventure completed, but as Bill always said, 'there's nothing like home, at the end of the day'.

## Visiting Southern Ireland

Bill has many fond memories of The Emerald Isle, laughing, when reminiscing on this part of the world. Here are a few true, but hilarious experiences.

The funny happenings began on boarding The Irish Ferries ship at Fishguard for the three and half hour crossing to Rosslaire. The ship sailed at 3p.m., but the film show on board, which one paid to watch, started at 2.30p.m.!!!! No way of watching the complete film, already started before boarding the ship.

On first trip to S. Ireland, the couple clocked up 2,500 miles, in their trusty Mercedes estate. Criss crossing Ireland as they did, they generally stayed in bed and breakfast homes, there weren't many hotels. Bed and breakfast establishments were like houses from the 'Ideal Homes Exhibition', a true compliment to the Irish, who are laid back, friendly, and funny. One bed and breakfast establishment, had everything until, Bill wanted to use his electric razor, but couldn't find anywhere to plug it in. He laughingly enquired of the lady, 'Don't men shave here in Ireland?' "Oh, to be sure they do", she replied. 'But not with an electric razor', said Bill. "To be sure they do", she said. 'Well, there isn't a socket in our bed-room", said Bill. "To be sure there is, it's in the double wardrobe, with a full length mirror". Bill not knowing where to look, doubled up laughing, he could imagine himself stood in a wardrobe, having a shave!!! Who would have thought of looking in a wardrobe, for the razor socket?

Next night, there wasn't a wardrobe to shave in!! Bill looked every-where, eventually finding a socket on the skirting board, next to the bed. He went out to the lady, saying, "I've just been lying under the bed". "Whatever for", came the reply. "I was having a shave", said Bill, hardly able to contain himself for laughing.

Back at that time, S. Ireland only had two TV channels, RTV 1 and RTV 2, and they really weren't very good. Carole asked, if the establishment had satellite TV, to help pass the evening. One reply, from a lady on the east coast, facing England was, "No, but don't worry, if the wind's in the right direction, we get Welsh TV, BBC1, BBC2, and ITV". A novel answer indeed, and they did get all those stations. I guess, the wind was in the right direction, that night!!

In another place they stayed, Bill noticed, as they were going out each evening, the owner would turn the TV on in the lounge, ready for when they returned, that's how long it took to warm up. Bill said to the lady one day, "I know what's wrong with your TV". Her face lit up, "Oh, do you, what is it?" "It's a Murphy", said Bill. That was true, it really was a Murphy TV. Staying in this town called Gory, Monday evenings, all the restaurants were closed, except one, a general take-away, or sit in. Bill fancied a curry, with chips, because they didn't sell rice. The curry arrived. It tasted good, but Bill couldn't find any chicken. Complaining and laughing to the lady that served him, she simply replied, "If you'd asked for a bit of chicken, I'd have put a bit in the curry". Bill learnt from this experience, always explain precisely what you want, when visiting S. Ireland.

Another place they visited, was on the west coast, close to Northern Ireland. The Irish lady owner, gave Bill and Carole the usual welcoming pot of tea and cakes. She stayed chatting, asking where the couple had been, and where they planned to go next. Carole explained, they'd already travelled through the west coast, and now planned to cross over towards the east coast next day, not intending to visit N. Ireland, because of all the

To be or not to be. A funeral Director in Southern Ireland

troubles witnessed on TV. The owner tried to talk Bill and Carole into visiting Northern Ireland. She laid out several maps on her dining room table, explaining how beautiful the country was. She said, she crossed the border to shop there every week. Now for the punch line, "Mind you", she said "Last week, they blew the check point up". Bill and Carole, could hardly keep straight faces, wanting to laugh, but couldn't because the lady was serious. Do you think she tempted them to visit N. Ireland, or put them off completely?

After a sumptuous breakfast at another house, cases packed in the car, and the bill paid, the lady looked up, asking if they had enough hot water for a shower, because she'd just turned it on, if they wanted a hot shower, now!!! No, they didn't stop for the tempting shower.

They visited a beautiful country hotel, after enjoying a Guinness, that took ages to pour, Bill laughingly asked the barman had he gone to Dublin to get it. They were proudly shown around this immaculate place, and decided they would stay the night. Bill asked how much it was for the two of them for the night. The young man shook his head, saying, the owner was away, and he didn't know how much to charge, saying, sorry, they wouldn't be able to stay, until a week later, when the owner would be back. What a reply!!

An Australian couple they met in Ireland, had a similar experience. They went to a garage, to hire a car, but as the owner was away, and no one knew how much to charge, they couldn't hire a car, until next week.

Staying in the Metropole Hotel in Cork, the fire emergency sign in the corridor points to the right, but the sign next to it, shows a man running to the left. Where's one supposed to go, if there's a fire? Confused, so were they.

Visiting a high class Irish restaurant, the young waitress brought Bill the large menu, saying, "Everything that's marked off, is on". So, what about the things marked on, were they off?

Driving in the Emerald Isle was also perplexing. Without exception, joining a main road from a minor road, there was always a sign post telling you where you'd been, but nothing to say where you wanted to go. The sign posts showed the distances in miles and in kilometres, so if it took a long time, one knew it was miles, if a short time, it was kilometres. It wasn't unusual to find a sign, with a workman's jacket covering it up. In which case, one didn't know whether, one was coming, or going!!

No good asking for directions either. They did this, when wanting to go to Tipperary. The old Irish gentleman, scratched his head, saying "That's difficult. If I were going there, I wouldn't start from here". Well, we all know, it's a long way to Tipperary after all.

Another time, they asked a barman how far it was to Shannon. The young man looked Bill seriously in the face, saying, "It'll take me 45 minutes, but it'll take you an hour". Bill left still not knowing how far away he was!!!

At Rosslaire they stayed at a farmhouse, in readiness to sail next morning. To boil a kettle, and fill their flask, ready for the long day ahead, Carole found the one and only electric socket, "No, it wasn't in the wardrobe". It was on the skirting beneath the middle of the double bed, so when the kettle boiled, Bill, still in bed, had steam coming up through his ears. He thought he was having a 'sauna'!! Worse was to come. After breakfast, packing cases in car, paying the bill. The owners knowing Bill was catching 9a.m. ferry, came out with a farewell punch line, saying, "We hope the ferry doesn't do what it did last week, It left half an hour early, without telling anyone, leaving half the passengers behind". Needless to say, Bill & Carole didn't hang around, it was the fastest drive they'd made since arriving in Ireland. Thankfully, the ferry left on time. Different to British Rail, which is usually late, but then, this was Ireland after all. I don't know which is worse?

Bill's visited the Emerald Isle several times, because he loves the Irish, with their laid back way of life. Where else can one go, and get tomorrow's newspaper today, and if you want today's paper, you'll be told, come back tomorrow. It was a true case.

An Irish couple, Bill had once spent a holiday with, called Patricia & Eric Dukelow, asked Bill & Carole to spend the festive season with them, they did and were really spoilt. Boxing Day's known as St. Stephen's Day, the children dress up, visiting houses for sweets.

New Years Eve, Bill and Carole decided to spend at The Bantry Bay Hotel. Bill asked the receptionist if his car was safe, parked, facing into the hotel foyer. Her reply was "Oh, to be sure, it'll be alright, but mind you, I left mine there last week, and when I came out, my windscreen wipers were tied in a knot". Bill then asked, if his car would be safe, in the large parking area across the road, her reply was, a definite, no. Not to be deterred, Bill strolled down to the local police station. The policeman on duty suggested it would be safe, if he parked outside the police station, adding, but mind you, he did that the other week, and by the following morning, his doors, had been kicked in. However, he insisted, it wasn't safe to park the car in the large parking area opposite.

Bill, realising, what they thought right, was wrong, and that therefore, what they thought wrong, was probably right, so he parked his car, next to a large bus, thinking it would make his car look insignificant. It did, and the car was still safe and sound the following morning. I'm not quite sure what the motto of the story is, except, when an Irish person says it's right, it's just as likely to be wrong.

That New Years Eve, Bill had already seen a lovely restaurant, that cooked muscles, seven different ways. Lovely thought Bill, I think we'll eat there tonight. The weather deteriorated. Bill thought, they might as well eat in the hotel. We'll sit at the bar, he told Carole. He'd already looked in the dining room, everything was laid up, all looked very inviting. He said, when they saw others arrive, they'd go in. Time ticked by. Soon it was gone 8.30 and still no-one had arrived. Bill asked the receptionist, when the evening meal started. He was told, the restaurant shut at 7p.m. Bill said, "So you didn't have anyone in tonight then?" She replied, "Yes, that's right". (Whereas she should have said no, 'if you see what I mean'. ha! ha!!) Realising they had had their chips, they went to bed, celebrating New Years Eve, with two packets of crisps, all they were able to get to eat. The next night, they stayed in a different hotel. The owners of that hotel, saying they'd had a marvellous dinner for the New Year, they should have stayed with them last night, but were very sorry, they didn't have anything on tonight!! Is this a case of, the luck of the Irish!!

## Driving Back From Portugal The Long Way

Bill and Carole were like the migrating birds. At the first sign of cold weather, they'd pack their car, catch the first overnight crossing from Plymouth to France, and head south, to their favourite destination, Portugal, a 1,550 mile trip. They never took the same route, always weaving their way through country villages, quaint Spanish fishing towns, across the Pyrenees, to unspoilt northern regions of Portugal, until finally reaching Monte Gordo, on the Algarve, just a few miles from the Spanish border. This really was an unspoilt spot. Their hotel, sat right on the beach. They'd book their usual apartment for months at a time.

It became, like a second home. They made friends, with Tomaisa, a seventy year old widow, always dressed in black, who drove her black mule and wooden cart into the local villages, selling her oranges, and other fruits and vegetables, she'd picked earlier that morning. Tomaisa, was always smiling, showing the one and only tooth she had, which was in the middle, at the front of her mouth. She had scales she'd balance in her hands, putting a weight one end, to weigh her produce. The couple met her, by buying oranges from her. Carole made meanings, that she wanted to give the mule a pear, Tomaisa nodded her head, but just as the mule was about to eat, she grabbed it for herself, making meanings, it was too good for the mule, but she'd enjoy it instead. Neither could speak the others language, but they were invited back to Tomaisa's single story, immaculate white washed three roomed village home, for a meal. The mule was housed next door, clean with plenty to eat, goats were kept in another outhouse for their milk, the next outhouse, had the automatic washing machine, what a contrast. She pointed up the green valley showing them her orange grove. The food consisted of spiced snails, Tomaiso had caught earlier in the week. No, she didn't run to catch the snails, they're just as slow as ours. It certainly was an honour for Bill and Carole to meet some of her family, also present at the meal.

Helena was a seventy year old French lady, who decided to spend her retirement in Portugal. Carole, able to speak a little French, made friends with this elderly lady, who invited them to her bungalow, situated on the edge of the village, by the main road, for French cooking. What an unexpected experience, French cooking in Portugal. The odd thing was, Helena couldn't speak a word of Portuguese.

Moored on the river Guadianna, was an Englishman, who'd sailed a huge yacht from England, and had decided he wasn't going to return, he loved the old fashioned, friendly village way of life, having become accepted as one of the riverside village community. Bill and Carole spent many happy moments, talking to this intrepid traveller, they all having so much in common.

They were invited to several weddings, all very large, with between two to five hundred guests. The guests would tie white ribbons on the aerials of their cars, hooting their horns all the time, as the long line of cars, followed the bride & groom from church to reception. The receptions consisted of several courses, savoury intermingled with sweet. Always plenty of free drinks, but never anyone drinking too much. The wedding cakes, were single tier, but huge, nothing for the cake to be 5 ft square, an iced creamy sponge, the guests lining up during the reception for their slice, after the traditional cutting by the bride and groom. They never managed to stay to the end of the receptions, which went on all night.

Just inland, in South East Portugal, are several mountain villages, with unmarked single track roads snaking through them. The food, clothes etc., for these villages were brought by various vans. The butcher would arrive, loudly sounding his horn, open his white van doors, then wait in the small village squares for his customers, finally moving on to the next village. The bread man would follow the same ritual, the fishmonger, clothes merchant, and so on, all announcing their arrival in the same manner. The most unusual one, was the arrival of a man on an old black motor bike, with a couple of solid brown leather cases strapped on the back. This man carried a gun. He was the jeweller, carrying everything one would normally see in a jewellery shop, hence the gun.

One day, visiting a local bar, come restaurant, which doubled up as the central shop for the few houses, the travelling dentist arrived. He set up his clinic in the kitchen of the restaurant, the locals waiting in the bar for their turn, for tooth extractions, etc. It was so obvious, that the locals didn't wear dentures, that Tomaiso with her one tooth and others like her, were a common sight.

The beginning of the nineties, brought a huge dam to the area, cobbled roads were tarmaced, the water wells, slowly replaced with water taps, either central to the village, or in the home. Electricity was also brought to the remote villages, large bridges built, new hospitals, all thanks to grants from the European Community. With all that modernisation, it was still a common sight to see a faithful old mule pulling a cart.

Talking about the new hospitals. The last time Bill and Carole were in Portugal, Bill suffered a stroke. He was rushed by ambulance, fifty miles to the new hospital in Faro. What a contrast, compared with the NHS in England. Ten hours after Bill had gone through a few basic procedures, it was proved he'd suffered a stroke. Carole, had to remain in a large room, with approximately one hundred others, all anxiously waiting for news of their loved ones.

Carole was shocked, when escorted to the specialist, who spoke excellent English, to be told, they wanted to keep Bill in a wheel chair for twelve days, in a corridor, with many others lining the corridors, on stretchers and wheelchairs. It was winter, the whole place windy and cold. Carole wondering how on earth, anyone could be expected to get well in such appalling conditions. All the beds were full.

She stressed that Bill hadn't worked all his life, to be placed in these horrid conditions, he was to go to a private hospital. He did, spending the next week in a small private hospital in Faro, Carole having to pay £2,000 up front, before he was allowed to be admitted. The cost was twice that of our private hospitals, and nowhere near as good as our NHS ones. The doctors and nurses were extremely kind, but very overworked in the Portuguese Health System. There wasn't a menu in the private hospital, the patient just gave instructions of what he or she wanted to eat and it was served at the next meal, but, at £500 a day, what do you expect?

Two weeks later, on the advice of the doctors, Carole drove the 1550 miles back To France. The first stop was in Spain, on the border with the Pyrenees. What looked like a modern, medium size hotel, turned out to be a brothel. With nightfall almost on them, with just the mountains ahead, Carole was furious, that this wasn't what it appeared. Fortunately, the first mountain village, had a perfect, restaurant, hotel, warm and cosy, so all was well after all. The rest of the five day return to France was uneventful. Bill immediately admitted to hospital on his return. The beginning of his recovery.

Until this last trip, their return trips each year from Portugal, some of which covered over 20,000 miles, have taken them through every country in Europe, right up to the Arctic Circle, all the Scandinavian countries, the borders of Russia, and down to the deep south of Greece and Italy, many memories, of kind people throughout the European Community, whatever their language.

## Plants and Seeds

As part of his extensive travelling experience, Bill loved nothing better, than to bring home cuttings, or seeds, from any unusual plants he found. Consequently, he has an Almond Tree growing in the garden, Prickly Pears that have grown into enormous plants, just from a few leaves, growing in his greenhouses, and garden. Orange tree, and various other specimens, he cannot name, they are just labelled with the country they originated from.

He's grown pineapples, by slicing the tops off fresh ones, the plant grows, producing more pineapples, which he laughingly says, he's going to sell to 'Del Monte'. Lychees, anything, even from England, that he thinks will grow, he gives it a go. A 'budding' Alan Titchmarsh!!

## The Far East

Bill and Carole were in Thailand, on there own. They landed at Bangkok, staying there for a few days. For any that don't know this city, the traffic in London is nothing compared with this place. A person trying to cross five lanes of traffic is a nightmare. Pedestrian crossings are ignored by the cars and three wheeled tut-tuts. A person has to step out, literally taking their lives in their hands by crossing one lane of cars at a time, the traffic weaving around the pedestrian. Lorries are not allowed to enter the city during daytime hours, but the roads are still jammed full.

To get away from this hustle, the pair hired a car, driver, and guide, going to the North of Thailand visiting Chiang Mai and Chiang Rai. This journey, was going to take 10 days, with Bill and Carole flying back to Bangkok.

On this journey north, they saw working elephants resting at the roadside, with their heavy chains hanging loosely around their bodies, with a boy sat on top also resting, this was their lunch break, before continuing to drag trees out of the forest. A man walking beside the road, stick in hand, with a dozen ducks waddling in front of him, an unusual sight indeed, and not repeated. Bill took a photograph of this unique scene, wherein the man made a small charge. Several people fishing, in the many small ponds beside the road. The ponds didn't have a river flowing into them, so where did the fish come from? A mystery Bill hasn't solved to this day.

They went to a wedding of a young village couple, the guests all sitting cross legged on the wooden floor, making sure not to show the bottom of one's foot, that is an insult and remembering to never pat anyone on the head, that is also deemed an insult. Then they followed the rest of the

Pineapple Plant, Bill grew. *Courtesy of The Evening Herald*

guests, by tying another piece of string around the couple's hands to join them together, thus by the end of the ceremony the bride and groom had well and truly tied the knot.

The country is mainly Buddhist, so they were shown plenty of Buddhas, of all shapes and sizes. Some had arms or legs missing, because raiders from Burma had deliberately done this to chastise the Thai people. They visited a stream of boiling flowing water, where the locals boiled their food in mesh baskets, and where one could purchase an egg, boiled in the river. The locals, with bare feet, stood on rocks, that were precariously poking out of the boiling water.

They finally reached The Golden Triangle in the far north, where three countries meet, Laos, Burma and Thailand, also a place where heroine was grown and sold. Although the couple were supposed to go on a river trip in that area, they declined after learning the fate of tourists the previous week. Apparently bandits riding water buffalo, had held up the boat, robbing the tourists, shooting and killing one poor person from Bristol. Although the river between Laos and Thailand looked so peaceful, surrounded by lush green trees, but with bandits in the area, that was one trip they could do without. There was a small bridge that people were constantly walking across, that led into Burma, but although they had their passports, Bill and Carole were not allowed to cross this simple border.

The young driver on this trip was called Mr. Tong, the guide was Manhole. Bill, never able to remember the guide's name, would often get mixed up, calling him 'Cesspit'. The young man always laughing at the mistake. When driving, and passing a spirit house, the drivers slowed down, tooted their horns, placed their hands together and then carried on. A spirit house, looks like a miniature house, on a 5 ft wooden stand, with room to place food offerings. On one steep winding road Bill noticed at

A Chinese hearse

A Chinese cemetary

least a hundred of these spirit houses beside one section of road, with a monkey swinging from one to the other house. The drivers slowing down, tooting their horns, quickly putting their hands together, and driving on. On enquiring why so many of these houses were in the one spot, they were told, a young boy had been killed by a car on that spot, which was a very dangerous section of road, where they were continually having accidents, and so, the parents placed a spirit house there in his memory, others followed, placing more houses in memory of those already killed on that section. Since which there hadn't been any more accidents. Bill, quick as usual said, of course you haven't had any accidents, you all slow down now, tooting your horns. They really believed, it was the spirits protecting them.

Thailand proved to be a very interesting country, full of surprises. One four star hotel they stayed at, had a gold, wrought iron winding staircase, leading from the ground floor bar and restaurant to the first floor. Bill, noticing many beautiful girls using this staircase, smiling to him as they passed, thought he'd see what the hotel had to offer on the mysterious first floor. He soon found out, the whole floor was used as a brothel. He returned to Carole smiling all over his face.

The floating market was also unique. Going up the narrow canals, with little boats laden with everything you can think of. There were even Chinese style burial caskets for sale in some of the little wooden shops beside the busy waterways. Everyone was wearing the typical sand pan hats, to keep the sun off their faces.

In Singapore, Bill was introduced to The Singapore Casket Company. Here he was taken out to lunch, eating cold, sweet and sour jellyfish. The wooden burial caskets are a very unusual shape. Bill saw false paper money, miniature paper houses, replica paper cars, etc. Apparently the more replica goodies the families could afford to have placed with their dead loved ones, the more the deceased was able to take into the next world. The cemetery was also very ornate, with fire crackers going off at intervals, to keep the spirits away. Singapore is very clean and modern, no smoking in public areas, no chewing gum in public, that way chewing gum isn't left on the pavements, with the inevitable consequences.

Malaysia appeared poorer. Here, Bill tried fish porridge for breakfast. Visited Crab Island, a village built on stilts in the mange-groves. The wooden structures all about 12 ft above sea level, with wooden roads joining the houses. There were prawn crackers, left to dry in the sun. A very hot humid country, but interesting with its' many varied cultures.

**The Pacific Islands of Fiji**

This is written, as if Bill is writing it himself. Staying in a beautiful hotel in Fiji, it had all kinds of engaging amusement every evening. We stayed there for two or three weeks, enjoying many of their strange different customs and amusements. We were one of the first tourists to see Fiji after a political uprising. Infact, we were the only two people to get off the plane.

Wanting to see as much of the Island as we could, instead of taking a taxi, we did the rounds in an old local bus, that didn't have a window in it, what a blessing it was, the weather constantly hot and humid. We were driven in and out of all the interesting little villages, taking much interest in the inhabitants, who were either Fijian, or Indian. The Indian population had been brought to the Island, by the British many years earlier, for general work purposes.

Being very interested in all religions, though it entailed a long walk in the scorching sun, we walked several miles to church, because there weren't any buses or taxis on Sundays. One doesn't immediately notice such things in the beginning, though it soon became obvious, that we two stood out like sore thumbs, all the natives so black, and we in comparison, so white. We were made such a fuss of, by grandparents, mothers, fathers, and an abundance of children. The morning service was taken by 3 ministers, each dressed in full length black gowns, with bare feet showing. There wasn't an organ, or piano, but the harmony of the singing, had to be heard to be believed. After the service, the large congregation, lined up, to shake hands with us, we really did feel special.

We were then invited to accompany the three ministers to the 'Bulla Hut', meaning, welcoming hut. This was a large circular building, in the

A change of suit in Bali

centre of the village, made of banana leaves, or similar, and bamboo etc. We all sat cross legged on the floor, which was made of, what appeared to be similar to the hut itself. Highly amused, and extremely interested, we watched one of the villagers, wearing a short sleeve shirt, and traditional long sarong which all men wore, he took two buckets, each of which appeared new, placed some black, dirty looking shoots in one bucket, and with bare arms to his elbows, washed and squeezed in that same bucket of water. To say least, it looked a right mess. He then strained it from one bucket to the other, when it became known as, 'Kava', a whitish liquid, to be drank out of half a coconut shell. After having drunk this not so pleasant liqud, the same shell was passed to the next person, and so on. We were told, it was good for the stomach, (you could have fooled me), and we should drink two lots. We were told, it was not intoxicating, which I didn't accept as the truth. When they brought my second helping, I laughingly said, "Oh, no, not another, thank you, my stomach is already rumbling". Actually, not only was it a vile taste, like drinking mud, but, without mentioning it, I very much resented drinking one after the other, out of the 'same coconut shell'. It was a known fact and very noticeable, that one particular minister was very fond, too fond of 'Kava', then they say, it's not intoxicating, not much ha! ha!! I'm glad I didn't like it in any event.

That same day, we were invited to lunch, by an Indian family. I really enjoy meeting different nationalities and customs, and so, although our food was provided at our hotel, the invitation was graciously accepted, and we very much enjoyed the food and the company.

Knowing who I was, and what I did, the next day, I had been invited to a very large funeral. Large, meaning, there were hundreds of the inhabitants involved. The deceased was apparently, extremely well known and highly respected by many people from different villages. The funeral, was very different to the thousands I had been involved with over the many years. Briefly, funerals in this part proceed as follows. Irrespective of whether death occurred at the home, or some other place, it is removed to a hospital. In this case, it was a fair distance away. It remains there until day of funeral, when, as in this case, it was brought back to the large village, where, with a number of bearers, each wearing a floral display on their arms, interchanging with each other, carried the coffin on their shoulders around to every house in the village, and eventually into the church for the service, which I thought was never going to end. They seemed to talk about all they knew of the deceased's life, each talking in turn. The burial took place in the adjoining cemetery. I always remember when going down to the grave, how it was closely surrounded by trees. At the bottom of these trees, were many fairly large holes, about the size of rabbit holes, which turned out to be, land crab holes. Although I didn't see any of the crabs, I was given to understand the crabs had one very large nipper, that enabled the crab to break open a coconut.

The most outstanding, notable thing to me, at this funeral, was the absolute abundance of fresh meat, to be consumed after the burial. There was more meat, than I had ever seen in a given place, more than I had ever seen, even at a meat market. I didn't stop to eat, knowing my wife Carole, wasn't very well. I made my way back to the hotel, from where, we got a taxi into town to see a doctor, after which, we called at a little music shop, to purchase tapes of the beautiful music, the band played at the hotel.

Infact, at a performance there one evening, I made an opening, by suggesting, on such occasions, the band, who were the ones that owned the little music shop, should always carry tapes with them, making it known at the time, such tapes were available from them, there and then. I'm always thinking of business, even on holiday, and for the aid of others. Liking the idea, they said, that's what they would do from then on. Thanking me for the idea, they gave me a couple of tapes, for my thoughts and suggestion

The best thing to look forward to now, was the cooking of a 3 ft 6" barramundi fish, and a large full grown pig, head and all, but that was to be done the following day. The procedure was as follows; a very large pit was dug out of the earth in the hotel grounds, wherein, a big fierce fire was lit, and large, square shaped stones left in the fire, until they were almost red hot. When all the wood etc., was burnt, both the pig, and the barramundi fish, which had been separately wrapped in banana leaves, were placed in the red hot pit, which was then refilled with earth, that had been dug from it, completely covering the fire, and left for three and a half hours, after which, we enjoyed the most succulent piece of pork and fish, we'd ever had.

Fiji was truly, an unspoilt tropical paradise, just as one dreams of, the people so friendly, making it even more special.

## Staying In Many Convents in USA

Earl of Plymouth Funeral Service were the appointed funeral directors to, The Little Sisters Of The Poor, Plymouth. The Reverend Mother, before coming to this country, was the Provincial Mother in USA. The Reverend Mother and Bill, got on exceedingly well with each other, infact at times, Bill took her to such places as, Buckfast Abbey, wherein, he was privileged to be invited to parts of the Abbey and its' grounds, where normally, the general public were prohibited. At a private conversation, the Reverend Mother said to Bill, she preferred the way The Little Sisters of The Poor funerals in America, were carried out. She went on to say, here they place the deceased in a casket, and just cover it with a cloth, thus when the coffin was placed in the chapel, prior to Requiem Mass, the old people, were unable to pay their respects, by viewing the deceased.

Bill, quickly explained, he being Devon and Cornwall's first qualified embalmer, having qualified and studied in USA & Canada etc., around the 1940's, he knew exactly what the Reverend Mother wanted, so he would

Leading a Centenary procession in Lambertville, USA

120

do the same for her from there on, enabling the elderly in the homes, to view their loved ones. She readily agreed, and was absolutely delighted. From there on, she was so pleased. Knowing Bill was going to USA again, in 3 weeks, she telephoned him one Sunday morning, asking him to come and see her. He said he'd be there in a few minutes, to which she replied, leave it for an hour, as we are just going to early morning mass.

When Bill arrived, he was taken into the big room he had been in many times. Laid out for him was an eggs and bacon breakfast, together with coffee, cigarettes, and a can of Coca-Cola. The good Mother sat chatting to Bill, giving him a very large envelope, full of invites to all their various convents, all over USA. The Provincial Mother went on to tell Bill, all The Reverend Mothers were expecting him as one of their benefactors, and that, if there was anything he wanted that they didn't have, he only had to ask.

Bill, looking at the number of invitations, gasped, saying to himself, with this amount, I'll have to stay there 3 years, or I'll never get round to them all. Instead, he said, "I don't think I'll be able to visit all of them, but I promise to do my best."

Each of the invitations read, 'As one of our benefactors, we welcome you to our convents throughout USA, where each of the Reverend Mothers are expecting you, and would like you to stay with them, for as long as you can.'

Going back to Buckfast Abbey, I must tell you, how Bill told me, he was also privileged, having already been through the private parts of Buckfast Abbey, he was also honoured to be welcomed into 'Zion Abbey', which is a closed order, not generally open to any of the public. Bill was taken to parts, where normally, one is strictly forbidden. He explained, the nuns could be heard but not seen. Infact, they are closed off by a sort of trellis work, which was completely covered with black curtain material. Being more fortunate, because he was with the Provincial Mother, he was able to see them and shake hands. To do this, he had to make his hand smaller, by only using three fingers, and pushing them through the trellis work. Bill was also taken to the L shaped chapel, where he was able to see the altar and priest etc., but the nuns, with whom he, and the Reverend Mother sang hymns with, were out of sight.

Bill's first stop from England was San Francisco, where he was met by an American couple, he befriended the year before, when holidaying in USA, having flown there with Plymouth Millionaires, Robert & Rita Daniel, and other of his business friends for three weeks, visiting, Plymouth Massachusetts, boarding the replica of the Golden Hind, which incidentally, he never bothered with when it was on his doorstep at the Plymouth Barbican.

However, although Bill's friends only stayed for the two weeks, as was planned for all of them, Bill stayed on for four months. Always one to try everything, he forwent his return flight ticket, and instead returned on the Queen Elizabeth.

Back to Bill's visits to convents across America. Bill was told by the Catholic fraternity, they had never known of anyone, who had ever stayed in as many convents, as Bill.

Bill arrived at San Francisco Convent for the Little Sisters of the Poor. During conversation with their Reverend Mother, knowing the nuns went to bed about 8p.m., and Bill, who of course, was on his own, told them he would like to go out for a short time that evening, saying, he wouldn't go far, as otherwise, he wouldn't find his way back. Bearing in mind, at this stage, he was only talking at the entrance. The good Mother, immediately took him right through the building to the rear of the convent, where the Mother pointed out which of the many doors, he was to use when he came in that evening.

Bill simply had a drink at the local, to pass away a little time, before retiring to bed. In the dark, as Bill walked back to the rear of the convent, to find, each door he tried was locked. Bill became quite concerned, trying so many different doors, all of which, led to nowhere, when suddenly, to his delight, he found one that opened. He then climbed the steep stairs. Bill feeling his way around, ended up in a dark room, with his hand right up under, one of the nun's skirts. It's true to say, that the nun never moved an inch, it's also true to say, there wasn't anyone in the skirt, and Bill, who was never known to shy away from anything, ran for his life, right into a lobby full of cubicles, where many more nuns gowns and cassocks were hanging. One might say, Bill had a hand in each. Whether he did or not, it didn't do him much good, for he was frightened out of his life. Eventually, he found a door that opened, into a warmly lit room, ah, his large bedroom at last.

Next day, Bill having told all concerned of the previous night's escapades, they all absolutely roared with laughter. He had a most wonderful time at this home. They took him here, there and everywhere; churches, crematoriums, cemeteries, funeral homes, casket makers, and hearse builders. One might call this a 'busman's holiday', to say nothing of the fact, that because Bill happened to say, he was very fond of corn on the cob, they gave him so much, day after day, it was taking root, and growing out of his ears.

Bill was of course, introduced to the Home's appointed funeral directors, and for a 'change', he spent much time with them, attending many funerals. He could hardly say any of it was exciting, could he, however, it was what he wanted. He found it enjoyable and educating, especially with the nuns, if you see what I mean.

Bill then moved on to other venues, and different convents, far too many to talk of each of them. However, he did describe a few more interesting instances, although he can't quite remember all of them, after all these years.

He does remember very well indeed, the extreme kindness the Reverend Mother bestowed upon him. Going from San Francisco, Bill drove right across the Arizona Dessert, 412 miles to the Arizona Convent. Wait for it, they even loaned Bill, their beautiful American Sedan, to drive himself there. Bill, so overwhelmed with their kindness, couldn't help wondering, how they would get their car back, and so he asked, only to be told, someone would be coming from there sometime.

Knowing of the extreme desert heat, Bill left 4a.m. Unfortunately, the car not having air conditioning, gave Bill the hottest ride of his life, and a thumping headache. What a lovely feeling it was, to walk into such a beautiful convent, which above all, under the circumstances, was air-conditioned. Bill said, he felt as if he was in heaven.

Greeted by the Reverend Mother, in the usual kindly manner, Bill told her, he would have to lie down, because of such a bad head. The Good Mother quickly explained, that the doctor attends every evening, so she would ask him to see Bill. Sure enough, as soon as he arrived, Bill was either sent for, or he came to his room. After taking Bill's blood pressure, he remarked, asking Bill, whoever sent him to that part of the world. Bill quickly assumed that his blood pressure must be high, apparently it was, so he gave him some tablets, and told Bill to consult his GP, when he eventually got home. Bill thanked him, and asked what he owed. To which he replied, you don't owe me anything. "But doctor", exclaimed Bill, "I come to you as a patient, and you tell me I've nothing to pay". To which he replied, "that lets you know, what we think of the British".

To Bill's utter surprise, he then asked to take Bill out to dinner, saying, he would collect him from the convent 6p.m.. 5.50p.m., the telephone rang, it was the doctor apologising, he would be a little late, however, he arrived 6.10p.m. Took Bill to a very posh restaurant. Apparently, the doctor knew the Italian proprietor, because, during the war, he gave him a place to live.

Bill said, he will never forget that evening. The proprietor was a famous opera singer, who had sang all over the world, including, Covent Garden, London. Without any warning, he suddenly burst into song, with his wonderful strong voice. One could have heard a pin drop, with everyone listening to his absolutely miraculous voice.

When they left, the doctor told Bill, he would like to call home at his house, explaining, his next door neighbour had 12 Pekinese show dogs, and that he had one. The neighbour arranged that the doctor would look after all the dogs, whilst she was away on holiday, and that he had to go back to feed them.

In his own house, he had a very large electronic organ, Bill's favourite instrument. Bill told the doctor, it would be a wonderful memory, if the doctor would play a couple of tunes, he did, making Bill's day so memorable.

The following day, which after all, was supposed to be Bill's holiday, he was introduced to the Convent's chosen funeral director, who, like all others, made a point of showing Bill his funeral home, and of course, their casket display room, which was, as with all American Funeral Directors, their focal point. Little did they realise, each firm's display was almost the same as any of their competitors, if based in the same area. The reason was, all USA funeral directors, purchased ready made caskets, from one or two casket firms in their area, and so each funeral home, had more or less the same as their competitors, because, as Bill said, caskets came mainly from the same makers. The main difference was, the number of caskets a firm displayed, and the size of their display room, example, one firm may only show 7 or 8 caskets, whilst another, much larger firm may have anything from 25 to 40 various caskets on show, for the public to chose from.

The general public, unless they shopped around, would not be aware of this fact, if they did, the larger firm would most certainly have most of the smaller firm's business.

Some of the caskets in USA were described as eg., half open couch, where only the head and shoulders of the deceased were shown, or, eg., the full couch, the whole of the deceased would be on display, because of the full open top.

At times, Bill got tired of seeing so many displays, bearing in mind, the abnormal amount of travelling Bill had done to various parts of the world, including, as already said, going right around the world 5 times. Yes, but wait for it, it was all for the same reason, to learn and improve his knowledge, to the advantage of himself, and all of whom he served. Very probably, the only man who has ever travelled so far and wide, for the one reason.

Being away so much, Bill's son would often be asked, where's Dad, he would reply, whatever country he happens to be in at the moment, you can be sure he is with funeral directors, or, he will be the only man on the beach, wearing a collar and tie.

## The Nuns Again

Bill told me of another time, when he was staying in a very large convent that, like all the other convents, they were so very kind to him.

Incidentally, every one of the very many convents, gave him fantastic living space. In every case, he had a very large room and bedroom, always furnished with every helpful possible convenience, TV, etc, you name it, they provided it, everything one might require. So friendly was each and every one of them, that Bill was given full freedom of each convent, enabling him, to freely wonder around, talking to the nuns, and asking questions.

One day, in the very large immaculate kitchens, Bill noticed, standing on a shelf, prominently placed in the kitchen, a very fine porcelain head and shoulders of Jesus Christ. Bill couldn't keep his eyes off it. Admiring and passing kind remarks, the nuns asked if he would like to have it. Hardly knowing what to say, Bill replied, "Well, it is nice, but I wouldn't like to take it from you." "Oh," they said, "You have it, we get fed up with him watching us every day, with every move we make, he never ever takes his eyes off us." Bill graciously accepted it, and still has it, after having carried it in his luggage for thousands and thousands of miles. Now it's looking at me, whilst writing this biography. Doesn't matter where one looks, for example, if one stands on a chair, the eyes follow and look up, sit on the ground, and it looks down, infact, wherever one turns, it looks at you. Everybody admires it.

Three of the nuns, came to Bill one day saying, "Come Mr. Earl, the car and chauffeur are waiting for us." As Bill knew, they were taking him to see some mausoleums, churches, cemeteries, convents, and their chosen firm of funeral directors, who Bill had already met, and spent time with, but it was no good, he had to see and go through it all again. The nun's chauffeur driven car, was a massive Cadilac, the envy of everyone, of course, but that was its' only failing point, because it made these 'little Sisters of the *Poor*' feel so embarrassed. Bill knows the feeling, because he had owned a whole fleet of Packards & Cadillacs for the "very reason, that they stood out", and is why Bill purchased the "whole fleet" of Reg Bougard's, and also his garage at Stonehouse, Plymouth, but the nuns had no alternative, because they were given a new car every year.

Infact, Bill's had everything, including the only large fleet of Rolls Royce hearses and limousines in Plymouth. There was a big difference between Bill's cars and the Sisters of the Poor. The Sisters had their Cadillac *given to them*, but it stood out too much for them, whereas, Bill had to *purchase* his, and did so, for the "very reason", that they "stood out a mile", which was so good for his business, and why he had them.

The more I write of Bill, the more amazed I become, it reminds me of the song, 'I've been everywhere man, I've been everywhere'. I think the song should continue with, 'and I've done everything', because he certainly seems to have.

However, as already said, the nuns, the chauffeur and the Cadillac, are still waiting for Bill, so off he went, taken to all the places already mentioned. It turned out to be a very long, interesting day. The best part for the nuns, was the return journey, home to the convent. On the way back, the nuns gasped with excitement, "Mr. Earl, we are going to call in at this parlour, for a Coca cola and some lovely ice-cream." Bill laughingly replied, "That's no good, ice-cream is too fattening." The nuns, made a sign of the cross, at the same time telling Bill, "This ice-cream, is not fattening."

That evening, Bill was taken out to dinner, by the Convent's priest, in an old mini, Bill thought it had come out of the Ark. Bearing in mind, Bill is supposed to be on a long holiday, all be it, a busman's holiday, it would be understandable, if readers thought, he was having a miserable time, on the contrary, he was enjoying every second, infact there is nothing he'd rather do, than study and learn all he could, from the various angles of his profession. Whether it was the business side, all the techniques, observing and helping the bereaved, or explaining his double value funeral bonds, whereby, one could go into Bill's office, purchase a funeral bond, that would immediately double its' value, eg., if one bought a £500 bond, *before* walking out of the office, it was worth £1,000.

Bill was always ready to try to help anybody, if he possibly could. If he didn't know the answer, he would say out straight, he didn't know, adding his famous words, let your yes be yes and your no, no.

## Staying in a Convent in Colorado

Father Ritter, who Bill said, was a dear old gentleman, and one of the most sincere, kind person's he's ever met.

On Bill's first morning at the Convent, Father Ritter, immediately after having taken early morning Mass, introduced himself to Bill, saying, he was going to take him to the top of the highest mountain in the world. Bill chuckled to himself, saying, "Every country claims to have the biggest mountain in the world."

The priest handed Bill the keys of his new car. Bill said, "But Father, you don't even know if I can drive." "No," he said, "But you can, can't you?" What a coincidence, for it was the very week, Bill had just taken delivery of a new fleet of 5 large, 7.5 litre American Sedans, all, exactly the same model, as the priest's.

Father explained, it's rather embarrassing, as his flock know, he's the residing priest for The Little Sisters Of The Poor.

Incidentally, it's worth readers noting, all the convents referred to, come under, The Little Sisters of The Poor. Father Ritter, was 'given' a new Sedan every year, by his sister.

Having eventually arrived at the top of the mountain, Father, was showing Bill around here, there and everywhere, until eventually he took him in to lunch, where there was so much to choose from, one hardly knew where to start.

Bill is a devil for meat, and so, of course, that's what he had. The priest decided on fish. It wasn't until Bill went to bed, back at the Convent that evening, thinking, as is usual for him, of all that happened that day, suddenly, he remembered it was Friday, and was probably why Father had fish.

Next day, Bill told him his thoughts. Father laughed his head off. For a week, he took Bill to one or other of his friends to dinner, every evening. Infact it was on one such occasion, Bill first saw a microwave oven.

Father Ritter, affectionately known to his many friends as 'A Night Bird', didn't usually get back to the Convent until early hours of the morning.

Many readers may know, Convents always have a large statue of The Virgin Mary in the grounds.

Irrespective of how late Father walked through the grounds, he never failed to lift his trilby hat when passing the statue.

Bill told me, that not once in those evenings, did he ever get bored, it was always such very interesting conversations, obviously everyone loved the Father. Infact, there's nothing Bill loves better, than talking and learning more and more about the many and different faiths.

Still on holiday, or is he? You wouldn't think so ha! ha!! Tomorrow evening, he'll be off to Chicago, and eventually fulfil, two more invitations, at the Chicago Convent, and the Chicago Monastery.

Next evening, Bill is on the all night train, having, with the help of Father Ritter, been taken to the station during the day, and reserved a sleeper.

Just as the train was leaving, Father quickly put an envelope, behind Bill's pocket handkerchief, and jumped off the slowly moving train, shouting, 'cheerio'. Opening the envelope, Bill sat back and read what Father had written, so very touched, big tears came to his eyes, whilst reading this message "written in gold", 'Please come again, as soon as you can, it's been a real pleasure having you. The dinner tonight is on me.' Enclosed in the envelope were several dollars. Bill continued to shed a few tears, for in a manly way, he loved that wonderful man. Yes, they kept in contact from there on.

**Staying in the Convent & Monastery in Chicago**

The Provincial Mother, here in the UK, had been the Provincial Mother in USA, and instigator of the new Convent & Monastery in Chicago. She was very keen on Bill being shown the new building. She personally arranged for the architect to meet Bill and take him to see same, and tell her all about it on his return to Plymouth.

Bill, sat waiting, in the reception area in the Chicago convent one morning, when a well dressed gentleman, strode in, with trilby hat in hand. Bill heard him say to one of the nuns, he was looking for Earl of Plymouth. On hearing this, Bill jumped up saying, "That's me". The gentleman introduced himself, giving his name, which Bill forgets now. However, he mentioned to me he was an architect

To Bill's surprise, he asked what sort of things he liked doing. Bill replied, saying, anything. "That's good", said the architect, telling Bill he would take him any and everywhere. First place they called at was, the 94 club, which was 94 floors high. Bill, having quickly weighed up this character, decided to play safe, and do the same as him, eg., if he drank whisky sour, so did Bill. He kept apologising for continually excusing himself, ringing different ones all the time. A surprising thing was, between many of the calls, he would order another drink, not having drunk the ones he'd already paid for. However, Bill in his usual alert and observant manner, watched every point, making sure he didn't drink too much, had he not done this, he would have become, as drunk as a Lord, especially, as he was not that sort of drinker anyway.

Bill soon realised, with so many dignitaries arriving and being introduced to him, what all the phone calls had been about. Bill met up with numerous people from high places, such as, the Aide to the Pope, Commissioner of Police, Highway & Traffic Controllers etc., far too many to mention. They all sat down to a sumptuous lunch, and were also taken out to evening entertainment, including musical shows etc. This went on for about a week. Bill was collected, and taken here, there and everywhere. By what Bill's told me, it was the longest week in his life, and he still hadn't seen the new convent.

Some of the things that stood out in Bill's memory (bearing in mind, all this took place many years ago), was at times, being taken to a particular place. The architect, who by now had become a close friend, would stop at eg., a filling station or garage, shout across to one of the attendants (obviously he was extremely well known), asking them to collect his car from the nearby hotel and park it. When ready to leave, he'd simply ring asking them to bring his car over.

Another thing that absolutely amazed Bill, was that mornings, an electric barrier would come up in the road, and allow eg., ten or so lanes of traffic coming into Chicago, and say, two lanes going out. In the evening, the whole procedure was reversed, for those leaving the city.

Bill still wondering when he was going to see the supposedly wonderful architecturally built convent and monastery, was eventually taken there, though not quite finished, they were magnificent. It was after all this, Bill met the architect's wife, when the three of them had dinner, and went to a first class show. They did correspond, then Bill sadly learnt, his architect friend, was very sick with a life threatening illness, which to be truthful, didn't surprise Bill, in view of his lifestyle.

Bill was eventually off again, this time to Canada, Ottawa, Toronto etc., and to the longest street in the world, Young Street, but by the time one got from one end to the other, it became more like, 'Old Street'. It was a bad job, if one wanted a no. 2, but started from the wrong end, if you see what I mean. Whilst there, Bill attended yet another International Conference and Exhibition for Funeral Concerns, they were more like huge Hyper-markets, displaying, hearses, cars, caskets, private ambulances, embalming tables & fluids, wearing apparel, automatic grave casket lowering devices, stretchers, known as one man cots. Infact, Bill was the first in Britain to have a one man cot. He brought his back from USA, on an earlier visit, when he was studying there. He became an agent for same, in those early days. It soon got around, and many many funeral organisations, including the Co-operative societies, were driving Bill insane to supply them. Bill never one to do half a job, or leaving a stone unturned, infact went to the Patent Office in Washington, so that he knew exactly how they were made. He often said, that next to the hearse, it was the most useful piece of equipment. Which is how he advertised it.

It was in the Canadian Exhibition, all those years ago, that he purchased, his special dermatology, cosmetic kit, specially formulated for facial restoration, which was another of Bill's studies in the States. However, there's just one thing in the funeral profession he regrets not doing, which was, 'facial masks'. Though I am told, he is thinking about it, even now.

Back to the Aide to the Pope, that Bill met in Chicago, he was a person, whereby nobody could contact the Pope or see him, except through the Aide. Infact later, Bill had an appointment with this Aide. Leaving UK, for Rome, where the sole purpose was, simply to meet him again and confirm through him, and various High priests, that Bill's understanding of the reason, Roman Catholics, all along, would not agree to cremation was correct, and why eventually, it had been accepted. However, even then, the priests, although they would agree to take a Mass at the Church, they would not even go into the Crematorium Chapel, and so, Bill would arrange for a minister of another denomination, to take the committal part of the service. Bill says, even now, he does not personally know of any Catholic priest that has been cremated.

Bill enjoyed his reunion with the Aide, and went on to spend much time with the largest funeral concern in Rome, where he was made so welcome and able to add much more knowledge to what he had already attained. It was there, he learned of a special valve for inserting in the coffins or caskets, before entombing them into a vault. This valve was to allow gases to escape safely. Incidentally, the firm referred to, employed special men for dressing the deceased.

I hope, like me, you've enjoyed Bill's trips around the world.

# 6
# In Search of Religion

**Thoughts on Belief**

Bill was always interested in Religion, from as far back as he can remember. Even as a little boy, he'd say in his prayers, "Please, please, God, give me a long and happy life whilst here on Earth, and an everlasting life with thee". Typical of Bill, to want the best of 'both worlds'. The long and happy life on Earth, is certainly being fulfilled.

His Mother was very religious, unlike his Father. She would take her children to Church every Sunday. It didn't matter to her, whether they attended Salvation Army, Methodist, Church of England etc., so long as they went. She ensured her children went to Sunday School. This gave Bill a good foundation in the various Christian denominations, and has been a wonderful help, enabling him to understand bereaved family's wishes, and why.

As you will recall from previous chapters, even when Bill was faced with imminent danger, whilst in the air raid shelter during The Blitz, his faith in God, was so great, he said to his two companions, whilst bombs were raining down on the city, "Pray to God to look after us all the time, don't stop, God wont take our lives whilst we're holding a conversation with him". They were the only three to come out alive from that terrible bombing. This gave Bill at the time, even more faith.

However, his faith was rather shattered, when he learned of a church full of people caught up in an earth quake. The Church collapsed on the whole congregation, whilst they were holding a Mass. Many were killed instantly, some suffered for as many as eleven days in the rubble, to be rescued, and then die. Bill said, 'They were also holding a conversation with God, like I did in the air raid shelter, but it didn't help them'.

Dealing with death and it's effects on others, all through his life, Bill can't help but think about religions and afterlife, every day, which is probably more than most.

Bill feels, when born into this world, we had no choice in the matter. We didn't ask to be brought into this cruel world, why then, should we be taught, we have to bear the sins of our forefathers.

It's our own life, therefore, we should be able to decide when we've had enough, and when to end it.

Almost everybody dies in the following manner. First we feel ill, then suffer pain, often more than one can stand for maybe, weeks, months, years and after all that, eventually die.

Some say, there's no need to suffer pain these days, with the abundance of pain killers on offer. Take it from one who knows, this is not always true.

We're taught we will be given punishment, for our sins, on the day of judgement. If that's true, we shouldn't be punished here on Earth as well.

We're taught, there's a magnificent place in Heaven, where all worries and problems are gone. How can that be, when example, we're told in Revelation, the devil and a third of the angels have been thrown out of Heaven.

Religious leaders don't agree with each other, example, some teach, we die and go to heaven, staying the same age, others say, we go, either forward or backward to the age of thirty, and there are those that say, we don't go to Heaven at all.

After sitting for hours studying and talking to teachers of many religions and denominations, these are Bill's thoughts; he would like to put all of them in a large room together, saying, when you can agree with each other, then teach me.

In his thirst, to learn about as many religions as possible, Bill has studied the Moslem & Jewish faiths, Buddhism, Hinduism, and many others, as well as studying most Christian denominations. Consequently, he is able to answer questions on most religions.

Bill doesn't agree with such tittles as, eg., The Very Reverend, His Eminence etc.

Bill says, whatever religion one has, hang on to it, you are just as likely to be right, as the next person.

Bill was in a fortunate position in his quest to study as many religions as possible, being the only funeral director to hold funeral services in his own Chapels. When the religious minister arrived, usually half an hour before the service, this allowed Bill to sit down, and learn as much as he could. Thus not only was he learning about the religions, but he was able to offer families, the very best, service possible, according to their religion.

He took instruction in the Roman Catholic faith, and to further his knowledge, stayed in many Convents all over America, as written elsewhere in book.

He's studied many religions in Sri Lanka, where one can find most of them, plus, Bill carried out many funerals in that country, as well as living and studying for that reason.

Seeing the lighter side, Bill is not afraid to die, he just doesn't want to be there at the time. Asked whether he wants burial or cremation, he says, neither, as he's quite happy as he is thank you.

Bill's advice now is, if you have a religion, and you're happy with it, that's all you want. If on the other hand, you don't believe and you're happy in your thoughts, that's good as well, because there isn't any proof one way or the other.

Do good to all, having a clear conscience at the end of every day. No-one can do better than that.

# 7
# Bill, Family and Friends

### Living Until 83, how did Bill do it?

Bill is the only one left, out of the five children. His eldest brother Tommy, died at the age of forty two. The second and third children, Florrie and Ethel, died in their mid eighties. Gordon, the youngest passed away when he was seventy nine.

A lot of the health giving advice we're given now, was not available in Bill's youth. Hence, as this advice has been made known, Bill has heeded the medical knowledge on offer, and does his best to lead a healthy life. One of his favourite sayings is, "If you don't look after yourself, no one else will".

To start with, Bill gave up his sixty cigarettes a day habit. Next, he took up swimming each morning, at Plymouth Hoe, all year round, to give him exercise, and help him overcome bronchial asthma, it worked. He always advises, anyone suffering with asthma, to take up swimming, to help with their breathing. Next, he took up a healthy eating routine, losing excess weight into the bargain, enjoying one glass of wine a day.

Finally, he says, whatever the doctors tell him to do, he does it. After all, what's the point of visiting a doctor, if you don't do, what he suggests.

Although Bill has had his health problems, he still leads a very active life, mentally and physically, still doing his 30 minutes exercise each morning, but on an exercise bike.

As the saying goes, 'The proof of the pudding, is in the eating', and all I can say is, Bill looks and acts a man twenty years younger than he is. I think we could all learn something from his way of healthy living.

### About the Personage of Bill

I think Bill was always very modest about his achievements, whereas I feel, he has a lot to be proud of. He says, "Infact, I left school at 14. A proper Devonshire Dumpling, and still am." Bill, so concerned about his broad accent, made far worse, after having had several strokes (which have also affected his memory), mentioned it to his bank manager, a close friend, saying, he'd arranged to take elocution lessons, to which the bank manager gasped, saying, "Oh, for goodness sake, Bill, don't ever do that, you will lose all your personality". However, anyone who knows Bill well, will also know, that if anyone lets him down, they only do it once. One of Bill's favourite expressions is, 'Let your Yes be Yes, and your No, No'. Well the elocutionist did let him down, hence, to this day, Bill remains one of the well known 'characters' of the City of Plymouth. No matter where he goes, everybody knows him. Infact, he made Earl of Plymouth, a household name, just like Harrods, effusing quality and a service second to none. Note, he never called himself, 'The Earl of Plymouth', it was others that added *THE*.

A funny experience years ago. Bill and his now wife, Carole, were visiting Plymouth Registry Office, to make arrangement for their wedding. Bill said to Carole, "I'll sit quietly on the seat in the corner, because I really don't want anyone to recognise me". All went well for a short while, until the lady registrar walked out of her office, glanced around the waiting area, walked straight over to Bill, saying, "Hello, Mr. Earl, how are you?" So much for anonymity, a little incident Bill often chuckles about.

Bill quickly expanded on his knowledge, after leaving school. He did a vast amount of travelling, having gone around the world, not less than five times, but wait for it, all that time spent studying, and learning from many hundreds of funeral directors, funeral homes, colleges of mortuary science, infact, any and everything to do with funerals. People would often ask his son, Christopher, 'Where's Dad?' Christopher would reply, 'Whatever country Dad's in at the moment, you can be sure, he'll either be with funeral directors, or, if he happens to be on the beach, he'll be the only one there, with a collar and tie on'.

Another thing about Bill's character is, he is always so unbelievably quick with answers, no matter how difficult the question posed, he always has an answer. It's no good arguing with him either, as annoyingly, he will always prove the other person wrong. As his friend Brian says, 'Bill is usually right, but the annoying thing is, he will prove it, which makes it even worse'. However, there is one thing for sure, if he doesn't know the subject, he will openly say, 'it's no good talking to me about, example, football, because I don't know anything about it'. He will explain, after much persuasion, the directors of Argyle did manage to get Bill, to attend a match with them. Bill always told them, he knew nothing about football. This point was proven, and Bill laughs his head off about it. After half time, Bill returned to the directors' box and started cheering the wrong side, forgetting they had changed over sides. Bill quickly explained, that since he was captain of 'The Muck-Ups Football Team', at school, the rules had changed. A

Bill gardening

favourite saying of Bill's brother Gordon about Bill was, that Gordon had had 130 fights and never once, did he ever even have a draw.

It was Bill's sure determination, that, as his office staff used to say, he saved his firm, thousands of pounds. Word, quickly spread to his various colleagues and friends, who, whenever they had a problem, sought Bill's advice. I've known him fight various cases both for himself and others, taking on unions, he even took on a judge and barristers, solicitors, large businesses and goodness knows what else, and although the odds have seemed stacked against him, believe me, Bill has won every case, a few examples are contained in another chapter.

In fairness to Bill, he is quick to say, that if he feels he is in the wrong, he will immediately admit it. Bill is very straight, one always knows where you stand with him, he abides by one of his favourite sayings, which is, "Let your Yes be Yes, and your No, No'.

### Some Tales of Friends & Family History

Bill married his first wife Sheila in his early twenties. Sadly, it was not to last very long. She was pretty and known as the best dressed lady in Devonport. He was busy building up his business during this period, working all the hours God gave him. In 1950, they adopted Christopher. At that time, their home was in the same building as the budding Funeral Business. Bill fondly remembers, playing with Christopher, chasing him around Coffin Creek, hiding amongst the coffins, all part of the home territory. Trust Bill to think of the name 'Coffin Creek'.

Bill was employing, amongst others, Brian McLoughlin, who lived with the family for many years, until his marriage to Nora. Brian spent all his working life with Bill, retiring at 65, the only job he had, or ever needed, lucky man. Brian would rather work than take a holiday, he was a man in a million. Bill taught him to make coffins etc., he in turn taught others. Christopher, was first educated at a private school until Bill put him to Plymouth College, giving him a head start in life. He became a partner in Bill's business at only sixteen.

In all fairness to Christopher, he passed the entrance exam, to get into Plymouth College. Although he had not been taught to pass the 11 plus, he took it and passed. With a father like Bill, telling him, you cannot have too much knowledge.

If it hadn't been for Bill's disastrous second marriage, he'd have been a multi-millionaire today. I can remember when Bill had so much money, he didn't know what to do with it. From this second short marriage, Anita, was born. With both these marriages, Bill fought the courts, and in each case, against all the odds, gained custody of both Christopher and Anita, giving them a good start in life. Very unusual, for a lone businessman to win one such case, let alone both. For Christopher and Anita, their well-being was paramount, but not without it costing Bill a fortune financially, in divorce settlements, however that was the least of his worries, he had the money.

Christopher had four children, Richard, Mandy, Jonathan & Charlotte. Anita has two children, Hazel and Tom.

His final and third marriage was to Carole, they have now been together for twenty four years. Bill says, the latter part of his life have been the happiest days of his whole life. Carole used to have shares in National Westminster Bank, he laughingly says, he thought when he married her, the bank went with it, sadly not so. With Carole, came his step-son, Jonathan, who excelled himself with anything he could make with his hands, and loves nothing better, than doing something in Bill's home to improve his Dad's life. Jon has two children, Courtney and Dylan. Life is hectic for Bill, with the young ones visiting, keeping him on his toes.

Bill's had many friends during his long life. In the late eighties he placed an advert in the Evening Herald, inviting his school friends to a party at his home, more than thirty arrived, including Miss Williams, his school teacher. It was a happy night with so many years to catch up on.

To keep Bill's hair in its' immaculate style, he only has to walk across the road to his trusty hairdresser Tony. Bill says, he's the best in town.

Tony never forgets, that at his wedding, more than twenty years ago, Bill never charged for the wedding cars. Another of Bill's good deeds.

To help keep Bill's Mercedes in good condition, he has an excellent garage, for neighbours. The funny part about the garage is, it has in large letters, right across the front, "Body Shop", next door to Earl of Plymouth Funerals. Many stop in disbelief, and laughingly photograph this 'odd' combination. The name of the really kind manager of this 'Body Shop', is Roy Rogers. Nothing's too much trouble for this big hearted man, a special friend of Bill's.

Bill had many business friends, who were directors of Plymouth Argyle. Stafford Williams in particular, kept asking Bill to watch a match with him. Bill, not having played football, or watched a match, since he was captain of 'The Muck Ups', at school, agreed to go. All went well for the first half. Bill returned to the director's box after the half time warming drink in the club house, he forgot the teams change sides at half time, and started cheering the wrong side. Something he never lived down, as explained earlier!

Bill, always enjoyed playing a harmless joke on others, decided to give Judy and Alan a Yule Log with a difference. His step son Jon, loved cooking, even at the early age of eleven, at Christmas he'd have orders for several cakes and Yule Logs. He gave Jon a real wooden log, to cover with chocolate, tie the normal red ribbon around it, and decorate in the usual manner. It really did look delicious. Bill presented Alan with two logs, telling him to use a certain one first as it had plenty of brandy in it. The other log, was for Alan's two children. Bill, not wanting to disappoint the children with a fake cake, giving them the real fruit log.

Alan had a new electric knife for one of his gifts. With several guests present, after eating their meal, the coffee served, Alan told his guests he was going to cut a very special log cake Bill Earl had given him. Poor Alan, he screwed up his face, as his new knife couldn't get past the chocolate coating, until he discovered, his beloved friend had played a joke on him again. Remembering his wife Judy's famous words, "You know Bill, Al." Everyone was roaring with laughter. Of course, Bill had made sure they had an edible log, anyway. A tale of a true 'log' cake, one that will last forever.

Talking about cakes, eighteen years ago, Bill was taken out for a surprise birthday celebration with many of his friends. The coffee was served, candles on the cake blown out. Everyone sat down waiting in expectation for a slice of this rich fruit cake to be placed on their empty plates, when Bill looked up and said "This is my cake, isn't it?" "Yes", said Carole. "Then I can do what I want with it". "Yes", said Carole. "Well, I've decided to keep it". And keep that cake he did. It has come out every year on his birthday, to be looked at, wrapped up and stored for another year. I don't know of anyone else with an eighteen year old birthday cake. More like a rock-cake by now!

When the children were young, and had, as children often do, bumped themselves on something, ending up crying. Bill would seriously look at the child saying, "Quick, quick, where did you bump yourself?" The child pointing to a door, or table etc. Bill would go over to the offending item, lovingly smooth it down, saying, "Poor door, poor door." The child would look so amazed at the door and forget to cry, it worked every time. A trick worth remembering.

That was O.K., until Jon, his step-son, came into Bill recently, rubbing his head. Bill said, "What happened?" Jon replied, "I've knocked my head". "Quick, quick, where?" said Bill. "Up there", said Jon, pointing to the top of a door opening. Jon knowing full well, that he at 6 ft 4", and Bill at 5 ft 3", he wouldn't be able to reach this time, saying, poor door, poor door, smoothing the top. Jon, too old to cry, they each doubled up laughing instead. A favourite tale often told.

## Robert Lenkiewicz & Embalming

Bill's business and travels were two of the most important things in his life, but intertwined within all of his adventures were his family and friends, all of which have been dear to his heart at various times in his life.

Bill became the first in Devon and Cornwall to achieve the British Embalmers' Society Diploma, and the British Institute of Embalmers' Certificate, both of which became, to him, the most important achievements in his profession, followed by the teaching of his son, Christopher.

His son was aged only sixteen and officially not allowed to start learning the profession so young, however with Bill's guidance he soon passed all his exams, including the BIE certificate and the NAFD diploma. In fact he soon achieved everything one could possibly achieve in striving to develop into his father's profession. He even passed the advanced motorists' driving test. Bill became very proud of his son, Christopher.

Robert Lenkiewicz, a famous artist in Plymouth, was a friend of Bill and once asked to paint the Earl of Plymouth funeral staff and family, including Bill. The work continued for many days with the subjects all solemnly stood in front of stacks of coffins. Chalk lines were drawn around the feet of each subject and day after day they had to return to exactly the same position for Lenckiewicz to continue his work of art. During these sessions, and on many other occasions, Bill and the unorthodox painter had many interesting conversations. He talked to Bill about suicide and death. He enquired about Bill's embalming career and the disposal of dead bodies. Bill explained quite clearly that there is no law against keeping a dead body, providing it does not cause unpleasantness. Robert and Bill had many closely guarded secrets, among which was Robert's wish for Earl of Plymouth to carry out his funeral, and this occurred shortly after his death in the summer of 2002.

Robert knew that Bill and his son, Christopher, were both qualified members of the British Institute of Embalmers and therefore contacted them when he was planning to preserve the dead body of his friend, Diogenes, who was a well known tramp in the Plymouth area. Bill and his son, thinking that the publicity might be detrimental, recommended a relatively unknown B.I.E. member. The whereabouts of Diogenes remained a mystery for nearly twenty years until his embalmed body was found in Robert's studio shortly after his death. It is true to say that Robert would never have been able to have done all he did with Diogenes' body if it had not been for the knowledge and advice that Bill kindly bestowed upon him.

When Robert first asked to paint the portrait of the Earl of Plymouth staff and family Bill was concerned as to where this infamous artist might display the finished work. Therefore Bill took the highly respected, late Rev. Walker as a witness to Robert's promise to treat the massive, nearly life-size, painting with the respect the delicate nature of Bill's profession deserved. This he did to the end of his days.

Robert, being a very fair man, presented Bill with two highly valued books entitled "R.O. Lenkiewicz", containing over one hundred pages of paintings and pictures, including the painting entitled "Mr. Earl, Funeral Director & Family in Coffin Warehouse", which permitted it to be included in Bill's own life-time book "Bill Earl, Funeral Director and friend to many, This is Your Life". This book contained over 80 years of memories and was presented to Bill at a special party held in his honour.

Bill has always treasured the memory of Robert and the mutually interesting and rewarding hours they spent together.

Bill's friends, too many to mention, engulf everyone from every walk of life, he loves people. There's nothing Bill loves more, than having a good conversation. Long may your conversations continue Bill.

Because of Bill's love of people, many have gladly contributed to this biography.

### What's Up Doc!

Bill was in hospital, having his first pace-maker fitted thirteen years ago, by his long standing consultant cardiologist, Dr. Andrew Marshall, who has become like a true friend to Bill. On the operating table, with local anaesthetic, he was asked, as they do these days, what music he would like. Quick as a flash, Bill replied, "Anything, but certainly not 'Abide With Me' ". He asked if he could keep his glasses on, to enable him to watch his operation on the TV monitor. However, the glasses had to come off. Bill said, "Oh, that's alright, I can see fine from here". I can just imagine Bill there instructing the surgeon, up a bit, down a bit, forward, stop. I don't know anybody who'd want to watch their own operation being performed. He's the only man I know, to sit in Dr. Marshall's examination room, using his own sphygmomanometer on one arm, whilst Dr. Marshall was using his own blood pressure measuring device on the other, so both arms were being pumped up together, all because Bill wanted to check his own machine was working correctly.

Another similar incident. Bill was on the operating table, this time having an angiogram, when Bill said, "Oh, I see you use the femoral artery", adding, "I'd like £5 for every time I've used the femoral in embalming". One of the nurses asked, how do you find the artery as there isn't any pulse in death. Bill simply replied, "You know where 'Scarpus triangle' is". There was deadly silence. No, they didn't know. Bill said, that even with his eyes closed, he could immediately find the femoral artery, and that infact, he'd demonstrated same, many many times when lecturing to students. By now the theatre staff were amazed, and so was Bill, hoping at least the surgeon knew ha! ha!! but it's true. By now, the operation was over, and so was Bill.

A few weeks later, when Bill saw his consultant, he explained his conversation with the theatre staff. The cardiovascular surgeon, Mr. Wilkins, immediately said to Bill, they didn't know, did they. Bill had to have two major operations, called carotid endortectomies, where the carotid artery in the neck (there's one in each side of the neck), for want of a better word, is cleaned out, whilst keeping the blood flowing to the brain, and is why the surgeon kept talking to Bill throughout the operation, to make sure that his brain was not being affected. These major operations likewise, were performed under local anaesthetic. One lasting 5 hours, the other 4 hours. The last operation was touch and go, whether Bill was going to survive. Bill having to stay in the high dependency ward for 24 hours each time. Each patient has their own nurse, constantly monitoring the body's functions. Although Bill had been so desperately ill, he remained cheerful throughout, and continued to remain friendly with his surgeon, writing an after dinner speech for him. Bill's parting words were, "Do you play golf?" He replied, "Yes". To which Bill said, "Well, I don't, but I'll get you in a hole in one, and will still be the last man to let you down".

Another occasion, Bill had just returned from presenting a cheque for £1,000, to the Lord Mayor for Leukaemia fund. It had been a busy morning, with the local press busy taking photos. Bill didn't feel too good, having a pain in the middle of his back. Thinking it was just muscular problems, he asked Carole to spray 'Ralgex', on the painful area. Several hours later, the pain hadn't subsided. Bill checked his pulse, only to find it was very low, thirty four beats a minute. Still not thinking there was anything serious, he rang his G.P., asking if it would improve matters if he took a drop of whisky. The doctor immediately said, "don't do anything, I'll be right there to see you". On examining Bill, the doctor wanted to call an ambulance, to have him admitted to hospital, in the intensive care unit. Still not comprehending the seriousness of his situation, Bill said, "don't do that, we've so many cars, I'll get someone to drive me". The doctor reluctantly agreed, telephoned the hospital, and gave Bill his hospital admittance letter.

After the doctor had gone, Bill went back to the kitchen, where he had been busy all afternoon, cooking up a feast of pigeons, in readiness for his close friends John & Pat Marriott, who were coming to his home for dinner that night. Bill had met John through all the advertising he did at the Herald, where John was a director of the newspaper. Bill rang John, explained what had happened, and asked him if he could drop him at the hospital, and in an hour Bill expected to be out again, when John could collect him, bring him home, and all sit down and enjoy the feast he had prepared.

Bill was dropped off at the hospital, with admittance envelope in hand. In Bill's typical manner, he ran up the entrance steps, and then thought, what a silly thing he'd done. The sister was waiting with a wheelchair, to take Bill to his bed. Bill always says, he must have looked out of place running into the intensive care unit. An hour later, the phone rang, it was Bill, telling Carole, he wouldn't be coming home, wired up to every machine imaginable, he asked, could he have his pyjamas, wait for it, and his carefully prepared pigeons, as he was hungry, and don't forget the wine.

Carole, Pat & John, arrived at the hospital half an hour later, laden with a bag of clothes, Bill's tray, with his evening dinner and wine. The aroma of his carefully spiced meal, wafted across the ward, the nurses came to inspect Bill's cooking, agreeing he could have his meal, saying, it looked delicious, they wouldn't mind some themselves. He did look odd, wired up to all those machines, amongst very sick patients, and him eating a substantial meal of pigeons. Bill remained in that ward for several days, until he was moved, to the end of a ladies ward, much to Bill's amusement. The nurse that had to do the inventory on Bill's locker prior to his move, couldn't stop laughing. Instead of a locker full of clothes, his was full of food. Well, that's how Bill was in those days, he really had a tremendous appetite. It was soon after this incident he was fitted with his first pacemaker.

Bill's G.P., Dr. Graham Walsh, has a similar sense of humour to Bill's. On one occasion, Bill said to Dr. Walsh, 'Please, whatever you do, don't let me become like a wet cabbage'. Just as quick with his response,

Dr. Walsh jokingly said, "Would a brussel sprout do?" He is another close and valued friend of Bill's. Trying to ensure Bill doesn't become like a 'wet cabbage', he has had written on a wristband on each arm, "If I pass out please don't revive me, I wish to die". To make sure nothing is overlooked, one band faces the opposite way to the other. Bill laughingly says, he did it this way, incase the surgeon is left handed. He's shown these to all his medical team, family & solicitor, who are fully aware of his wishes.

Another hospital escapade happened, when Bill woke up one day, unable to urinate properly, as Bill knew, this was a real emergency. He immediately went to hospital, where the urologist, Mr. Hammonds, tried unsuccessfully to remove the offending stone. Bill was informed, he would need an operation that day. Asked if he had eaten, Bill said, "only a few prunes", hoping he could get his operation over immediately. Unfortunately, because of his prunes, Bill had to wait several hours before he could have a general anaesthetic. Carole left as Bill was wheeled down to theatre, she busied herself making one of Bill's favourite foods, 'Cornish pasties'. As anticipated, 7p.m., the phone went, it was Bill, he'd come around, and could he have something to eat, he was starving, would she please bring him his pasty. Needless to say to his delight, he enjoyed an extra large home-made pasty that evening, much to the amusement of the nurses, and was home next day.

**A letter Bill wrote was to his doctor:-**
who asked Bill for an update on his health, this is exactly what Bill gave him, it's entitled, "Just Exercising My Brain".

Remember, we old folks are worth a fortune, with silver in our hair, gold in our teeth, stones in our kidneys & lead in our feet.

My preacher friend called the other day, I thought he came, just to pray. Instead, he said, at my age, I should be thinking of the hereafter. I told him, I do that all the time. In the living room, study, or upstairs, and ask myself – "What am I hereafter".

I'm living not among the dead, but I'm getting more forgetful, mixed up in my head. I've got used to my strokes and jokes, to dentures I'm resigned, I can put up with bifocals, but oh, how I miss my mind.

At times I can't remember, when standing on the stair, should I go up for something, or have I just come down from there. Before the fridge, my mind filled with doubt, did I put some food away, or come to take it out?

Sometimes at night, with my night cap upon my head, I don't know if I'm retiring, or just got out of bed. Now I'm stood beside the box, my face has sure got red, for instead of posting this, I'm off to bed.

Bill's life story wouldn't seem complete, without including these two letters, which describe him to a 'T'.

## A West Country Dialect Letter

This is an exact replica of a letter Bill wrote to a Cornish Inn, to book Sunday lunch, using West country dialect. He was always up to something for a laugh. See if you can understand it, the landlord did, saying it was the best letter he'd ever received.

"Arken to me, me anzums, uz knows tiz a brave way to down alonga we, but uz wont rin word, usle be there Sunday, 12.30p.m. Please reserve a table for two, amongst Cornish people, if possible.

I nows yoda savise. Usl spake youl member me, the one warein sparticles and all triggered up zmart.

No need to get vussled, shall ave me wive with me, hers lookin some vorwood to it.

Didee yer zaid about that young varmer, Tom Cobley, down longa wee. They da tell me thats near yo. He yerd strange noises comin from a rabbit hole and zed to tother varmer, 'Yer maister, put yer yer yer, and yer wot yo can yer' ha! ha!!'"

No wonder Bill says he is very broad in his speech, and is happy to say, 'he's a Devonshire Dumpling'.

Couldn't resist including that little gem in the book.

## Swimming & Food

Bill, always an all the year round swimmer at Tinside, Plymouth Hoe (men only area). Every morning, winter months and all, Bill and two others, would take a running dive into the sea, so early, it was pitch black, he could barely see the water he was diving into. At lunch time, he, with the rest of the all year rounders, such as Bill Lippel and others, about a dozen of them, all of whom, Bill has photographs of, when he took them all out as his guests to evening dinner, would love to picnic. More about that later.

Bill Earl, though only a little chap, was known for his gourmandising. The restaurants used to remark, and still do, to Bill's wife, that they had never known anyone eat as much as Bill. No matter, what part of the world, or country he was in, he always wanted the meats that were different. He relished everything he ate, whether crocodile, witchety grubs, kangaroo, which he cooked himself in Alice Springs, whilst another kangaroo looked on. He's also eaten, EMU (Bill always laughs, saying one leg was plenty), wild boar, jelly fish, cold, which he said, slid down lovely, mud crabs, water buffalo, a very large Australian fish, he had in Fiji, cooked, first by digging a big pit in the soil, then lighting a large fierce fire, to which large stones were thrown in, until they became almost red hot, to which was added for cooking, a Barramundi fish, head and all, completely wrapped in banana leaves, as was a whole pig, also with its' head on, and similarly wrapped in banana leaves. The big fire and pit, was then completely filled in, with the earth that had come from it, and then left for about 3 1/2 hours, by which time, it had become sumptuous and delicious. By the time Bill had finished, he felt like the pig himself, but unlike the pig, he hadn't lost his head. Needless to say Bill attended funerals whilst in Fiji, more about that earlier.

When it comes to food, you name it, Bill's had it. Wherever in the world he is, it doesn't matter if he can't speak the language. For he either made motions, to look in the kitchen, then point to anything bubbling away, that looks and smells good to him, often trying several dishes in one evening. Another favourite of his, is to use sign language, he made up himself, example, if he wanted pig's trotters, he would snort like a pig and point to his feet. This always broke the ice, wherever he was, invariably causing much laughter he always got what he wanted, except once. Bill wanted fried egg, so he clucked like a chicken, made a sign, as if cracking an egg in a frying pan, the meal arrived, but instead of getting his fried eggs, he was brought a cooked whole chicken. He always laughs and says, it was nearly right, it's simply that the egg had been allowed to grow, that's all.

Back to Bill's lunch times at Tinside. First they would play a game with a ball on an elastic, affixed to a lead weight, before diving back into the sea, after which, Bill would take out his lunch from a very wide thermos flask. Laughingly, they would all shout, Look out, Bill's getting his lunch out, each saying, I am going to sit on the Leigh side of all the spicy stuff, together with loads of garlic and herbs.

Well, of course, his daily lunch varied, it was all sorts of odd things, sometimes he would take out a very large flask, and withdraw from it, a whole duck, spiced up with garlic etc. Next day, it might be a flask, of spiced up udder. I remember, Bill always said, it had to be well swung. He always had something exotic, and different every day.

After his lunch, he often had, either a brandy and coffee with cream, or whisky, or gin with coffee and cream, or a nice Tia Maria, Bill loved Tia Maria. Bill always generous, usually, saw that the swimmers had a little of his warming drinks as well. Some remember when Bill was going to have, specially baked Cornish pasty. Honestly, it really was, over a foot long. Bill wanted it, like the old Cornish clay workers had their long Cornish pasty. Made extra long, then part way down, a piece of pastry was placed across, separating say, a quarter from the rest. The portioned part, held the desert, which was example, cooked apple.

A couple of the swimmers, had arranged for two newspaper reporters to be there one very cold lunch time, to see Bill come in from his swim, and eat this enormous pasty. It wasn't as simple as that. The Sunday Independent Newspaper reporter, wanted to take a photo of Bill with his mouth wide open, trying to eat a huge piece from the side of the pasty. Bill wouldn't have any of that, always conscious, it just wouldn't look right for his profession, and anyway, he didn't eat like that normally, as he laughs and says, he's got a dainty little mouth.

## Eating & Eating Out

Bill wouldn't dream of eating so much food in one go now, but many years ago, I remember a group, including Bill, were eating in a small restaurant. Everyone ordered fish and chips, except, Bill, who ordered fish, chips and two faggots, with plenty of gravy. His meal served on a large oval plate, all the others, were normal round plates. Everyone cleared their plates, the food was always good at Perrillas. The waitress arrived to take down the desert order. Again, everyone ordered a normal desert, except Bill, he wanted the same again. Everyone's eyes popped out like organ stops, unable to believe their ears He ate the lot, a hearty eater indeed.

Another example. Bill had just enjoyed a lovely four course evening dinner at The Glazebrook House Hotel. Everyone had had more than enough to eat, and at 11.30p.m., were pleased to go back to their homes, full and pleasantly tired. Not Bill. He drove into the city centre to his favourite spot, The Grecian Tavern, to eat all over again, as if he hadn't eaten for a week, instead of just minutes earlier, an appetite that's hard to beat.

## Diving in The Pool

Bill was a keen outdoor, all year round swimmer, until the latter years, when due to his health, took to swimming in the local pool, 7a.m. every morning, always first one in the pool.

The rules of the management were, 'no diving'. Bill with his injured foot, found it hurt to walk down the iron steps into the water, so always with a respect for safety, with no-one close to him, would dive in every morning. The attendants told Bill, you're not allowed to dive, pointing to one of the many notices. Bill's quick response, was, "I didn't, I fell in". He's been swimming in this pool for years, "slipping and falling in the pool", every morning, ha! ha!!

## Just Bill

Because of Bill's strokes, and subsequent loss of memory, he can't remember all the names of the various ones he came in contact with during his life.

If Bill's about to give a speech, he always starts off, by saying, "I'm a Devonshire Dumpling", then it doesn't matter how he speaks. Because he is a Devonshire Dumpling, and proud of it. Infact, he used to teach people the Cornish and Devonshire dialects. It is the accent that promotes Bill's character. For he certainly is one of the old, established 'characters' of Plymouth.

However, don't be fooled by his West country speech, as you can tell by this book, he is no fool. His response is sharp witted, he's led a successful business life, as well as fighting his own and others court cases, all without solicitors. He would have made a first class solicitor, he never lost a case. He was so well known, others would come to him for advice, which he freely gave. He loves helping anyone in need. More about that in another section of the book. A very versatile man.

### This Is Your Life at Sixty Five

For Bill's sixty fifth birthday, a surprise party was held in his honour. On this special day Bill was presented with a book entitled, "Bill Earl, Funeral Director and Friend To Many, This Is Your Life". Friends flew from Toronto, Canada, and various parts of the world specially to be with Bill that night. There certainly were many many friends at the reception, and a talk followed by evening dinner.

Tony Beard, the well known, 'Wag from Widecombe', who is a close friend of Bill's read the letters contained in this book; for your enjoyment, here are some copies of those scripts:-

### From Christopher Earl (son)

So much has happened that only you and I know of and for which I shall always be grateful, it is so difficult to speak of any one instance. There's so much in the distant past that you have done, that I shall never know about. Only now, with all I have been through, can I fully appreciate what you have been through yourself and still did for me.

I wish to finish, with a big thank you, which I hope you understand, is a small way of trying to say, thank you for everything. With love, and I hope you have a very special birthday.

### From Anita Earl (daughter)

I remember when Dad was trying to teach me, 'manners'. I said, "Look at that man over there". I pointed to him. Dad said, not to point, it's rude, so I clenched my fist, and said, "Look at that man over there".

So that I wouldn't be frightened of spiders, he used to tell me to say, "Little Miss Muffett sat on a tuffett eating her curds and whey, along came a spider and sat down beside her, and they all began to play", instead of saying, frightened Miss Muffett away.

Dad was always teaching things like that, for example, he told me that Peter Pan wasn't true, so that I wouldn't jump out of the window and try to fly.

Life might be full of ups and downs, but you know I'll always love you, happy birthday.


## From Jon Lendon (step-son)

Here are a few incidents Jon can remember. Jon was nicknamed Noj by Bill as a little boy, because at age four, he would write Jon backwards, spelling Noj, and it stuck.

We were in France on holiday, Jon was six years old, badly wanting to go to the toilet, there was nowhere to go on the beach, just a few rocks. Bill told Jon, to take some paper and hide behind the rocks. Eventually Jon disappeared, a little head just visible above the rocks. After a while he returned, carrying something, saying, "You didn't give me enough paper to wrap it up properly!!"

Another occasion in France, in the middle of a country village, Jon badly wanted to go to the toilet again, but there were none in sight. "That's alright", said Bill, "Just stand here and whistle, and look at the plants, no one will notice". "That's alright for you Uncle Bill", said Jon, "But I can't whistle."

This time we were in Wales, Jon was swimming in a river. Bill shouted to him, "Jon, if I were you, I'd cover up those shoulders, or you'll be sorry". Jon took no heed of the warning, carrying on swimming. Next morning he was sore with sun burn. Bill looking at Jon, said, "What did I tell you yesterday?" Jon answered Bill, repeating his warning, adding, that Uncle Bill never tells him anything wrong. Bill said, "So why didn't you cover up your shoulders?" To which Jon replied, "Because I didn't hear you, as I was in the water at the time!!"

Another laughable incident, Jon came home from school asking Bill, if he could make a private phone call to his girlfriend. Bill said to him, "Girlfriend!" Jon replied, "Well, everyone's got to have a girlfriend". As he went out to make his call, he closed the door. Bill, the aggravate shouted, "Jon, open the door, or I wont be able to hear what you say!"

There was a time, Jon had said his headmaster had died, coming home from school, crying. A few months later, when he wanted Xmas cards, he asked for an extra one for his headmaster, Mr. Uglow. "We thought you said he was dead, Jon". "I know", said Jon, "But he's alright now".

And there are more, but the main thing Jon always says, "Whatever Uncle Bill tells him, is always right". Happy birthday, love Jon (Noj).

## From Florrie

Bill was always up to mischief. I remember the time he ran away from home on a 'cycle', going to St. Austell. He told me, he wanted to spend a penny on the way, but rather than get off the bike, he did it whilst cycling.

One of his school pals, Alf Brooking, told me, how he bought a pigeon from Bill for 6d, and when he let it out, it flew back to Bill's loft. Alf never saw it again, not knowing one bird from another. I think this was the time, young Bill would sell these pigeons, knowing they would fly home to him, allowing him to sell them again. No wonder he always had plenty of money, even as a little boy.

## From The Rev. Reg. Walker

The thought of Bill being 65 leaves me speechless. Somehow I think of him in terms of perpetual youth. I would like to recall his humour ... especially his uncontrollable delight at my downfall.

It happened like this. We were all involved in a funeral service, at which there was only one mourner, an elderly gentleman who had lost his wife, and for a reason I can't now recall, he was the only person at the funeral service, apart of course from Bill, his entourage, and myself. I felt very sorry for the old man, so I walked with him to the grave, in a notoriously unkempt graveyard.

Bill Earl, 'This is Your Life', 1985

At the grave, the coffin was lowered on to the two bars, and the bearers waited for my signal to lower the coffin … when, for an inexplicable reason the grave digger hurried away, leaving Bill and three others holding the coffin, but with no chance of lowering it, because of the bars across the grave.

Well, it was an unusual funeral service in any case, so always valiant, I stepped forward, pulled the bars away, and was about to say the committal, when the side of the grave fell in, and down I went!!

The coffin was put on the ground, whilst I was hauled out, cassock, gown and all. How we ever got through that committal, I shall never know.

And Bill … walking back to the cars … whispered, "How like you, to try to get two burials for the price of one!"

I have seen Bill cry at funerals, but that day … the day of my downfall … his laughter was almost out of control.

We join with all your friends in wishing you a happy 'retirement'.

### From Pam & Lou Glanville

In this book, I feel I must pay tribute to Bill, for all the kindness he showed my father, who was very ill during the war. Several months before he died, he would often visit my father with gifts which were difficult to obtain.

I remember once, my father mentioned how he liked tomatoes, which were very hard to get. One morning, on opening the front door, a large box of tomatoes was there, from Bill. It seems, nothing was too much trouble, Bill would go out of his way to help anyone, and the pleasure he had from doing a good turn, was so obvious.

I have known Bill all my life, and I can honestly say, that's the way he's always been.

Many times, whilst working the late shift on the buses, during the war, Bill would be there, at the depot in his car, to pick me up, making sure I got home safely. Also, not forgetting my rides in Bill's trolley when we were kids, and now, here we are celebrating your 65th birthday. In conclusion, I hope this book gives you as much pleasure, as I've had knowing you.

### George Bougard & Margaret

I hardly know where to begin mentioning the times Billy and I experienced, most of them unfortunately are unprintable. You name it, we did it. However, I will do my best to tell you a few tales.

One such tale that springs to mind, was the time Billy flagged me down, about midnight, near Derrys Clock. "George", he says, "I've got a Yank here, who wants to go to Yelverton, there's fifteen quid in it". "Why can't you do it Bill?", I asked. "I'm already booked up", he says. "Infact, I've been driving around looking for you, because it's too good a job to miss". Of course, Billy already knew, that the road to Yelverton was fog bound, because he had just come back.

So off I went. Needless to say, I had not gone very far outside Plymouth, before I realised (as usual), he had b ... well caught me. When I could no longer see the hedge, I stopped, and said to the Yank, "Your camp is just around the bend mate". "Thanks buddy", he said, and paid up, not knowing that a seven mile hike lay ahead of him. Billy was surprised to see me back so quickly.

Another time, we picked up a girl, and Billy promised to drive her home. She had not been in the car two minutes, before she asked if Billy, would take her to the nearest toilet. "Of course my dear", he said, "As soon as I've dropped this fare at Crownhill". By the time we returned to Plymouth, she was in agony, and pleaded with Billy to stop anywhere.

He finally stopped at the Brickfields, and in those days, it was just open space. She sped off into the darkness to relieve herself. Billy was laughing so much, he could hardly drive. He mounted the kerb and turned all the headlights on, focusing the lights on the poor girl. She was unable to stop what she was doing and tried desperately to get out of the light, by moving along like a crab, her skirt was around her middle, and her pants around her ankles. When she asked Billy why he did that, he said, "I thought you couldn't see what you were doing". We nearly died of laughing.

I wish Billy the best, to me he is the "Tops", God bless and a healthy retirement.

### From Ron Jess

To me, Bill is a very dear friend, we have had wonderful times, dinners, or a glass of wine together. He has given me good advice and help at times when needed, and I hope I have helped him in times of stress as well. There has not been a time when we have not enjoyed each other's company. I look forward to many more happy times in the future.

He has always kidded me along, that I was the elder because I am a little taller, now the secret is out. I wish Bill all the best for the future.

### From Brian and Nora

I think a look back over the years is called for, and just like the song goes, "We've been together now for forty years", seems appropriate at this time. But, how does one sum up a forty year relationship in a letter, well, it all started on an errand to the Co-op.

Going back to my first day at work, I was left in charge of the garage wearing my step-father's ex-navy bell bottomed trousers, in which I had to take two steps before they moved. The phone rang (so called office in corner), I climbed over the chair and desk, trying to avoid a vicious looking Alsatian dog, called "Rinty", who became my friend for many years. An hour later, the roof blew off, so ended my first day.

My wages were £1.50 a week, but not as easy as that. I had £1.00 on Fridays and ten shillings on Tuesdays. What a difference now, and how laughable, when the youth of today talk about hard times.

The next day, saw the beginning of our long association together, taking our equipment (one hearse and clapped out car and hose pipe) to Capera Terrace, where we made many friends, including the Gilbert family. Doris the maid and her "know all" bus driver husband, and grumpy Mr. Berry, and what about the everlasting tea pot, I don't think it was ever empty, with the number of people coming in the back door; Henry Buzzer, Claud West, Harry Farrow, Frank Bloom, Jan Gilbert and Sam Burgoyne (with petrol tanker). It was there I was given the name of 'Belson Kid'.

Our next stop was Redlands Garage at Hartley, where we grew tomatoes in the back of the hearse. We also made more friends, Bill Wright, Gwen, Edgar Dennley, among many others.

From there, Valletort Road must be mentioned, where our first printing press came into action, plus our 'leaflet round', and what about the Christmases when we worked around the clock, more times than I like to remember.

Albert Road and, Mount Street was our next stop, where I lived with you as a family for many years. We certainly have a wealth of memories to look back upon. Remembering all the so called "housekeepers" we had to endure. Remember the soggy dumpling lady and Mrs Hayes, when she sprayed the house with the pressure cooker, also, the numerous maids, whose names I can't recall? (Quickie), remember the motor bike you bought in St. Austell? We charged up and down Albert Road all day, and took it back the next day.

We have come a long way since those days, I'm glad to say, and it's only for your unending concern for the business, the long hours in days gone by, that has brought us to the successful firm we are today. There is so much more I would like to say, many names that come to mind, which are impossible to mention here, but as you know, the crew of the ship, is only as good as the example set by the captain, and our ship has sailed into calm and stormy seas, but like the good captain, you are, we have come through the storms, and are now in peaceful waters, which I hope, we will never sail out of again, and as a Captain leaves his Ship after a commission, I salute you Sir, but I'm sure you will always be running up the gangplank, keeping a weathered eye on your crew.

We hope you have a happy retirement (at work).

## From Sylvia & Ken

I have known W.A.E. for many years, during which time, I've always held him in high esteem for many reasons, of which I will mention a few:-

He thrives on achieving perfection in everything he does, always ready to point out any discrepancies for the benefit and learning of all concerned. A good example to all. If one took notice of all he said, you couldn't go wrong, as has been proved many times. Much can be learnt from his criticisms, during which time, he can get very excitable. However, he is equally as quick and never fails, to give praise where due.

I have never known anyone to have so much patience, and get so much enjoyment in letter writing (mind you, the typist needs patience at times!) A most familiar sight, sitting at his desk, writing letters. Many is the time one can get rather excitable oneself with his writing, after a couple of hours. Then, when thinking, you realise, he is right. As many people will know, results have proved, and, he derives so much pleasure from it.

He is dedicated to business, nothing is too much trouble. Any question asked, he is always ready to answer, with help, and means so well by all. As he comes in the office, curtains are neatly placed, doors shut, check on thermostat (little does he know, we have them out of place, to give him something to do).

Staff party with Tony Beard, circa 1981

I have always enjoyed working with him, along with the rest of the staff, one only has to think of the length of time we have been with him. I wish him health and happiness for many years to come, which he truly deserves.

## From Alan and Judy

Since the first time we met in the Cooperage, you have been a kind and loyal friend, your sense of humour never fails to raise our spirits from the doldrums. Do you remember the night you taught me the biggest lesson of my life, when we went to Stockton Manor?

You said to the both of us, "If you can eat everything that's put in front of you, I'll pay the bill, if not, you pay".

I said to Judy, "What do you reckon Jude?" Judy said, "Well, you know Bill, Al".

The most fantastic meal arrived, a huge rice cake in all the colours of the rainbow, complete with curry. Needless to say, we were unable to eat such a vast amount, and I had to foot the bill.

This gave me nightmares and I couldn't wait for the morning to come to call you Bill, little dreaming that you were awaiting my call, and laughing all the way down the phone. You certainly taught me a lesson, I shall never forget.

Stockton Manor has since been burned to the ground, but thank goodness there are numerous good eating houses where we have enjoyed the pleasure of your company, and considerably broadened our culinary taste. May we have many more enjoyable times together, I know, 'you're the last man to let me down'.

## From Cyril and Myrtle

At 10.15a.m., a removal van arrived outside a house. On the side, in large letters, was written, 'G.C. Covington, Removals and Storage'.

At 10.30a.m., a hearse arrived at the house next door. On the name plate was, 'Earl of Plymouth'.

Cyril started to move the furniture from one house, whilst Bill went into the house next door, to remove the body. Cyril got on with the job very fast, and was on the pavement, holding a piano on his back, when Bill came out, and said, "Hold on there a minute Cyril". Cyril stood holding the piano, and Bill and the hearse moved off. However, when the funeral procession drove back, after the funeral, poor Cyril was still there holding the piano, waiting for Bill. It nearly broke his back.

May I add, that during Cyril's latter years, when he was confined to a wheelchair, Bill would regularly drive up to take us out. One of the few friends who still cared. Cyril so looked forward to seeing you. Thank you for your kindness.

## From Reg Collicot

I first met Bill in the 1940's, when he was still in Albert Road, and we teamed up for a night out with two nurses. We met them at their homes in the Laira area. Away we went to the George Hotel at Roborough for a few drinks, finding out what a 'bloody Mary' was. I thought it was a nun who suffered with high blood pressure. After a few drinks, we cruised across the moors, until we stopped at another, but higher class Inn. A few more drinks, and the time was around 10p.m. Nurses are great company anytime, but this wasn't my night.

Near Roborough, we stopped yet again, but with a difference. Bill said to me, we are going for a walk, so enjoy yourself. He left with his nurse, and disappeared into the Moorland, with a smile on his face. I was left in the back of the car with my nurse.

After nearly an hour of absence, Bill returned to the car with his nurse, still smiling. Bill never had any flowers in his hands, so I guess, when you go walkies with a nurse, you don't stop to pick flowers.

Bill and I went out for a drink many years ago, when we were returning home via Milehouse. Bill said to me, "Look at those kids carrying a punnett of blackberries". He stopped the car, lowered the window on my side, and said, "What have you got there kids?" They said, "We've been picking blackberries for our mum, to make apple and blackberry pie". Bill said, "I'll give you sixpence for them". The kids said, "No mister, our mum wants them for the pie". Bill said to me, "Offer them a shilling, Reg". I said to them, "I'll give you twice as much, and give you a shilling". They looked at each other and smiled. I knew I had won my bargain. They offered the large punnett of blackberries to me, and so Bill got his blackberries.

When we asked the boys where they'd picked them, they said, "Up the cemetery, at the back of the bus depot". I'm sure the punnett jumped on my lap for laughter.

Whilst under the driving orders of Bill, we went for a run around, at the Grand Hotel, Duke of Cornwall, and ended up at Perillas. Bill is one person, who really and truly loved his food, and it was good to see eating at its' best. One idiosyncrasy Bill always had was, to sit at any table, facing the way he could see who came into the restaurant and going out. His friends had to turn their necks. On this occasion, he offered me the menu, and said, "Order what you fancy, Reg., so I ordered fish and chips with a cup of tea. I knew Bill would have a good meal, so I cut down on my expenses, not wanting to put too much of a bill on his plate.

My meal was very good, and so was the tea. Bill had mushrooms, tomatoes, and all the best of the trimmings, plus his glass of wine. After having his main meal, he surprised me, by asking the waitress, if he could have a plate of chips and two eggs (hardly cooked). When all was done, he surprised me even more, by saying to me. "What does your bill come to?" I said it came to £1.20. He then said, being an aggravate, "Alright Reg, you pay your bill separate, and I'll pay mine. "So much for being invited out!" ha! Ha!!

We went to Ford Hotel, for a drink one night, Bill was driving the American saloon, silver grey and very eye catching indeed. After a lemonade and lime for me, which I drank most times with Bill, we were just leaving, when a little boy came into the pub, with a number of fresh mackerel for sale, at 1d each. Bill said, "How many have you got there?" The boy counted his fish, and said, "There's eighteen fish, so that's 1s-6d." Bill said, "I'll give you 1s-3d for the lot". The boy, seeing all his fish going in one effort, duly handed all his mackerel over to Bill, who immediately, put them in the boot of the American car. A good night's work done, thought Bill, until two days later, when a whiff of fish crept into the car. Boy, did he realise, he'd forgotten to take the fish out of the car … phew …

The boot was washed out with disinfectant, but the smell remained for nearly a week after. I often wondered, what the wedding guests and funeral mourners thought, whilst riding in the car. Sounds "Fishy" to me.

After travelling at a slow speed for a funeral at Minehead, we decided to get back to Plymouth, as soon as possible. Going through the Exmoor forest, we came across a pheasant in the middle of the road. Bill said to me, "Reg, he's mine". Like a Brands Hatch maniac, he shot forward and went over the pheasant, leaving him motionless on the road. Bill got out of the car to pick up the bird, when a farmer came out of the field, by the side of the road. "Lucky for me, I came up", said the farmer. Bill looked at him, like daggers, and said, "It may be for you, but not for me, I was going to put him in the boot of my car".

In 1973, I was disabled, and on crutches. Bill Earl visited me at my home, to see how I was getting on, being on my own at the time. He gave me a new life, when he took me out for a friendly social evening, in his American saloon car. I felt great, when I realised, I could drive these cars, and with weddings, I really got the feeling for living again. Bill Earl, put me on the road, even to the extent of driving V.I.P.'s, such as the Mayor of Perth, Australia, executive directors of Marks and Spencer, and other occasions. He gave me the willpower to live, and I started to dance again.

Time is the healer of all ailments. I wish it to go on record, that my life was given a boost by Bill Earl.

## From Pat and John Marriott

How good it is to be blessed with a friend such as you. It is so rare, to find a complete person, with a soul, a heart and imagination. So rare, for characters, as ardent and restless as ours, to meet, and to be matched together, that I hardly know how to tell you, what happiness it gives me, to know you.

## Brian Jones

Having known Bill for so long, and had so many funny times together, it's hard to recall all of them.

One I remember is, the time Bill and I were driving back from Helston, many years ago. It was winter, very cold, and drizzly rain. We were travelling in Bill's Rolls Royce hearse, which did not have a heater. We also had a passenger in the back (you know what I mean), and it was my first time helping Bill in his work.

We had just left Helston (Bill was driving), we had travelled about ten miles, when all of a sudden, the hearse started to spit and splutter. I, Brian automatically thought, we had run out of petrol, but could not understand it, because Bill had filled the tank up before he left. As luck would have it, we were on a downward slope, and there was a small country garage at the bottom. We free wheeled down, and managed to pull up at the forecourt and asked the attendant to fill her up.

After putting in 2 gallons, the tank overflowed, but the engine still would not start. Then a mechanic came over and started stripping this down and that down, but still could not find the fault.

All this time we were shivering in the cold, and still had to get all the way back to Plymouth. After some considerable time, the mechanic thought of an idea, and said to Bill, "Have you got a separate ON, OFF switch to the petrol tank?" Bill said, "Yes, down there", which was by my feet.

On investigation, it was found, I had accidentally pushed the Lever to Off, with my foot. You can just imagine Bill, and what he said to me, but after that, we laughed all the way home to Plymouth.

That is typical of Bill, always sees the funny side of things. I wish him a happy birthday, with many years to follow.

## From Barbara

I remember one day, when W.A.E., came into the office, smiling like a Cheshire cat. He sat at his desk, which is directly in front of mine, and started to read his mail. After a while, he turned around to me, with the biggest smile on his face, and kept looking at me. After a while, he turned around and carried on reading. After a short while, he turned around again, still smiling like a Cheshire cat. This continued all morning, every half hour or so.

Eventually, I asked him, if he was feeling alright. His reply was, that he intended to make someone happy during the day, and was going to keep smiling at someone every half hour.

One thing I would like to say, is that, he is a very straight man, and even when he tells us off for something, he goes to town and makes sure we understand what he means, at the same time, listening to our points of view, it is then forgotten.

He is highly respected by all the staff, said with the utmost sincerity.

## From Annie, St. Austell

He used to love coming down here weekends, going to the clay works, with my husband, Phil, accordion in sack, playing to the men during crib time (that is meal times). Wanting a whole rabbit to himself. Also, he liked brains, cooked.

My husband had a motor-bike and side-car, which he loved to drive up the lane. One day, he took June, who was a toddler, when he came back, we could not find her. She had fallen off the seat, and rolled up the front of the side-car, he didn't know she had gone.

He used to cycle down here, very often. The first time, was when he ran away from home. His father, being very hard on him, made him cycle back, it was a long way to go.

One day, he was on the station, when Ethel saw him, and said, "We didn't expect you until next week", so he caught the next train down again, going home the following week. He loved it down here. Have a very happy birthday Bill.

## From Carole

Through the years, Bill has been a very good friend and counsellor to me, as well as to the several friends of his, who seek his advice in times of trouble. He is always there, to give unlimited time to listen and help. I shall always be indebted to Bill, for, without him being so concerned about my health in the early days, when I had pneumonia, I wouldn't be here today, it hardly seems enough, thank you.

Not only was Bill concerned about my health, but he also noticed, Jon was visiting the bathroom frequently, hence a visit to the doctor, and a hernia repair operation.

Bill always enjoys a laugh, here are a few occasions that spring to mind.

We were at a restaurant. The waiter gave Bill the menu to study. He told the waiter, he'd write down the order for him, which he did. He ordered, crabs' eyelashes on toast, followed by filleted frogs elbows, then the normal order. Bill was chuckling about his joke, when the surprise came. On a piece of black toast was an aubergine skin, cut into the shape of eyelashes. When the waiter asked if everything was alright, Bill's reply was, "Next time, don't get them from darkest Africa". Next, up came a pile of bones, which were quail's wings. Bill ate the lot, asking the waiter, where the wish bone was. Eventually the main course arrived. After Bill had finished his duck, the waiter asking if everything was alright. "Lovely", said Bill, "But would you ask the chef, if he would reupholster these bones". It wasn't long before a plate was placed infront of Bill, of thickly battered bones. The chef certainly wouldn't be beaten. However, when it came to paying, Bill had the last laugh, by writing his cheque on the menu, the owner having to take his large menu to the bank, to get his money. A few days later, Bill said to the restaurant owner, "I was at the bank today, they were all studying your menu, they want to know if it's cheaper if they make a booking for 36!"

From there on, Bill would write out his cheques, on anything that came to hand. I remember him writing one out on a greasy paper bag, presenting it to an Indian Restaurant owner, he knew well. Every time Bill asked if he'd paid his cheque into the bank, he'd laugh and say no. Eventually he plucked up enough courage to present this unusual cheque, to be pleasantly surprised, the bank accepted it. Bill wrote out numerous cheques in various languages, like Chinese, all for fun, all accepted. He always likes to do something for devilment.

There was the time, I was supposed to introduce myself to a certain pub owner, as the deputy Lord Mayor's chauffeur, telling the poor man, to clear a room for the Deputy Lord Mayor and his dignitaries, who were waiting in a Rolls Royce outside. The Landlord had a room emptied of a rather large crowd of people, making a gangway, for the entry of, non other than, Earl of Plymouth. A good time was had by all.

Bill loves to introduce the unsuspecting to Indian ice-cream, done his way. He'll ask, haven't you had 'hot' ice cream before. It's hot alright, covered in chilli powder.

The waiter offering Bill a drop of wine to taste. Bill tastes it, then screws up his face. The waiter looks so worried, saying, "Is it off?" Off, you say, it's lovely. When the waiter tries to pour wine into my wine glass, Bill turns it upside down, saying, she doesn't drink, she's Mohammedan, but to give Bill plenty, as he's Church of England.

We always know when Bill is home, rather than on one of his numerous business trips abroad. The 7.30a.m., yodel from the front door, as he comes home from his early morning swim. His operatic singing throughout the day. The occasional cook ups, with mounds of delicious food, but me, as the chef's skivvy. To the late night music from the tape recorder. Not exactly peaceful!!

If Bill is out of an evening, which is often, I always know where to find him, ring his favourite restaurants.

The day Bill took me to the doctor's. I didn't know it then, but I had measles. Bill was waiting so long in the car, not realising the doctor was late. When I eventually walked back to the waiting Bill, he said, "Don't tell me why you're late, the doctor couldn't find your chest".

In Spain, with the topless sunbathers, Bill said, "I shouldn't go topless if I were you Carole, they might think you're a man".

If we go shopping, Bill always ends up walking in front, with his hands in his pockets, with me carrying the goods. When I protest, he looks around, and says, "People have been looking at us, they say, it's funny, but wherever that little man goes, that big woman is always following".

There was an occasion I'll never forget. Bill had been to a Masonic evening, and had obviously had a good time. I had been asleep, when suddenly, I was awakened by a noise from the bathroom. There was Bill, hanging on to the radiator, trying to get his trousers off. I steered him into the bedroom, removed his trousers, handed him his pyjamas, and went downstairs, to check he'd locked the front door. He'd locked it alright, but I had to laugh, sitting at the top of the steps were several full bottles of wine, and a wet box containing 4 glasses. Worse was to come, I carried his prizes into the breakfast room, there, stood in the middle of the table, were two glasses. He'd managed that, but forgot the rest. I went back upstairs, still laughing, and there, prostate on the floor, was Bill. He had put his legs into the armholes of his pyjamas, and of course, when he tried to walk, he fell over.

Well Bill, comforter, counsellor, thank you, for being you. Happy birthday, with many more to follow.

### From The Wag From Widecombe

I was thrilled to think that I was to be numbered amongst your close acquaintances, and especially, as I have only known you a few years, and yet, because of your warm personality, I feel I've been a 'pal' for years.

It was due to our common interests (good food and a good laugh), that we first met. I well remember, that we immediately found the happy 'banter' between us, made for such a happy evening. Since that, I've had the pleasure of meeting you, and enjoyed your company on many occasions.

So often, when one meets a successful business-man, one finds him to be a bore and self-centred, but with you, you always have so much to add to a conversation, and also, show your concern for others.

I say this with the greatest respect Bill … You are a little man, with a Big Big heart. Good luck.

### From Gerry & Peggy, Canada

It seems like a miracle, Bill, the way that our friendship has developed, since that day, over twenty years ago, when I first spoke to a funeral director from Plymouth, England, who wanted to talk to someone at

The family that loves Bill so much

Dominion Manufacturers Ltd., Toronto, about purchasing equipment for his business.

That was all we knew about each other. You were a stranger in Toronto and we got together. That was the beginning. You had dinner that night with our family, and since then, our friendship has just kept growing. Our family have visited you at different times, and accepted your most gracious hospitality, creating memories often talked about and greatly cherished.

All in all, the crossing of our paths, has resulted in many changes in our lives, for which we are most grateful. We sincerely hope, our friendship will continue on a personal eye-ball to eye-ball basis for many years to come.

## The end

The above is a taster of how Bill's many family and friends feel about him, giving an insight into this Big character of Plymouth.

To finalise this chapter, the following is how his son Jon, feels about Bill:-

"Bill is a man in a million, a wonderful, warm loving guy, a mentor, a friend and a teacher, who's worth more than money can buy.

In my childhood, he was my real hero, defender and champion too, who shared all my good time and bad, and watched over me with care as I grew.

He's been a shining example of just how a father should be, though you make the role seem so simple and always so matter of fact.

I know that the job isn't easy, for along with the joy we know, comes a lot of hard work and commitment. All the worries that that he never showed.

I thank you for all of the times Dad you have been there for me come what may. To help me make the right choices and guide and show me the way.

You deserve to be showered with praises, for I want the whole world to see, that you are a Dad to be proud of, the most wonderful Dad there could be."

*Jon and Lisa*

# 8
# Pearls of Wisdom

There's Chinese proverbs, and King Solomon's wise words, here are some of Bill's thought provoking sentences he uses most days, and are well known by his family and friends, who've adopted them to use in their own lives, try them, 'the proof of the pudding's in the eating'.

'It takes a wise man to invent, but any fool can improve'.

'Laws are made for the strict adherence of the foolish, and mere guidance of the intelligent'.

'The Earl hand of helpfulness is ever extended, infact sometimes it gets stretched to the limit, but then he uses the other hand.'

'I'm sometimes EARLy (excuse the pun), but never late', never a truer word was spoken, Bill's never late. Arriving at a restaurant, or anywhere Bill's made an appointment, he often points to his watch, saying, in a jocular manner, 'Sometimes early, but never late'.

'Let your Yes be Yes, and your No, No'. A favourite saying of Bill's, when explaining he always does what he says he will, eg., 'If Bill tells you, he will be in the middle of Central Park, 3am in the morning, stood on his head, he will be there, 3am, and stood on his head.' Bill will only say "he can and will, if he knows he can fulfil", and he doesn't take kindly to those, promising to do something, and then don't. You only let Bill down once, there's no second chance.

A person asking Bill the time, will often be told in a jovial manner, 'It's a quarter to half past'. "Thank you", comes the response, and they walk on, Bill laughingly says, "And they still don't know the time".

Another favourite saying of Bill's is, 'One's business is only as good as one's staff'. Bill always making sure all his staff were properly trained, making them an asset to his firm, and to themselves.

A favourite piece at the end of Bill's adverts, now used by many, is 'One call we do it all'. That really was Bill's motto, to do all that was humanly possible to help bereaved families, using his funeral service, and to lift the burden.

'One cannot have too much knowledge'. How right that's proved for Bill. Throughout his eighty three years, he's continued to gain more and more knowledge, following another of his sayings, 'You're never too old too learn'.

'Talk about me, good if you can, bad if you must, but talk about me'. Whilst talking about me, they can't be talking about anyone else.

Bill says, 'Turn all adversities to your advantage', look on the positive side, and it usually comes up 'trumps'.

Another favourite, "Fool me once, shame on you, fool me again, shame on me".

When you believe in yourself, others believe in you.

It's nothing to do with what I do, who I am, or what I am; short, long, fat or tall has nothing to do with, what I know, or don't know.

I may have changed, but the main thing is, I am still the same inside.

Today's news, is tomorrows chip paper.

I must not hate you, but you don't help, do you!

There's no law against being stupid. If you're daft, they can't touch you for it.

I am not afraid to die, but don't want to be there at the time.

Without a purpose in life, you're merely a lost soul, wondering here and there and never reaching any objective and getting nowhere.

There's nothing as frightening as knowing what the other person is saying, is right.

The child's every inch a fool, but luckily for him, he's not very tall.

We outlive our friends, or they outlive us. Few would hesitate about the choice.

Most people at my age of 83 years, are dead.

If the cap fits, I made it!

To write to you, I had to think of you first, so here's thinking of you.

'A picture speaks a thousand words', says Bill, hence all his advertising, included at least one picture, either of Bill or his son Christopher, and the chapels and vehicles. Infact, to prove his point, Bill laughs, when people still come up to him in the street, saying, 'I see your picture in the Herald every night, good old Bill'. He chuckles to himself, saying, "My picture hasn't been in there for fifteen years, and they still haven't realised it". A great believer in the power of advertising, naturally people came to recognise Bill with his immaculate grooming, well cut black hair style, not forgetting his trade feature, his well known black moustache. Infact, Bill's brother, Gordon, always said, "If an incendiary blew your moustache off, you would be out of business". (Infact, that's what did happen during the war.) People would say, they knew it was Earl of Plymouth that did the funeral, because it was that short chap with a moustache, and all his cars were grey. When telephoning the business, often the public would ask to speak to Bill, feeling they knew him as a friend, just by regularly seeing his picture.

Bill's style of dress code, never alters, even in sweltering temperatures abroad. Infact, he's the only man, I know, who rode a camel in the Sahara desert, wearing a full suit, and a collar and tie. He dresses just the same fishing, in Australia, or climbing Ayers Rock. He certainly is a character that stands out from the crowd.

When with Bill one day, someone came to him, as they often did, asking to borrow a tenner. Bill, with usual quick response, simply said, "Yes, but hang on, there's a little story attached to this. I keep a ten pound note, especially for people like yourself, but at the moment, it's out, however, be assured, as soon as it comes back, you will be the next in line". Needless to say, he gets his point over in a polite manner, never borrow, he never did himself. Bill, always tells youngsters, to enjoy themselves, "Get as much out of life as you can, but always save enough for a rainy day, as none of us knows what's before us".

If something looks as if it's about to fall apart, but Bill realises it's OK, he'll say, 'Don't worry about it, a little dog's tail wobbles, but it wont drop off'. This came from a memory of what Bill's father said, when told the wheel on his horse and trap was wobbling. His father replied, 'a little dog's tail wobbles, but it wont drop off', saying to the horse, 'get up my beauty', and off he went. Like father, like son.

Another saying, of Bill's is, "I want half a pound of mixed nuts please, and not too many coconuts". This always brings a smile to faces.

On returning from the hairdressers, Bill loves to tease, he drops his chin and says, 'What's the matter couldn't they do it?' The general public often asks his wife, is he always like this? The answer is, yes, he's always bright from first thing in the morning, until last thing at night.

Bill's belief is, it doesn't matter how corny a joke is, as long as one or the other, gets a laugh. Laugh, and the world laughs with you. It's being so happy that keeps one going. How true.

Knowing he has a heart condition, in all seriousness he's told his wife, if in France, and he died suddenly, just sit him up in the front seat, say nothing and drive on the ferry, as if he's asleep. Adding, it's much easier to arrange a funeral at home, than in France.

Bill's heart specialist said, "You're looking well". To which Bill immediately replied, saying, "I have a gold fish at home, he looks absolutely wonderful, but he's dead".

One who gives what he can't keep, to gain what he cannot lose, is not stupid.

It's unnecessary to wait for my death, to talk about me, I can do it myself whilst I am alive, and perhaps, enjoy some of the pleasure others may get.

I am already in the minority, as most people my age are dead.

We are all different, but all have one thing in common, we all die, and none of us will go any sooner by talking about it.

98% of deaths are brought about by sickness, pain and suffering, followed by sorrow, and bewilderment for those left behind. Don't bottle it all up, it's better to talk about it.

It's better not to wait till your deathbed to forgive others, or recognise the purpose of your life.

Here and now's the only place to begin, because the only way to heal the world and our families, is to begin with ourselves.

The first moment of every day, is a new beginning, of the most important day of your life.

This is what you should do: love the Earth, the sun and the animals, despise riches, give alms to everyone who asks, stand up for the stupid and the crazy, devote your income and labour to others, hate tyrants, argue not concerning God, have patience and indulgence toward the people, take off your hat to nothing known or unknown or to any man or number of men. Re-examine all you have been told at school or church or in any book, dismiss what insults your own soul, and your very flesh will be a great poem.

"Don't be a yes man for your 6d tip, like a taxi driver". Bill always practices what he preaches, even if it makes him a little unpopular with a person, because he disagrees with a certain subject, he will always stick to his guns, not agreeing with someone, just to make them happy. One always knows where you stand with Bill, he always speaks his mind.

He is not a friend, simply because you agree with him, and he's not an enemy, because you disagree with him. Bill knew a gentleman, that no matter what one said, he always agreed, by saying, 'zactly'. That sort of character was no good to Bill.

Another well known saying of Bill's, "Don't leave a stone unturned".

When he wants to remember to take letters, or any written material somewhere, he drops the documents, on the floor, just beside his front door, hence, the items can't be overlooked.

Another saying of his, 'Cleanliness is next to godliness'.

'It's being so cheerful that keeps me going.'

## We Complain About This & That But What's The Use, If We Do Nothing About It

We have seen so much on TV, regarding filthy restaurants, when in general, we remark, eg., it's terrible, it's disgusting, in a minute I'll be afraid to eat out, and so on.

We've watched, read and seen, the grime, muck and even vermin associated with many restaurants and production of our food, and yet personally do nothing about it. Not in Bill's case, whose favourite saying is, 'Cleanliness is next to godliness', and so, he does something about it. However, if one is an introvert, it's perhaps harder to do, than for the extrovert.

Well, what is it that Bill does? He will walk into a restaurant, seek out the manager, and with a 'smile on his face', say, "Please, will you to take me into your kitchen, right now". If they refuse, Bill assumes, that in which case, it can't be very clean, and so, he doesn't eat there. On the other hand, another manager will often agree, saying, "just a minute", because he's going into the kitchen first, but Bill quickly intervenes, saying, "no, no, don't do that, you must take me now, to coin a phrase, 'take me just as I am, clean and pure' ha! ha!" A friendly smile on Bill's face helps the situation, which once met with the remark, "But my staff will wonder what you're there for". Quick as a flash, he said "That's alright, tell them I'm thinking of buying the place".

In the instance referred to, when in the kitchen, Bill found everything satisfactory, except for one thing, the open top bin, where all waste food was thrown. Bill pointed out this was incorrect, and attracted flies. He suggested an industrial pedal bin would solve their problem. The only other fault, he immediately noticed, on entering the restaurant, was that, the large mat was filthy. Bill remarked, the only good thing about the mat, was that all the muck trapped on it, was at least on the mat, rather than in the restaurant. Bill then suggested, if he had two mats, interchanging one with the other each week, whilst the first was being cleaned, this would solve the problem. The owner, noted Bill's remarks, acted on them and Bill eats there often.

Another incident Bill and his wife encountered, was going into an upstairs restaurant. The stairs were beautifully carpeted, but extremely filthy. Bill, immediately remarked, "If the stairs are like that, I dread to think what the state of the kitchen is like", and so, he immediately retraced his steps, vowing never to return.

Another kitchen Bill 'inspected', was very clean, but spoilt by the owner's pet Alsatians allowed to roam freely in all the food preparation areas. Bill, years ago, had toxocara, brought about by the worm from dog's faeces having travelled behind the pupil of the eye. He's never visited that restaurant again. Bill was told by his eye specialist, he's the luckiest man in Plymouth, not to have gone blind. A point of interest, Bill hasn't a dog these days. It was the result of dog faeces, eg., being dried by the sun, and blown with the wind. All brought about, by thoughtless owners, not worming their dogs.

A final thought on restaurants from Bill. If the toilets are dirty, which the public see, it doesn't say much for the kitchens, which the public don't see.

As the saying goes, "and there's more," but that'll do for now.

**The following is a letter Bill wrote, to advise others on how to improve their lifestyle, with the aim, to live longer:-**

"My name is Bill for short, but not for long, however, my aim is to try to stretch it to as long as possible, by taking notice of the brains of the 'whole world', eg., doctors and professors, who freely advise us against sunbathing, smoking, over-eating, or drinking to excess.

I've often heard it said by doctors, a drink wont do you any harm, but I've never heard them say, if you don't drink, start. We are given a free mind to do as we please, but what do we invariably do.

If we smoke, we say the doctors are wrong, making such excuses as, 'I know a doctor that smokes, and Churchill did'. Slow down, I've also heard it said, that it's the slow drivers that cause accidents, but I've never heard of a steam roller causing one.

40% of the population die before their time. Ask yourself, do you want to do all you can to be one of them, or all you can not to be?

There's a saying, nobody goes before their time. If you believe that, then eat up, drink up, and frizzle up, as the grass does in the sun.

When tempted to have another portion of food, stop, think about it for 5 minutes, then one will find, one doesn't want it. Stick this on your mirror and think of me, for it's being so cheerful that keeps me going.

From a sincere friend, who's always here when wanted, and even when not.

**Words of Wisdom on Funerals**

Bill says, funerals were once a taboo subject, now some, can't get to the TV fast enough to watch post-mortems etc., a long way from the sentiments of people when Bill first started in the profession. Bill's thoughts are, 'One doesn't go any sooner, through talking about it'. Which is right of course. He's a great believer in one pre-arranging their own funeral, lessening the burden on those left behind, at such a sad time in their lives, often unable to think properly. Far better to have everything put in order, when feeling happy, and the mind is functioning properly. Good sensible, sound advice.

Bill Earl is thought to have been the first person in the world to have introduced "Double Value" Funeral Bonds. A client could purchase a bond for any amount, and immediately its value was doubled! That is £200 would become £400 instantly, and even £1,000 turned immediately to £2,000. What an investment! Competitors thought it a ridiculous idea; they could not imagine the benefits to both the client and the business. However, it is very interesting to note that firms throughout the country later tried to copy, but with a difference. Their bonds did not increase in value, and they were mainly administered by insurance companies, who, naturally, were only in it for profit. They were not in the least bit interested in the client's funeral wishes, or in helping them.

There were numerous advantages of the Earl of Plymouth Bonds, which others found difficult, no, impossible, to imitate. The bonds not only doubled in value instantly, but Earl of Plymouth staff were with the client throughout, to offer guidance and provide help before, during and after the funeral, which was carried out by them exactly to the wishes of the deceased.

Some wondered and asked how could Earl of Plymouth possibly double your money? As well as competitors even Bill's solicitor found it difficult to understand. No-one allowed for the fact clients did not die immediately they invested in a bond. Bond-holders considered the investment foolproof and not a gamble. Their money immediately doubled in value. They made a sound provision for their funeral, easing the burden on relatives at the time of bereavement. Earl of Plymouth could not lose either; because, with tens of thousands of pounds of 'bond-holders' money invested in high interest accounts, and many guaranteed clients for years to come, it made Earl of Plymouth Funeral Bonds a unique success. Bill had people lining up to purchase bonds. Even his own staff, bought bonds, and people to this day, are still cashing in the funeral bonds, when the occasion arises.

Literally hundreds of families personally thank Bill for his help, his bonds, and personal touch. They all benefit from Bill's determination and drive, which made him a true pioneer in the funeral profession.

Today his advice to people considering funeral bonds, as currently being advertised, with enticing free gifts, such as eg., a clock or pen, is don't. Instead, invest your money and keep the interest. That of course, doesn't stop one from pre-arranging their own funeral, without having to part with money at that stage.

### Helpful Hints For Pre-Arranging One's Own Funeral

Bill feels it a helpful, loving thought to one's family, to pre-arrange your own funeral, especially if it's at a time, when there's no sorrow, thus making sure, your wishes will be carried out. Whether you pre-arrange your funeral with, or without a funeral director, make your wishes known to as many as possible, eg., your next of kin, executor, solicitor, etc.

Some of the questions to be considered carefully; your full name, date of birth, occupation and home address. Name and address of your doctor. Do you wish to be removed to a Chapel of Repose. Have you a pace-maker fitted. Do you want the coffin left open for viewing your body, or closed? Are you to be dressed in your own clothing. Have you any dentures? Do you wear jewellery, if so, do you want it left on, or given to specified loved ones, if so, state their full names and addresses, sign your request and have it witnessed.

What, if any, is your religion. If example, Roman Catholic, is it your wish to be received into church on the eve of the funeral, followed by Requiem Mass the following morning?

Is it to be earth burial, sea burial, cremation, etc., or any of the lesser known means. Where do you want the funeral service to be held, state name of place. If cremation, do you want your sacred remains to be kept at home in a suitable container, urn or casket, scattered to the four winds, buried in a certain place or an existing grave, or scattered at sea, scattered in some particular place, locally, or anywhere in the world.

Is a Memorial Required, organist, and particular hymns. Do you belong to any organisations, eg., Masonic connections etc. Do you want a crucifix affixed to the coffin, obituary notice in a certain paper. Chapel to be opened at a particular time for relatives and friends to pay their respects. The funeral director to provide flowers, what sort of flowers, if any, and/or money to go to a certain charity, give the name and address.

Bill trusts the above will be helpful giving food for thought, when thinking of pre-arranging your own funeral.

**Paying for the Funeral**

If you are in receipt of certain benefits, you may be eligible for help towards the funeral account, or financial help after the funeral.

Some of the benefits available are; **Bereavement Allowance**. This is a taxable weekly benefit for 52 weeks after a husband or wife dies, as long as the survivor is over 45 and meets the conditions.

**Bereavement Payment**. This is a tax free lump sum of £2,000, payable as soon as a person is widowed, as long as the conditions are met.

**Widowed Parent's Allowance**. This is a taxable weekly benefit paid, as long as the conditions are met.

For full details, and to find out if you are eligible, get in touch with the local DSS office, look for Benefits Agency advertisement in phone book.

**More Sayings**

Little sayings and expressions, with meaning, have played a large part in Bill's life. His home is full of cards and plaques with words of wisdom. They are constant reminders of important beliefs and provide regular motivation and inspiration. The following are just a few examples of his most frequently used sayings and expressions.

We all know it is important for a business to have publicity. It was even more so before television and the internet took control of feeding our minds. However, most businesses, then and now, grow through "word of mouth" recommendations, or at least gain customer awareness through receiving publicity, good or bad. An often used expression is "there is no such thing as bad publicity – any publicity is good for business". For Bill publicity about him reflects on him. He was his business, whether Earl of Plymouth Funeral Service, his driving school, very large taxi service, own newspaper, clothing business and general hardware or wedding business etc. Bill would say "talk about me, good if you can, bad if you must, but talk about me". The benefits to the success of each of his businesses were there for all to see, or talk about, and each one advertised the other.

Bill's always seen punctuality as a virtue and clear demonstration of someone's character. As such he's always prided himself on his attention to the clock. He has always been very particular in arriving for appointments, meetings or social events prior to the time agreed, barring of course, sickness. I would go as far as to say he has never been late for anything, just as his saying goes. he is "sometimes early, but never late" (please note the deliberate pun).

Some people tell lies, promise to do something, knowing they'll never "get around to it", others will say they'll do it to keep somebody "off their back" or falsely to impress. Bill doesn't fall into any of these categories, his word is his bond. Throughout his life he's lived by the expression "don't say you'll do something if you are not going to do it". He would rather tell you bluntly, or be told straight, it cannot be done. That way you know exactly where you stand and are not disappointed when delivery does not meet expectation.

Equally concerning to Bill is the situation where someone nods in agreement, says "yes" and "I agree" to every question and statement. The person may have no sinister intent. They may only wish to appear friendly and accommodating, not realising the consequences of their actions and words, or of more concern, they may be deceitful. Truth has been a strong and cherished quality to Bill and he's regularly said "don't say yes if you mean no, and no if you mean yes". That way you don't let anyone down, or damage your credibility; if anything, you enhance it. People don't feel let down by one who says "no", but they do by someone who says "yes", when later they find that was not the truthful answer. Blunt talking can jar, but it doesn't hurt like lies. Saying truthfully what you think can lead to debate, a difference of opinions, and ultimately to learning on both sides. Truth can build wisdom, whereas lies prevent learning.

On one occasion Bill tried to help an individual, who came to him for employment. The person was naturally unaware of Bill's exceptional support for her when she was offered an opportunity to work. Bill's support manifested itself in the fact that she was paid the same rate for the job as another employee, who had been in Bill's employment for many years. Bill also purchased two outfits for his needy employee, as she did not look the part when she first started. The second person complained through a third party it was unfair an inexperienced worker should be immediately employed on the same rate as the experienced one! Bill's response was profound. He asked his experienced employee, "If I reduce the amount paid to the inexperienced worker, tell me, would that make any difference to you? Would it make you feel happier if I pay less to the one I know needs the money?" The reply was, "I suppose not." Bill, always known for his preaching, which often became protracted, but always made sense, told her the story of the Prodigal Son, which summed it all up, and all three continued to work together happily for many years afterwards.

Bill's motto at work was "Good employees should remain loyal, even after their employer, who gave them their start, may have retired". He was often known to say, "If it wasn't for your employer, you wouldn't have had the start. And if it wasn't for you I wouldn't be where I am today." He would add, "One's business is only as good as one's staff".

Bill used to delight in little remarks and sayings. His favourite was, "Remember, as you go through life, everybody likes nice things said about them." It always works, say something nice about someone and they not only feel good about themselves, but also about you.

It was a standing joke with the girls in Bill's office that his letters were always so very long. They used to joke together when given another exceedingly long letter to type. They were so long, they went on and on, but never missing a single point. However it was through the thought that had gone into the letter and the strength of his arguments that Bill always won and saved his business thousands of pounds year after year, as the girls so often remarked.

Bill's management style, as an employer of many, was that he would always be forthright in letting his employees know if anything was not done to his standards or liking. Each employee knew exactly where they stood after being told in such a straightforward manner, and they always knew what was required in future. Bill set the standards and all his staff were very much aware of them. However once Bill had told an employee that there had been a shortfall in their work he would immediately drop the subject and allow the atmosphere to return to normal.

What a way to gain publicity? People were creeping past Bill's house, having read the large sign outside. His house was simply being repaired, but it caused a standstill for traffic and pedestrians. They wondered at the sign. Some could not believe their eyes and returned to gaze. One dear old couple kept looking from each other to the house and back again. They were heard to say, "It's disgusting." Nobody will ever know what they were thinking, or imagining. The sign simply said, "Silence, please, this house is being reborn." To demonstrate the extent of the publicity caused, Bill's bank manager sent him a letter in an envelope, upon which he had drawn a house with a man climbing a ladder, paintbrush in hand, but no address was written. The letter found its way to Bill the very next day! Good advertising, as proven by prompt delivery of letter, brilliant!!

## Debt Collecting

These are just a few ideas of Bill's, when, after using all the usual methods, the bill still hasn't been paid, but please note, these are extreme cases, when all else has failed.

One method Bill successfully used, was to send an open postcard addressed to the correct person, but to the next door neighbour's address. It would have 'Unpaid Funeral Account', stamped in Red. Very embarrassing indeed, to have this brought to one's home by your neighbour, knowing very well, the neighbour couldn't help but read it, but hard people call for hard tactics.

One lady hadn't paid her funeral account, had left her home without a forwarding address. Bill, not one to be beaten, placed an advert in the 'personal column' of the paper, saying, that if Mrs. X, would like to contact box number Y, she'd find something to her advantage. The greedy lady, couldn't resist replying, giving her new address. Bill certainly gave her something to her advantage, her long outstanding funeral account, which she paid.

Sometimes, he'd have outstanding accounts, from friends of a bereaved family who'd ordered flowers for the funeral Bill was carrying out. Again, if he was unsuccessful in retrieving the money owed to him, he'd write, asking them if he'd made a mistake and should have sent the account for the flowers to the family, adding, if he didn't hear anything within seven days, that's what he would do. They always paid up without delay.

Bill did a big wedding, supplying many cars. No matter how many times he sent the account, they ignored it. Never one to be beaten over anything, on the way back from the cemetery with his hearse, called at their house, presenting them with their reminder. The embarrassed family not wanting a repeat immediately paid up.

A different type of case, entailed a butcher, who kept borrowing money from Bill, repaying him over a period of time until he'd cleared his debt, then he'd immediately borrow again. This went on for a long time, but on this occasion he ignored the demands. Bill wrote out a large sign, simply saying, 'Please be sure to pay me the money today, in the "early hours" of the morning'. Bill driving one of his Rolls Royce limousines wouldn't want to be seen, sticking a large notice right across the large plate glass shop window, very late of a night. Result, the money was repaid 9a.m. same morning. Of course, Bill didn't put any names on the sign, especially his own. One could understandably say, Bill must have been silly.

Not Bill, he's never silly. He always knows what he's doing. In this case, he was having double the value repaid to him, in meat every week. In other words, he was living for nothing. The butcher was backing horses, but backed the wrong one this time, when it came to Bill.

Repeat, these were extreme cases, but the methods worked, thus Bill never accumulated any bad debts.

## Some of Bill's Unique Inventions

This invention came about, through Bill's intense love of food, together with his equal love of travelling with his car. Him and his wife loved to go on the overnight ferry crossing from Plymouth to France, at the drop of a hat. He loved the freedom. Bags packed into back of car, with food and flasks for picnics in wild remote locations. He'd never plan where he was going, so long as they had their AA road map of Europe, the 'world was their oyster' as they say. It was nothing for the intrepid pair to be gone for months at a time, visiting Portugal, then, when it got too hot there, to move on to cooler climes like, Eastern Europe, the borders of Russia, Scandinavian countries, anywhere that was different, often covering 20,000 miles on one trip.

Food cooked off the engine of the car

Bill thought of a novel way of having a hot meal, whilst on their travels. He made up a small metal oblong 'cooker', with removable metal top, that he fitted onto the manifold of the engine. He would place bacon, chicken, pasties, whatever took his fancy, into his cooker, before setting off, in the morning. At about 12.30p.m., he'd look up to Carole, saying, 'We'll pull in now, lunch is ready'. They'd pull into the nearest lay-by, Carole busy putting up the picnic table and chairs, whilst Bill opened the bonnet. People would stare, thinking the pair had trouble with their car. To the onlookers amazement, Carole would stand by the hot engine, with two dinner plates, waiting for Bill to serve their lunch. It really must have looked a very odd sight indeed. Carole says, she can never forget the look on people's faces, wondering what on earth was going to come out of the engine onto dinner plates, of all things. It certainly would have been worth watching this unusual happening.

Only Bill could ever think of an idea like that.

Another time, thinking of how he could vacuum his car whilst on one of his travels, Bill came up with the perfect solution. He had a metal pipe made to his specifications. The pipe had a hole pierced part way down its' length, with another metal pipe welded to it, at right angles. On the end of this piece, a long length of rubber tubing was fitted. The metal tube, slide on to the end of the exhaust, when the car needed vacuuming. With the engine working, the exhaust caused a vacuum in the rubber pipe, making it a very easy way of cleaning the car. The bits of rubbish were sucked up and blown out with the exhaust. A case of 'Gone With The Wind'!! Again, I don't know of anyone else, who's ever thought of such an idea.

Bill should add, that he's an innovator, to his long list of qualifications.

**Beetroot for Pen Refill**

Bill had found the perfect red pen. It slid over the paper effortlessly, with a very fine point. He found it very useful for squeezing small writing in between main script. Lovely, thought Bill, he bought many of these pens. Their only downfall, they didn't use refills. Everything went well, until one day, the last one dried up. Unable to purchase more, Bill, not to be beaten, took his precious pen to pieces, finding the centre contained a solid rubbery strip. Bill put his thinking cap on. Unable to obtain red ink, what could he use? He had to have red. He visited the indoor market, bought one small beetroot, sliced it almost in half, and carefully placed the rubber strip in the middle of the beetroot, covered the lot with hot water and a few additives. Next day, he retrieved his experimental refill, placed it back in the pen, and hey presto, success. Bill now writes, 'in beetroot', for want of a better word. Beetroot goes off, quick thinking Bill, with nothing else at hand, added a mere drop of embalming fluid. What will he think of next?

## White Marble Table

Thinking of the future, and deciding to make his garden almost maintenance free, like his house, Bill had the lawn cut down to a minimum, replacing the rest of the land, with paths, and many colourful shrubs, that only needed a trim once a year. Bill had many large trees in his garden, some were getting very old, so for safety, he engaged two friends, Jim (nicknamed Jim'll fix it) and his wife Paula, to cut them down. All went well, except for one very tall tree, close to the house. When it was cut down, it brought down the telephone wires, crashed into the greenhouses, smashing Bill's garden table in half. The ladder falling to the ground, leaving poor Jim stranded halfway up the remaining tree trunk. What a mess. Everyone was doubled up laughing. When, all had been tidied up, phones reconnected, glass replaced in greenhouses, Bill decided to repair his garden table himself. An old disused cemetery had been cleared, leaving many old headstones. Bill used one white marble headstone about 3 ft by 5 ft for the top of his table, delicately placed on white cemented concrete blocks. That's one table that will never be moved, it's so heavy, and 'different'.

To complete the coordination in his garden, he used other wasted spoilt grey headstones for paths, and bases for his greenhouses.

To add a little variety, he travelled many miles to dig up buckets of a very colourful gritty sand, from Slapton Sands, to make two more paths. He made many journeys to get his special sand, until one day, a warden spied him, and gave him the news, that sand was not permitted to be removed from the beach. Never mind, because Bill already had the paths he wanted, covered in sand from Slapton Sands. A garden with a difference I think.

## Final Thoughts

Bill says, it is an advantage to be an extrovert in business. He didn't get where he is today, by not speaking out, standing up for himself.

If in business, it's wise and sensible to deal with local private businesses as much as possible. After all, it's the local businessman that feels the benefit of the trade, and eventually it will be that same local man's family that will use you when in need. Example, if having doorstep delivery of milk etc., the large firms don't appreciate the business but the small local man does. Bill always had his milk etc., delivered by local firms. It makes business sense.

Bill fondly looks back on his long colourful hardworking life, saying, there's lots I did in the past, that I wouldn't do now.

No matter who, or what you are, there's one thing for sure, you could learn a lot from this book.

Bill's had so many, deep, varied experiences. It should be borne in mind the majority of people are dead before they reach their eighties; a period of his life in which he is only too willing to offer yet more help and advice, and also to share some of his vast array of experiences and his many pearls of wisdom.

# 9
# Fond Memories

## Funny Incidents

Bill always chuckles when he tells this story, he was an ardent ball-room dancer, and was in The Duke of Cornwall Hotel, enjoying a glass of wine with his old friend, Brian, between dances. The girl behind the bar, was very well developed, showing off her assets by wearing a very low cut top, with a large flower in the middle. Brian, knowing how quick Bill is with his answers, said to Bill, "I bet, you can't just walk up to that young lady behind the bar, and say something to her, right off the top of your head?" Bill, eyeing up the situation immediately answered, "Yes, I can", and off he went to the other end of the long bar. Brian, at the other end, listening intently. Bill called the girl over, admiring her, eyeing her up and down, said "You do look lovely". "Do I", she said, really pleased with Bill's obvious admiration. "Mind you", said Bill, "If I had known I'd have brought you a better flower than that". The young lady's face lit up, looked down at her pretty large flower perched between her rather enormous, half exposed breasts, said "Would you. What would that have been then?" Bill could hardly contain himself, when he said, "A snowdrop".

Another time, Bill walked into the same hotel, a similar girl was serving the drinks behind the bar. Bill looked at her, coughed, patting his chest, saying "Chest trouble. Do you ever get any chest trouble." The poor girl didn't know where to look.

Yet another prank of Bill's. He wore a pair of spectacles, from which he had carefully removed the lenses. Looking seriously into a girl's eyes, he poked his finger straight through the glasses frame, saying, "I think I've got something in my eye, can you see it". The girl in question replied, "Look up a bit, look down a bit. No I can't see anything". No, she certainly didn't see anything, not even noticing he'd poked his finger through the frame.

Bill always loves a joke.

## More Funny Incidents

Bill, always liked to keep himself fit. Not satisfied with just his early morning swim, he'd bought himself a metal bar exerciser, that had a wheel in the middle. The idea was, to lie on the floor, face down, and try and do push-ups, but still holding onto the metal bar. He'd religiously go up and down, doing twenty or thirty of these push-ups, every morning, in his office, smartly dressed in full suit, collar & tie, infront of his secretary, Mrs. Alford. He certainly looked unusual, all dressed up, whilst exercising, but, that was Bill. She had got used to this ritual, trying hard to concentrate on her typing, whilst Bill was puffing away.

One day, this all came to an abrupt end. Bill had pulled the exerciser back too far towards him, and of course, without any control on the free running wheel, the bar with Bill's hands still tightly clutching it, went right back past his waist, Bill hitting the floor head on, with an almighty thump. I can just see poor Mrs. Alford, trying so hard to be serious, when she really, couldn't hold back the tears, with uncontrolled laughter.

Needless to say, Bill never did that again, following the example he'd learnt from his father, never to get caught twice.

His father would constantly remind Bill of the true story, about his Uncle Willie, whom he had been named after. Uncle Willie, would enter a room, trip over something, leave the item in the same place, return and trip over it again, never moving it. This went too far, when his Uncle Willie emigrated to Australia. He had a habit of standing right on the edge of the pavement, with one foot in the road, ready to cross when the traffic had passed. He'd had several close shaves with cars coming too close, but never learning from the experience. One day, the inevitable happened, a car ran right over his foot, resulting in the loss of that foot. A true story, but one Bill fondly recites, when reminding people, never to get caught twice. Needless to say, the family always copy Bill's example.

Mrs. Alford, fondly remembers, Bill kept an enormous book, that was specially made for him. It was placed in the main office, next to the telephones. It was used like a diary, containing each day's events, including wedding car bookings etc. Bill always insisted, anything that was said or done, had to be written in that book.

Mrs. Alford, had just been reprimanded, for not putting a message of importance in this book. He said to her, that even if someone called Bill, a b ... fool, to write it in the book. Little did he know, how soon those words would come true. A couple of days later, Dr. Skeins arrived to arrange his daughter's wedding. Mrs. Alford dutifully, gave him the wedding booking forms to complete and sign. He refused to sign, taking his wroth out on poor Mrs. Alford. She explained, there was nothing she could do about it, as it was Mr. Earl's regulations, to which the doctor replied, "Mr. Earl is a bloody fool". consequently, to finalise this true story, Mrs. Alford, with tongue in cheek, wrote in The Book, "Mr. Earl is a bloody fool".

After that, whenever they were looking for a certain date, the staff would remark, it's just after Mr. Earl's a bloody fool. That page becoming a special marker point for that year. After all, she'd only written down what she had been instructed to do, hadn't she!!!

Mrs. Alford told me, she could always tell when Bill was about to enter the office, rather than any other member of staff. There were ten slate steps leading down to the office, from the garages. When Bill was coming down the steps, his feet would travel quickly, making a fast tapping sound on the stone, whilst all the others were slower, making a clip clop noise. Bill always quick off the mark, even coming down steps.

## Copycat Businessman

Les, built houses, Bill knew him quite well, he thought of him as a nice hard working man. He came to Bill one day, saying, he was going to start a funeral business, and wanted Bill to supply him with the hearse, cars and bearers. He said to Bill, that as Bill was so successful, he was going to copy him in every possible way, right down to the minutest detail. He did. He even had a swallow tail morning suit made, and as Bill always had white edge piping (removable for washing), on his waistcoat, Les even copied that. As Bill said, he was a nice person.

Typical of Bill, it gave him much pleasure, to help him get started in the funeral profession, especially as he wouldn't be in competition with Bill, as he lived in an outer area of Plymouth. Bill posed the question to Les, "How do you expect to get started? It's no good thinking all you have to do, is to put up a sign, and families will come to you. You have to become recognised somehow."

Les replied, "I'm a Roman Catholic, and get on well with our priest, who's promised, he will do all he can to recommend me to bereaved families". Whenever Les had a Roman Catholic funeral, which were the only ones he ever had, instead of going to the Roman Catholic church in the normal manner, example, arrange for the deceased to be received into the church without any fuss, on the eve of the funeral in readiness for mass the next morning, the priest would give out the message to the congregation, asking them to meet the hearse, at a particular point, not too distant from the church at, eg., 7p.m., and walk behind the hearse to the church. This way, everybody knew who the funeral director was.

All went well for a while, with Les hiring his vehicles and bearers from Bill. Bill even giving Les business, by way of Bill buying coffins from Les. It came about like this, with Les being a builder, he was able to obtain plenty of Chestnut timber, very suitable for making coffins. Bill always with an eye to business, could see how he could be helping both himself and Les. Bill ordered many such coffins from his friend. This way, by Les delivering the coffins to Bill on an 'open' flat deck lorry, it gave the impression to Les's church congregation, that gosh, Les is busy. Of course he was, but only delivering coffins to Bill. You couldn't blame Les for that, in business, you have, to coin a phrase, "use your loaf". As will be seen, Bill often used his 'loaf'. Infact Bill's expression often was "Bill's Bread was often Buttered, but never Bettered".

Bill would ring Les, saying, "I want six 5 ft 8" × 20", and three 5 ft 4" × 15" coffins. A few days later, Bill would ring Les again and order a similar lot of varied sizes. Les would say to Bill, from time to time, "I said to my misses, what a business that man has, I had no idea he had such a large business".

Having delivered Bill's coffins in his 'open' lorry, yet again, which don't forget, kept Bill in the limelight as well. Bill would pay Les, with one of his especially printed cheques, marked 'Earl of Plymouth', making each cheque an advertisement in itself. Bill always believing in paying everything possible by cheque, even when dining out. All bringing his name to the forefront, and it worked. The moment Les had left, Bill would ring a wholesale coffin supplier, saying "I've another lot ready for you, will you please collect them immediately, as I need the room". The whole-saler would pay Bill, at the same time as collecting the coffins.

Bill, immaculately dressed as usual, hadn't even taken a hand out of his pocket, having made £25 profit on every load he sold, which was a lot of money in those days. This business enterprise continued for many years. Going back to Les, and his funeral business, no, it never really took off, although he tried to imitate everything Bill did. It wasn't long before Les, was back concentrating on building houses, for which he had an excellent reputation, and not forgetting making coffins for Bill. He never did know about Bill's enterprising scheme with all those coffins he made.

### Telephoning for estate car after holiday

After a cruise, which docked at Plymouth, Bill's home port, he tele-phoned from the ship to his office, asking for a driver to come and collect him in an estate car, bringing plenty of rope.

The staff, knowing Bill so well, started wondering, what coffin or cas-ket he'd brought home this time. However, on this occasion, they were 'way off course'. He did bring home something, it was a four piece cane furniture sofa set for his sun lounge. Different though, not the normal holiday souvenir!!

## Breakfast At The Duke of Cornwall, in Aid of Business

Bill's manager, asked him, if he would attend an early morning break-fast at The Duke of Cornwall Hotel, at the ungodly hour of 6.45a.m.? David, the manager, explained, the meeting was for businessmen and women, and he would appreciate Bill's opinion, as to whether it was worth becoming a member, from a business point of view.

Knowing nothing about it, but always ready to learn, even at 82 years, Bill agreed to go, realising, David, sincerely appreciated Bill's business mind, and friendship. David collected Bill, next morning 6.15a.m. Bill, was always an early riser anyhow, until recently, swimming every morning by 7a.m. Reaching the hotel, in the centre of Plymouth, Bill was surprised to find over 200 others there for this business breakfast club. The idea was, to chat and meet each other first, exchanging business cards. Every business had to be completely different, thus no competitors. After this exchange, everyone sat down to breakfast, after which each stood up in turn, simply stating who they were, name of the business they represented and sit down, immediately, the next person imitating the same procedure. As one sat down, the next was already stood up, thus no time waste.

Apparently, Bill's manager purposely hadn't told Bill the procedure, to enable him to note Bill's response, he certainly wasn't disappointed. David stood up, and said, "I am David Fowell, manager of Earl of Plymouth Funeral Service". Bill, as usual, quick off the mark, got up and said, "And I am he, and if he doesn't get you in the beginning, I will in the end." It went down like a bomb, and so did Bill, because they were all having a good laugh. Bill living up to his usual quick wit.

## Skeleton Staff & Free Funerals

One of Bill's friends, called Jack, said, "Come on Bill, we've known each other, all our lives, how about giving a good discount on my funeral".

Bill looked around, making it appear, as though he didn't want anybody else to hear him, and said, "For you Jack, I'll do it for nothing, but how about next Wednesday, will that be alright?" Jack, laughed and said, "Why next Wednesday?" Bill quickly retorted, "Because we're stock taking, and only working on a skeleton staff".

Odd, but no-one has ever taken him up on his offer, I wonder why!!

## Rebirth of a House

None of us know how we would react under similar circumstances, it had to be seen to be believed. Bill always with an eye to business, and ready with an innocent bit of fun, erected a large printed sign, placing it at the top of his house, it read, "Silence please, this house is being reborn". This drew attention to his home, which, because he had been out of it for some time, the person living there during Bill's absence, allowed it to deteriorate to a poor state. Bill was having new double glazing installed, together with other home improvements, the house really did look as if it was being reborn.

It became so amusing, people were amazingly surprised, they were creeping by, stopping and gazing, slowly moving on. Even more surprisingly, cars were stopping, their occupants staring at the house, driving up a bit, back a bit, eventually driving on. The picture made a full page in the Herald. What an advert, especially with all his white doves.

Bill's bank manager, who had moved from Plymouth, happened to pick up the paper, saw the picture, and said, there's only one man who'd do that. He immediately sent a letter to Bill. Instead of an address, he drew the house, with a man going up a ladder, in the front of the house, holding a large paint-brush, on the envelope, challenging the Post Office to, "Find This House". They did. Bill receiving the letter first post next day. Obviously the house had become a well known advert, for Bill, as intended.

## Being Painted By Famous Artist

Robert Lenkiewicz, asked to paint Bill with his Earl of Plymouth Funeral staff, meeting, day after day, he painted Bill and his staff, also showing stacks of coffins.

He drew a chalk-line around Bill's feet, where he was to stand, over long periods of many days. He talked to Bill about suicide etc., he talked all the time, learning about Bill's embalming career and disposal of the dead. Bill explained, there's no law against keeping a body, providing, it doesn't cause unpleasantness. Robert and Bill had many, closely guarded secrets, least of which, Earl of Plymouth, was to carry out his funeral, eventually. Robert, knowing Bill and his son were both qualified B.I.E. members (British Institute of Embalmers), contacted Earl of Plymouth Funeral Service, to embalm Diogenes. Bill and his son thinking publicity might be detrimental, recommended an unknown B.I.E. member to embalm Diogenes, but Earl of Plymouth did Robert's own funeral in 2002.

True to say, Robert would never have been able to have done all he did with Diogenes body, had it not been for the kindly knowledge, Bill had bestowed upon him.

Not knowing Robert as Bill affectionately came to know him, conscious of the delicate nature of Bill's profession. When he asked to paint Earl of Plymouth's portraits, Bill was concerned where a notorious painter, might display the finished product. Consequently, Bill took the highly respected, late Rev. Walker, as witness, to Robert's promise, to treat the massive, life-size painting, with respect, as he always did.

Painting by Robert Lenkiewicz. *Courtesy of Lenkiewicz Foundation*

Robert's being most fair, presented Bill with 2 highly valued books entitled, 'R.O. Lenkiewicz', containing over 100 pages of paintings and separate pictures, including a life-size painting, entitled, 'Mr. Earl, Funeral Director & Family in Coffin Warehouse', enabling Bill to include it with Bill's own life-time book, which was also presented to Bill, of over 80 years of memories, entitled, 'Bill Earl, Funeral Director and friend to many, This is Your Life'. What an interesting ending to Robert's life, and eventually Bill's life.

Bill will always treasure the memory of meeting Robert, and for the mutually interesting hours spent together. True to say, some females were scared to stand unaccompanied with Robert, as can be plainly seen, by the lady in the front of the picture, who appears scared, however, it all adds to the value.

## Enjoyment of Good Food

Bill always loved cooking, the more unusual, the better. Once a week, was Bill's cook up night. He'd invite some of his loyal friends around to dinner, of a similar disposition to himself, to enjoy something a little out of the ordinary. Some of his creations have been, cow's udder, slowly boiled with herbs and seasoning. Bill always laughingly asked for an udder that had been well hung and well slung, without the fingers. Sheep's riddies was another favourite, fried. When asked what they are, he'd say, all he knows is, each animal only has two, leaving you to guess where they came from. Pig's chitterlings and natlings, again fried, nice and crisp, and surprisingly tasty. Curried tripe, and curried crabs, as done in Sri Lanka, were another favourite. Nothing to see Bill cooking twelve crabs, he'd bought at the Barbican fish market, straight off the boats. Another delicious meal, and a great favourite was muscles, cooked on the half shell in the oven, each with a drop of oil, crushed garlic, tomato & parsley. The trouble was, Bill never content to buy just a few pounds, he'd come home with a sack full, which meant all day preparing the food. Most of the muscles after cooking, were kept in the deep freeze.

He loved pigeons and rabbits, all cooked with herbs and spices. Carole went into a butcher's at Liskeard, Bill driving past, noticed several rabbits hanging up. He asked Carole to buy a couple. She did, telling Bill the butcher said they're lovely, just like chicken. Bill, jokingly said, then take them back, I don't want chicken, I want rabbit. Using his faithful pressure cooker, a tasty meal that came out of this item was, oxtail. I don't know how he cooked it, but I can only say, it was 'more-ish'.

One night, up to his tricks, he cooked a sheep's head, he'd specially ordered. He steamed the head, until every fraction of meat came off, which he made into a brawn. Leaving a meatless, skinless skull. He carefully presented his dish to his faithful friend, John Marriott for dinner. In the eye sockets, he'd placed a boiled egg, with a sultana in the middle, for the pupil. Some rosemary was delicately placed in its' mouth. The meat, 'tongue 'n cheek', by this time brawn, he artistically arranged around the base of this tasty concoction, saying, if the sheep hadn't lost it's head, it wouldn't have been on the dinner plate.

His experimenting, didn't end with the savouries. A friend happened to mention he couldn't stand beetroot "in anyway whatsoever", this presented Bill with a challenge. He boiled a combination of tomatoes and "beetroot", with sugar etc., and allowed to cool, offering this concoction on a meringue nest, topped with ice-cream, and clotted cream. It did taste good, his friend not realising what he was eating until he'd 'cleaned' his plate, then Bill dropped the bomb-shell, delighting in telling him.

From Southern Ireland, Bill learnt how to boil carrageen moss (a type of seaweed), strain, mix the strained fluid with milk, add a coloured jelly to some for variety, allow to set. A colourful, healthy unusual desert. Not one person was ever able to guess what they were eating, although it was always enjoyed.

Bill has cooked all over the world. Even on holidays, if the opportunity arose, if he could show his talent at cooking, he liked nothing better. Even in Alice Springs, he was barbecuing kangaroo steak in the hotel grounds, whilst a young orphan Joey looked on.

One little delicacy, Bill really enjoyed, on his winter vacations on the Algarve, was prickly pears. One winter, eating thirty every day for one hundred days, he'd eaten three thousand of them, virtually clearing all the Algarve, of their prickly pears. Prickly pears are about the size of a kiwi fruit, and grow out of cactus leaves. The outer covering is carefully removed. One of the ways of removing all the little prickles from the outer green skin, is, if on or near a beach, roll the fruit in the sand, using a brush, and hey-presto, they're all gone, the outer skin is cut and peeled back, leaving a green fruit, similar to a kiwi. Another type of prickly pear, is smaller, the fruit red, like a raspberry. These fruits were delicious, with a plain yoghurt, cool and refreshing. Bill enjoyed this fruit so much, he brought some of the cactus leaves home, after doing a tour of Europe. They are in his greenhouses, huge, and producing the precious fruit, an edible reminder of Portugal.

He loved to pick up unusual cooking tips from any part of the world, and taste different foods, he'd never tried before, to use at a later date.

To go with the food, there's nothing nicer, than a relaxing glass of wine. Bill made his own. Some were popular favourites like, a light slightly sparkling elderflower wine from trees in his garden. Later in the year, the same trees produced berries, for a full bodied red. From two home grown marrows, he'd hollow out the seeds, keep filling with brown sugar, suspended in a pair of Carole's tights, over a large white plastic wine bucket, and allowed to drip. The resulting nectar, was extremely alcoholic. When Bill first made this, he carefully placed his wine hydrometer in, expecting it to float, showing the alcohol content. Instead, it sunk like a stone. At first, Bill thought, he'd failed. He rang up his friend and G.P., Keith Protheroe, who explained, as alcohol is lighter than water, what he had made was stronger than any wine, more like a liqueur.

Another white wine Bill made, that was very unusual, to go with his unique cooking, was garlic wine. He made this wine in the usual manner, but with crushed cloves of garlic and sultanas in the making. Delicious, no one ever guessing it was Bill's favourite, 'Garlic Wine'.

These are just a taster of some of Bill's culinary arts, as the comedian would say, and there's more.

No-one ever knew with Bill what they were going to eat next, but one thing was guaranteed, his meals were never dull and everyone enjoyed whatever he cooked, never knowing what to expect.

Bill always enjoyed going out with friends and colleagues for meals, and often he would ask one of his female staff to reserve tables for dinner, always in the name of Earl of Plymouth. On one such occasion Bill was going to have a meal with two friends Alan and Julie Hambridge. A lady from Bill's office had booked a table for three, in the name of Earl of Plymouth, at a hotel in Launceston. When they arrived in one of Bill's Rolls Royce limousines the three of them were ushered gracefully to a special table adjoining the hotel's main dining area, where they enjoyed their pre-dinner drinks and tit-bits, the latter being served on beautiful silver trays.

Some American couples were there at the time, enjoying an after dinner drink. Much to Bill's surprise, when they began to leave, each couple came over and curtsied or bowed, saying, "thank you, sir." Bill and his friends could not understand what was happening. Why this sudden regal attention? They were dumbfounded, almost spellbound by the continuous stream of courteous Americans. That was until the account was presented at the end of the evening. It included not only the bill for their dinner, but also for the tit bits and after dinner drinks, which had been consumed by the grateful Americans, courtesy of the Earl of Plymouth!

It had been Alan who had wanted Bill to use one of his Rolls Royces, because he loved the thrill of driving one. So, Bill, grinning all over his face, handed the account to Alan, saying, "It was you who wanted all the flannel and attention. So now *you* can pay for it."

On another, somewhat similar, occasion, Bill had received a couple of invitations to attend a dinner at the five star Imperial Hotel in Torquay. Bill and Alan, enjoyed an exceedingly high class dinner. The wining and dining was out of this world, and as Bill said later, that with all the free drink he had consumed, so was he!

The whole evening was of the highest possible calibre. It was one of the best dinners Bill had ever attended; all courtesy of Cunard Millionaire Cruises. This organisation specially organised cruises just for millionaires to enjoy. They were very exclusive. Bill, being a highly respected citizen of Plymouth, had been given the extremely rare and prestigious invitation, which included not only the meal and wine, but also liqueurs, aperitifs and a top class show. It was a very auspicious occasion.

Cunard Lines, besides providing the dinner, also took the opportunity to show some magnificent films, advertising their fantastic cruises to idyllic, far-off countries. Bill has always said that the whole event was one of the most wonderful experiences he ever had.

The laughable part of the evening was, as usual, Alan had insisted on driving the Rolls. When they had arrived the commissionaire promptly took the keys and parked the magnificent, gleaming limousine. Bill had laughingly said to himself at the time, "wait until we come out. The commissionaire will collect the car and then expect a decent tip." That is exactly what happened and guess who was made to pay the tip? Alan.

## Christmas In Summer

Bill, always feeling hearted, and gaining immense pleasure from helping others, thought of a novel idea to raise money, for those not so fortunate as himself.

In the middle of summer, each year, Bill would send out Christmas invitations to between 40 to 50 of his friends, to come to his home, for a sit down 6 course traditional Christmas Dinner, including wine, Xmas

The summer 'Christmas' party

pudding, complete with crackers and after dinner drinks, having completely decorated with Xmas decorations and a tree for Christmas, with the seasonal music in the background. Except for the weather, on entering Bill's house, one could be forgiven for thinking it was December 25th.

How did Bill raise such substantial amounts for various charities at these Mid-summer Xmas celebrations? Well, although the meal and all that went with it was completely free, each guest had to bring a Christmas present, wrapped in gift paper. After the sumptuous meal, with the Lord & Lady Mayoress present and other dignitaries, it was followed by a talk given by a representative of the chosen charity, then all the presents, still wrapped were each auctioned, no one knowing what they were buying, making it more interesting. Many thousands of pounds have been raised by Bill for several good causes every summer over the years, using this tried and tested unique method. The evening was always enjoyed by all, to give to all.

## Red Pigeons

Bill, always a devil for the 'birds', developed a passion for pigeons as a school boy, and carried his knowledge to adulthood. His family home, was deliberately located in a busy area of Plymouth. No-one could miss it, with his name in large gold letters. He thought that an added, and pretty, though unusual attraction, would be, pure white doves. A symbol often used to signify peace. Bill had about fifty, which certainly drew attention to his house, as they flew in and out of their home, built into the front of the house.

All went well for many years, until finally Bill noticed some of his newly hatched doves were becoming a little speckled. Next, he noticed the cheeky pigeons were jumping in on the band wagon, getting free food, free housing, and free sex. To let this continue, Bill would soon lose his pure white doves.

He decided to trap the intruders, after which, he sprinkled red food dye on them, to mark them, telling his friends, Pat & John Marriott, who were going to Padstow, that they were going to take the pigeons with them that day, and let them out at their journey's end. The four travelled in John's car, with a box of 'red' pigeons. On reaching the pretty Cornish fishing village of Padstow, Bill quickly opened the box, stood back, expecting them to take flight. To their amazement, the birds just stood there, not moving, with a dazed look on their faces. Bill, not expecting this, quickly scooped his birds up, placed them back in the box, for fear cats might get them, as they were like sitting 'ducks'.

They took the birds to the top of the cliff and let them off there. Again, they still stood as if frozen to the spot, but eventually they flew away. Bill thought he'd finally got rid of those troublesome birds, and that was the last he'd see of them.

Next morning, to Bill's surprise, all his red pigeons had returned home again, for all their freebies, like visiting MacDonalds, only better.

To get rid of them for good, knowing they would have plenty of company, he took them to Piccadilly Circus. Whether it was the distance, or the company, Bill will never know, but at last, he'd got rid of his red pigeons, aptly nicknamed the red arrows, for their continuous speed of return.

## A Taxi Fare

It was a pleasant, albeit cloudy, evening in late September. The air was still and, as the World War 2 black-outs were still in operation, it was very dark. Bill was driving his taxi, a big black, 7 seater Buick, around Plymouth taking taxi fares to and from city centre ballrooms and restaurants. As was a regular occurrence in those times Bill had another driver with him. Claud's own vehicle was off the road through a lack of petrol, but because of the enjoyment gained from Bill they usually took such opportunities to ride with him.

That evening had been fairly busy. It was just after 11.30p.m. when Bill was about to set off from Union Street, in the heart of Plymouth, to collect two army officers from Yealmpton, a few miles away on the outskirts of the city. As the engine quietly sprung into action and Bill engaged first gear a pleasant looking young lady with long, dark hair approached with her hand raised in a gesture to stop the car.

Bill, always a gentleman where pretty young ladies were concerned, eased his foot off the accelerator and wound down his window. The young lady, in a clear Plymouth accent, requested whether Bill's taxi was for hire. Bill smiled to himself, looked at the young lady, shivering slightly in her pretty, red, cotton frock, and without hesitation opened the driver's door and beckoned her into the middle of the front, bench seat. Seeing her concerned expression he quickly explained he could certainly take her to her destination, but that he was going to have to take her via Yealmpton, where he would be collecting two army officers, who would occupy the rear seat.

Having been reassured the young lady climbed through the driver's door, perched carefully on the bench seat beside Claud and waited whilst Bill returned to his driver's seat, before introducing herself as Mary, and requesting she wanted to go to Ford, a suburb of Plymouth. The Buick gently eased away in the direction of Yealmpton.

After driving five minutes, with some flirtatious chat between Bill and his new passenger, Mary asked whether there was a public toilet nearby as she was in desperate need. Bill, having already recognised that Mary had obviously been drinking, as well as dancing, smiled to himself and responded by pulling over to a large old marble building, by the side of

189

the road. Fortunately they had been driving through Prince Rock and were just approaching the marble building, a public toilet, just as Mary had made her request.

Bill and Claud waited patiently for their fare to return, relieved of her excess liquid. They exchanged a few whispered remarks about her pleasant appearance, that she was good company, and that her bladder was obviously very full and that they may be required to make further unscheduled stops before this journey was complete. Eventually she returned to the car, with a satisfied smile upon her pretty face, and announced that Bill could resume the journey, as she was now much more comfortable.

Later, after collecting the two army officers and dropping them at their destination in Richmond Walk, back near Plymouth's centre, the weak bladdered passenger requested a further stop. At that moment the car was entering the Brickfields area of Plymouth, which was very open, and also very dark in the black-out at this late time of night. Although Mary had requested a public toilet, Bill grinned wickedly, winked at Claud, and told her there were none nearby. However, because of their location and the lack of any light she could use the patch of wasteland just ahead. As she was desperate to relieve herself she agreed quite readily.

Bill pulled the Buick quietly over to the side of the road and Mary disembarked. Feeling the now chill air and darkness around her, she turned her head and asked hurriedly that they should not leave her in the dark. She had only taken a few steps up a small, grassy bank when she disappeared into the night darkness. After a very short wait Bill reversed the car, lights off, and then eased it gently forward onto the grass and a little way up the bank, until the rear wheels were just touching the kerb. The car came quietly to rest pointing slightly uphill.

At this stage Claud, looking puzzled, enquired as to what Bill was doing. Bill replied by putting his finger to his pursed lips and pointing, with his other hand, through the front windscreen, up the bank in front of them. Then, quick as a flash (no pun intended), Bill switched on the headlights to reveal the young lady's dress pulled up around her waist, and knickers dropped around her ankles. At first she looked quite white in the bright light, but quickly her face turned scarlet. Her eyes widened and she froze for a second, like a rabbit caught in the light, and then she made a dart for the darkness. Unfortunately her feet could not travel as far, or as fast, as her legs, because her knicker elastic was holding tight around her slim ankles. She fell, gathered herself up and stumbled forward again. Bill and Claud were laughing uncontrollably at this amusing scene.

A few minutes later the red-faced passenger returned to the car. She regained her composure and climbed back into her seat in the front of the car. Bill was just sliding back into the driver's seat when Mary, trying to adjust herself so as not to sit on a damp patch, demanded an explanation. To which he replied in his ever quick thinking manner that he had been concerned she might be scared in the dark or might not have been able to see what she was doing, and therefore he had thoughtfully given her a little light.

As was usual with Bill's practical jokes the three of them laughed heartily about the whole episode and parted on good terms when he dropped his fare safely at her destination behind Ford Bug-house Cinema, as it was known in those war days.

### Eckard

Bill was with his men and outstanding fleet outside St. Andrews Church. The cars, all bearing the words, 'Earl of Plymouth', on each number plate. A young German student, called Eckard, asked Bill, who Earl of Plymouth was. Bill giving his usual response to such a request, that he's a short man, with black hair and a moustache. The young man, realising, he was talking with 'Earl of Plymouth', asked about the Earldoms. Eventually, Bill invited the young man to stay at his home for a holiday, providing he gave Bill some references, and when he arrived, he brought a 'collar and tie'.

The young man asked all he came into contact with in Germany, what was a 'collar and tie', because it didn't make sense to him. He still didn't know, when he arrived for his one month's holiday. Just showing, the simple phrases we take for granted, make no sense at all to others in different countries. Eckard enjoyed his holiday, compliments of Earl of Plymouth. Going home with his favourite tape 'Welcome to my world, wont you come on in'.

### Conclusion

I hope you've enjoyed Bill's world of memories, spanning 83 yrs. I feel sure you will agree, he's certainly led, a very interesting, and varied life.

Carole Barkell,
5 Outland Road,
PLYMOUTH,
PL2 3BZ.
Tel:- 01752-567813.